Applying the Standards

Student Edition

by Paul R. Lawrence

Lawrence Educational Services Inc.
Bridgewater, New Jersey

Lawrence Educational Services Inc., Bridgewater, NJ 08807

Applying the Standards
Student Edition

Printed in the United States of America
10 09 08 07 1 2 3 4 5 6 7 8

ISBN: 978-1-59699-644-1

Cover design: James Ticchio, Direct Media Advertising
Editorial Services: Steve Andriolo, James Carr, Brian Rawlins

Lawrence Educational Services Inc. and its partner LLTeach, Inc. are dedicated to excellence in education for all children and provide high-quality materials and professional staff development in mathematics education K-12.

800-575-7670 www.llteach.com

Number Sense – Day 1

Name: ______________________________ Date: ______________

Create four different problems, one containing only the operation of addition, another with subtraction, and the remaining two with multiplication and division. The digits can be used in the ones or tens places, which permits the creation of one two-digit number and one one-digit number. Each digit can only be used once in each number sentence, and each number sentence can have only one operation. When finished, plot the numbers on the segment provided. Remember to show the scale and label the points. Calculators may be used to complete the problems.

1. Today's Digits: 6, 3, 0   Today's Answers: 5, 24, 63, 180

2. Label the segment and plot today's answers.

3. Use the digits 2, 6, 7, 9, 8, and 1 to create an addition problem consisting of two three-digit numbers whose sum is the greatest possible that can be created with these digits.

4. Use all the digits 2, 6, 7, 9, 8, and 1 exactly once to create a division problem with a two-digit divisor whose quotient is the largest possible that can be created with these digits.

Number Sense – Day 2

Name: ______________________________ Date: ______________

Create four different problems, one containing only the operation of addition, another with subtraction, and the remaining two with multiplication and division. The digits can be used in the ones or tens places, which permits the creation of one two-digit number and one one-digit number. Each digit can only be used once in each number sentence, and each number sentence can have only one operation. When finished, plot the numbers on the segment provided. Remember to show the scale and label the points. Calculators may be used to complete the problems.

1. Today's Digits: 8, 7, 2 Today's Answers: 9, 64, 80, 576

2. Label the segment and plot today's answers.

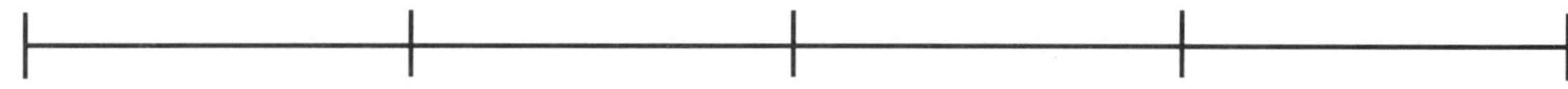

4. Use the digits 4, 2, 8, and 3 to create a multiplication problem consisting of two two-digit numbers whose product is the smallest possible that can be created with these digits.

5. Use all the digits 7, 4, 2, 8, and 3 exactly once to create a subtraction problem with a two-digit subtrahend whose difference is the smallest possible that can be created with these digits.

Number Sense – Day 3

Name: ______________________________ Date: ______________

Create four different problems, one containing only the operation of addition, another with subtraction, and the remaining two with multiplication and division. The digits can be used in the ones or tens places, which permits the creation of one two-digit number and one one-digit number. Each digit can only be used once in each number sentence, and each number sentence can have only one operation. When finished, plot the numbers on the segment provided. Remember to show the scale and label the points. Calculators may be used to complete the problems.

1. Today's Digits: 8, 0, 2, 5 Today's Answers: 55, 56, 132, 2000

2. Label the segment and plot today's answers.

3. Rewrite the problem below so the product will be 2646.

$$\begin{array}{r} 62 \\ \times\, 43 \\ \hline 2666 \end{array}$$

4. Use all the digits 9, 4, 7, 8, and 3 exactly once to create a 3-digit times 2-digit multiplication problem that yields the greatest possible product.

Number Sense – Day 4

Name: ______________________________ Date: ______________

Create four different problems, one containing only the operation of addition, another with subtraction, and the remaining two with multiplication and division. The digits can be used in the ones or tens places, which permits the creation of one two-digit number and one one-digit number. Each digit can only be used once in each number sentence, and each number sentence can have only one operation. When finished, plot the numbers on the segment provided. Remember to show the scale and label the points. Calculators may be used to complete the problems.

1. Today's Digits: 4, 6, 9, 8   Today's Answers: 52, 83, 117, 4094

2. Label the segment and plot today's answers.

3. Use the digits 8, 1, 5, 3, 2, and 7 to create a division problem with a two-digit divisor whose quotient is the smallest possible that can be created with all these digits.

4. Which arithmetic operations are commutative?

Number Sense – Assessment – Day 5

Name: ______________________________ Date: ______________

Create four different problems, one containing only the operation of addition, another with subtraction, and the remaining two with multiplication and division. The digits can be used in the ones or tens places, which permits the creation of one two-digit number and one one-digit number. Each digit can only be used once in each number sentence, and each number sentence can have only one operation. When finished, plot the numbers on the segment provided. Remember to show the scale and label the points. Calculators may be used to complete the problems.

1. Today's Digits: 7, 8, 2 Today's Answers: 4, 19, 80, 196

2. Label the segment and plot today's answers.

3. Use the digits 5, 6, 7, 2, 3, and 1 to create an addition problem consisting of two three-digit numbers whose sum is the greatest possible that can be created with these digits.

4. Use all the digits 5, 4, 7, 9, 1 and 8 exactly once to create a division problem with a two-digit divisor whose quotient is the largest possible that can be created with these digits.

Number Sense – Computation in Context – Day 6

Name: ______________________________ Date: ______________

Estimate and then calculate the answers to the following problems.

		Estimate / Exact Answer
1. $6\overline{)4771}$	2. 3,234 + 1,732 + 12,812 + 687	1.
		2.
3. 8,456 − 6,498	4. 435 × 97	3.
		4.
5. 43 + 39 + 51 + 55	6. 43 × 69	5.
		6.
7. $26\overline{)7432}$	8. 10,000 − 2,432	7.
		8.

Numbers: Masters of Disguise – Day 7

Name: ______________________________ Date: ______________

Use the Fraction/Decimal Equivalence Bars and a Communicator® clearboard to answer the questions below.

1. Use the fifths bar to show $\frac{3}{5}$. Position the Communicator® clearboard to find as many equivalencies on the sheet as possible. List them below.

2. Use the twentieths bar to show $\frac{16}{20}$. Position the Communicator® clearboard to find as many equivalencies on the sheet as possible. List them below.

3. Use the tenths bar to show $\frac{7}{10}$. Position the Communicator® clearboard to find as many equivalencies on the sheet as possible. List them below.

4. Use the twenty-fifths bar to show $\frac{13}{25}$. Position the Communicator® clearboard to determine as many equivalencies on the sheet as possible. List them below.

5. If $\frac{1}{25} = 0.04$, what is the decimal equivalent of $\frac{9}{25}$? __________

6. If $\frac{1}{20} = 0.05$, what is the decimal equivalent of $\frac{13}{20}$? __________

7. If $\frac{1}{5} = 0.20$, what is the decimal equivalent of $\frac{4}{5}$? __________

8. If $\frac{1}{10} = 0.10$, what is the decimal equivalent of $\frac{7}{10}$? __________

Numbers: Masters of Disguise – Day 8

Name: ______________________________ Date: ____________

Use the Fraction/Decimal Equivalence Bars as needed to determine decimal approximations for each of the fractions.

1. $\frac{1}{7} \approx$ ________
2. $\frac{1}{16} \approx$ ________
3. $\frac{1}{9} \approx$ ________
4. $\frac{1}{15} \approx$ ________
5. $\frac{1}{6} \approx$ ________
6. $\frac{1}{3} \approx$ ________
7. $\frac{1}{12} \approx$ ________
8. $\frac{1}{8} \approx$ ________

Based on the approximations above, determine approximations for each of the following fractions.

9. $\frac{3}{8} \approx$ ________
10. $\frac{9}{16} \approx$ ________
11. $\frac{2}{3} \approx$ ________
12. $\frac{5}{6} \approx$ ________
13. $\frac{11}{15} \approx$ ________
14. $\frac{5}{12} \approx$ ________
15. $\frac{4}{9} \approx$ ________
16. $\frac{4}{7} \approx$ ________

17. List the fractions above that are greater than $\frac{1}{2}$. ______________________

18. Explain how you determined the answer to Number 17.

Numbers: Masters of Disguise – Day 9

Name: ______________________________ Date: ______________

Use the Fraction, Fraction, Fraction Discovery Template to answer the questions below.

1. Record the approximate decimal values for all of the fractions in Set B.

2. Record the decimal values for all of the fractions in Set C in the order in which they are given.

3. Record the approximate decimal values for all the fractions in Set D in the order in which they are given.

4. Which set of non-unit fractions appear from the greatest value to the least value?

5. Rewrite all the fractions in Set E so they are in ascending order.

6. In which set do all of the fractions have exact decimal equivalents and appear in order from greatest to least?

   (A) $\frac{1}{3}, \frac{9}{11}, \frac{7}{15}, \frac{3}{4}$ (B) $\frac{2}{3}, \frac{3}{10}, \frac{1}{5}, \frac{1}{4}$ (C) $\frac{3}{4}, \frac{3}{5}, \frac{1}{10}, \frac{1}{20}$ (D) $\frac{1}{5}, \frac{4}{25}, \frac{1}{2}, \frac{3}{4}$

7. Which of the following is a true statement?

   (A) $\frac{5}{5} = \frac{101}{101}$ (B) $0.27 \approx \frac{3}{4}$ (C) $\frac{2}{3} > \frac{4}{5}$ (D) $\frac{1}{2} = 0.66$

Numbers: Masters of Disguise – Day 10

Name: ______________________________ Date: ______________

1. Record the decimal equivalent or approximation (rounded to the nearest hundredth) for each fraction in Set A and Set B on the blank next to the fraction. Then use a calculator and divide the numerator of each fraction by the denominator and record what is shown on the calculator's display.

Set A			Set B		
$\frac{1}{2}$	________	________________	$\frac{1}{11}$	________	________________
$\frac{1}{4}$	________	________________	$\frac{1}{15}$	________	________________
$\frac{1}{5}$	________	________________	$\frac{1}{12}$	________	________________
$\frac{1}{10}$	________	________________	$\frac{1}{7}$	________	________________
$\frac{1}{20}$	________	________________	$\frac{1}{9}$	________	________________
$\frac{1}{25}$	________	________________	$\frac{1}{6}$	________	________________

2. Which of the following generate a terminating decimal?

   (A) $\frac{7}{8}$ (B) $\frac{2}{3}$ (C) $\frac{4}{15}$ (D) $\frac{1}{12}$

3. Which of the following has a value of $0.08\overline{3}$?

   (A) $\frac{1}{6}$ (B) $\frac{1}{15}$ (C) $\frac{1}{12}$ (D) $\frac{1}{9}$

4. Which of the following is equal to 0.0909090909090909…?

   (A) $\frac{1}{9}$ (B) $0.\overline{09}$ (C) $\frac{1}{12}$ (D) $0.\overline{1}$

Numbers: Masters of Disguise – Assessment – Day 11

Name: ______________________________ Date: ______________

1. Study the values for the inputs and outputs in the table. One of the outputs does not follow the same pattern as the others. Which one is it?

Input	Output
$\frac{4}{5}$, 0.75, 0.43, $\frac{1}{16}$	$\frac{1}{16}$
0.03, 0.18, 0.5, 0.51	0.51
$\frac{4}{5}$, 0.66, $\frac{1}{3}$, $\frac{2}{9}$	$\frac{4}{5}$
$\frac{1}{9}$, 0.3, 0.02, 0.4	0.4

(A) $\frac{1}{16}$ (B) 0.51 (C) $\frac{4}{5}$ (D) 0.4

2. In which set do all of the fractions have approximate decimal equivalents and are in order from least to greatest?

(A) $\frac{1}{15}, \frac{5}{12}, \frac{2}{3}, \frac{7}{9}$ (B) $\frac{3}{5}, \frac{2}{7}, \frac{1}{11}, \frac{1}{9}$ (C) $\frac{1}{2}, \frac{2}{5}, \frac{3}{4}, \frac{1}{10}$ (D) $\frac{1}{5}, \frac{1}{4}, \frac{3}{10}, \frac{19}{20}$

3. Which of the following generates a terminating decimal?

(A) $\frac{7}{12}$ (B) $\frac{1}{3}$ (C) $\frac{4}{15}$ (D) $\frac{3}{16}$

4. Which of the following has a value of $0.\bar{1}$?

(A) $\frac{1}{6}$ (B) $\frac{1}{9}$ (C) $\frac{1}{12}$ (D) $\frac{1}{15}$

Numbers: Masters of Disguise – Computation in Context – Day 12

Name: ______________________ Date: ____________

Estimate and then calculate the answers to the following problems.

		Estimate / Exact Answer
1. $\begin{array}{r} 4{,}655 \\ -\ 2{,}320 \\ \hline \end{array}$	2. $\begin{array}{r} 4{,}201 \\ 2{,}837 \\ 10{,}730 \\ +\quad 288 \\ \hline \end{array}$	1. ______ / ______ 2. ______ / ______
3. $8\overline{)5589}$	4. $\begin{array}{r} 8{,}655 \\ -\ 4{,}389 \\ \hline \end{array}$	3. ______ / ______ 4. ______ / ______
5. $\begin{array}{r} 12{,}099 \\ -\ 8{,}123 \\ \hline \end{array}$	6. $49\overline{)99{,}921}$	5. ______ / ______ 6. ______ / ______
7. $\begin{array}{r} 49 \\ 64 \\ 46 \\ +\ 72 \\ \hline \end{array}$	8. $\begin{array}{r} 66 \\ \times\ 33 \\ \hline \end{array}$	7. ______ / ______ 8. ______ / ______

Fraction, Decimal and Percent Equivalencies – Day 13

Name: ______________________________ Date: ______________

Each of the decimal equivalencies or approximations for the sets of fractions below were shaded on the grids shown. Match the grids to their respective problem by placing the letter of grid next to the correct sequence of fractions. If necessary, use a Fraction/Decimal Equivalence Bars and a Communicator® clearboard to determine the decimal forms of the fractions.

1. $\frac{1}{6}, \frac{1}{25}, \frac{1}{3}$ ________

2. $\frac{1}{7}, \frac{1}{5}, \frac{1}{4}$ ________

3. $\frac{1}{20}, \frac{1}{9}, \frac{1}{12}$ ________

4. $\frac{1}{3}, \frac{1}{20}, \frac{1}{4}$ ________

5. $\frac{1}{25}, \frac{1}{20}, \frac{1}{4}$ ________

6. $\frac{1}{4}, \frac{1}{9}, \frac{1}{7}$ ________

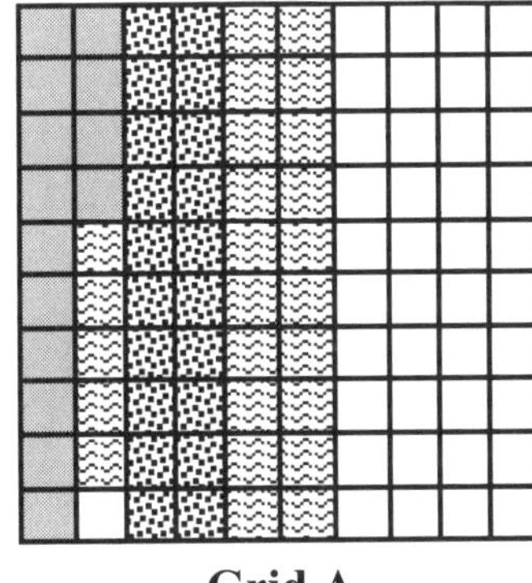
Grid A

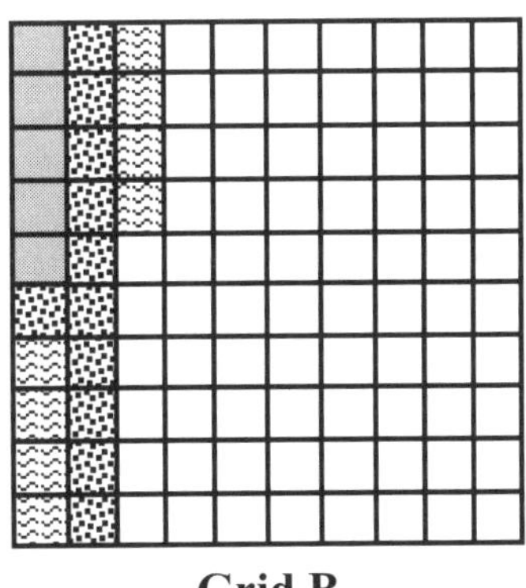
Grid B

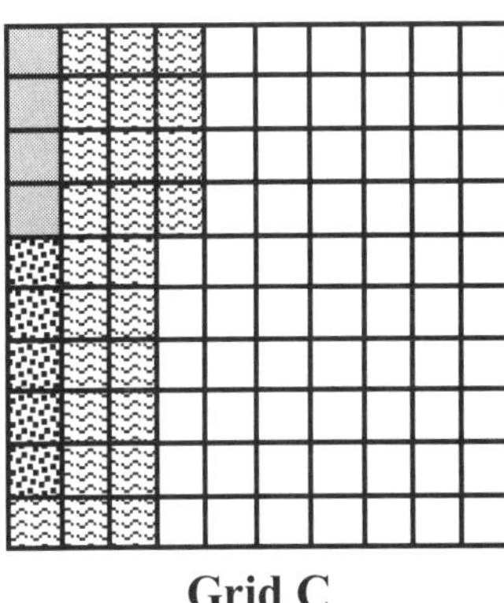
Grid C

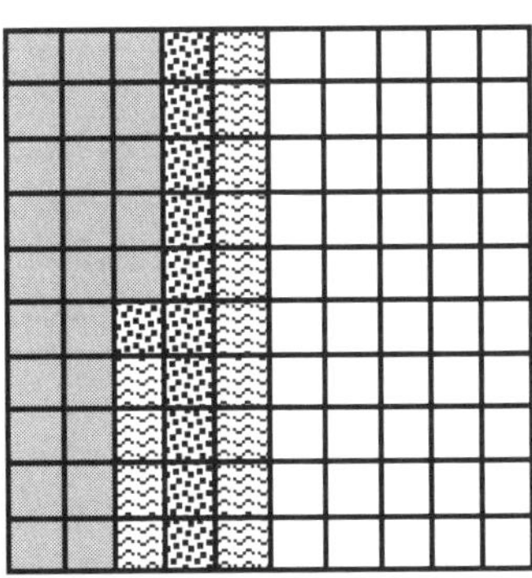
Grid D

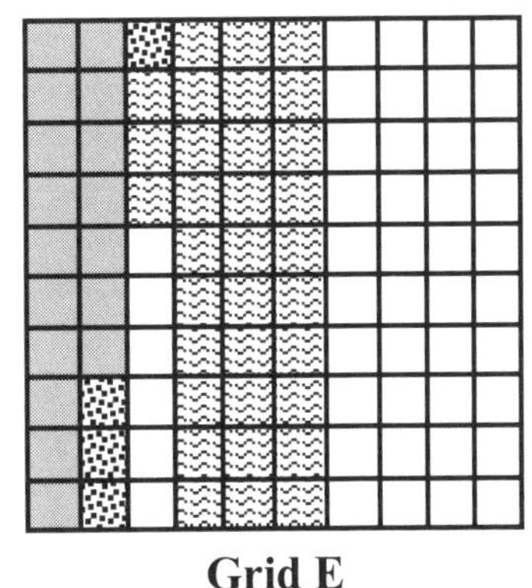
Grid E

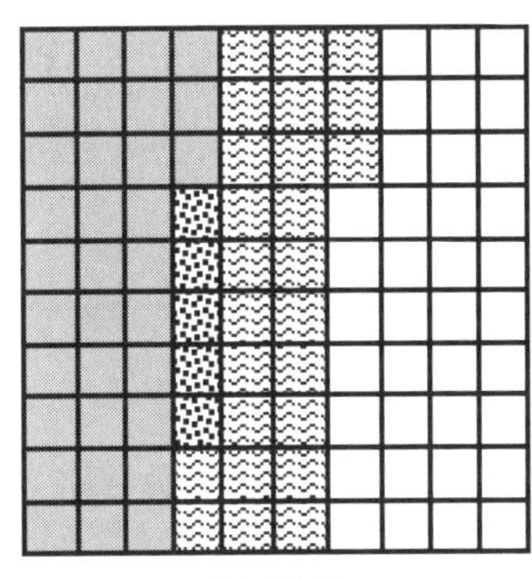
Grid F

Fraction, Decimal and Percent Equivalencies – Day 14

Name: ______________________ Date: ____________

Each of the decimal equivalencies or approximations for the sets of fractions below were shaded on the grids shown. Match the grids to their respective problem by placing the letter of grid next to the correct sequence of fractions. If necessary, use a Fraction/Decimal Equivalence Bars and a Communicator® clearboard to determine the decimal forms of the fractions.

1. $\frac{1}{6}, \frac{3}{25}, \frac{2}{3}$ ________

2. $\frac{3}{7}, \frac{2}{5}, \frac{2}{11}$ ________

3. $\frac{7}{15}, \frac{1}{9}, \frac{9}{25}$ ________

4. $\frac{3}{11}, \frac{7}{20}, \frac{1}{4}$ ________

5. $\frac{6}{25}, \frac{11}{20}, \frac{1}{16}$ ________

6. $\frac{1}{12}, \frac{5}{9}, \frac{2}{7}$ ________

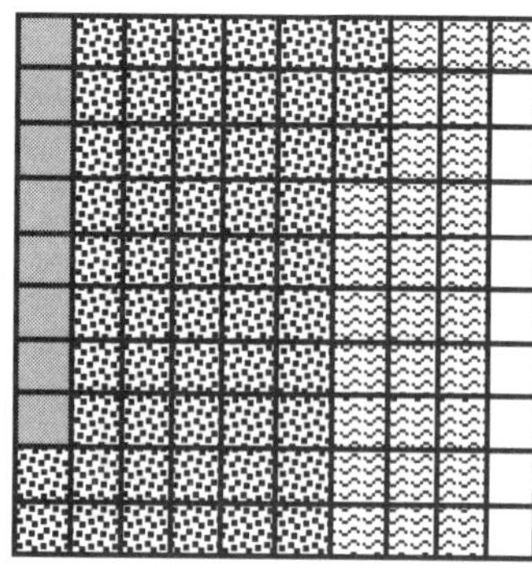
Grid A

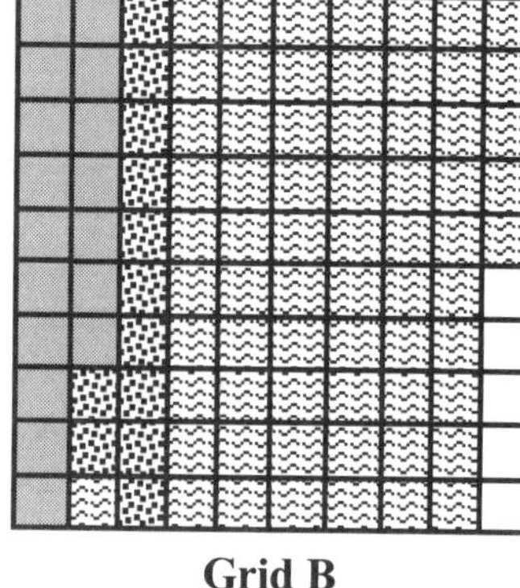
Grid B

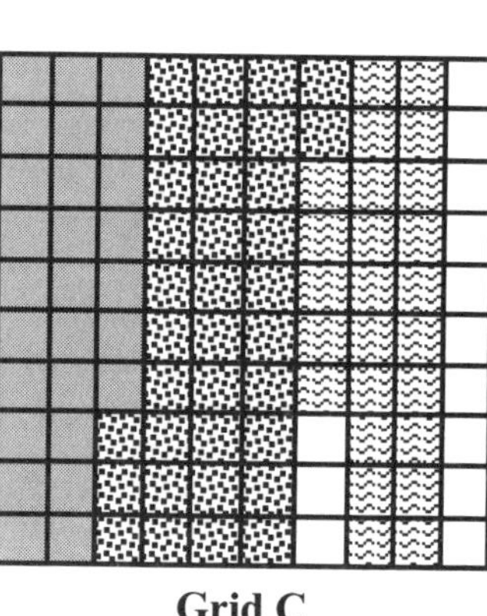
Grid C

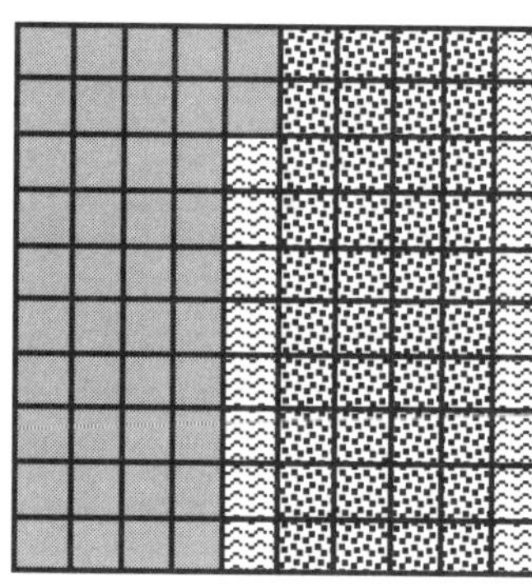
Grid D

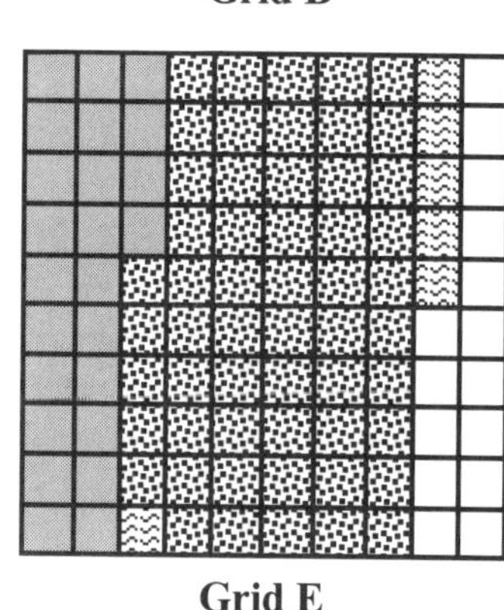
Grid E

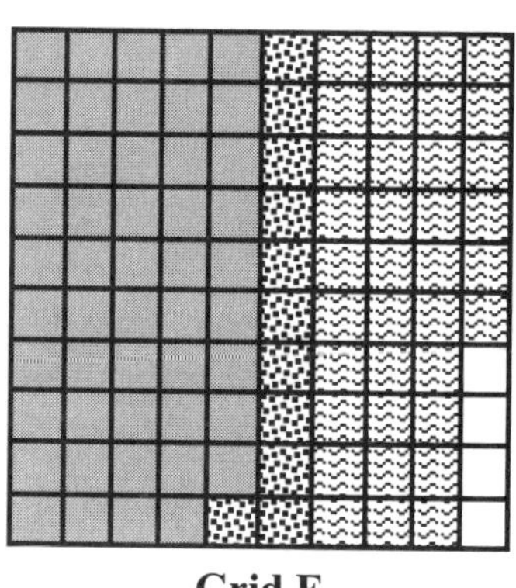
Grid F

7. Study the total number of hundredths shaded in each grid. Record the letters of the grids and their total decimal values in order from the least decimal value to the largest.

Fraction, Decimal and Percent Equivalencies – Day 15

Name: ______________________________ Date: ______________

Provide the missing equivalent forms for each of the following:

	Fraction Simplest Form	Fraction Hundredths Form	Decimal	Percent	Model
1.	$\frac{9}{25}$				
2.					
3.			0.16		
4.	$\frac{13}{20}$				
5.				75%	

Fraction, Decimal and Percent Equivalencies – Day 16

Name: ______________________________ Date: ______________

Match the percent circle with the fraction circle below by placing the letter of the fraction circle in the blank along with symbols that relate the two quantities.

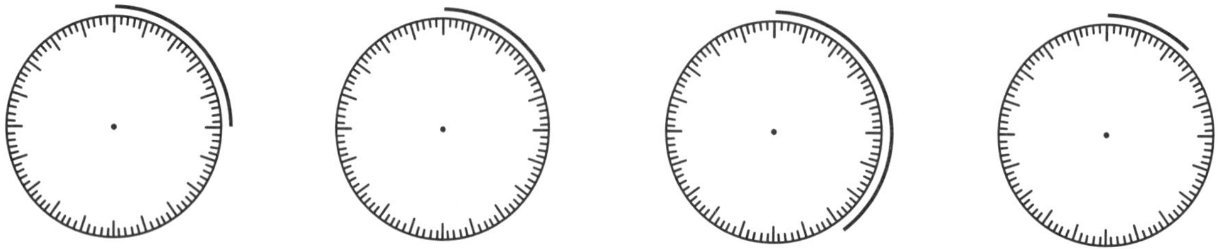

__________ __________ __________ __________

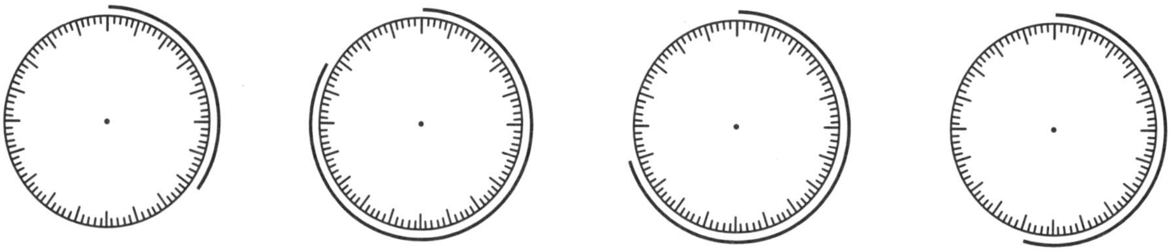

__________ __________ __________ __________

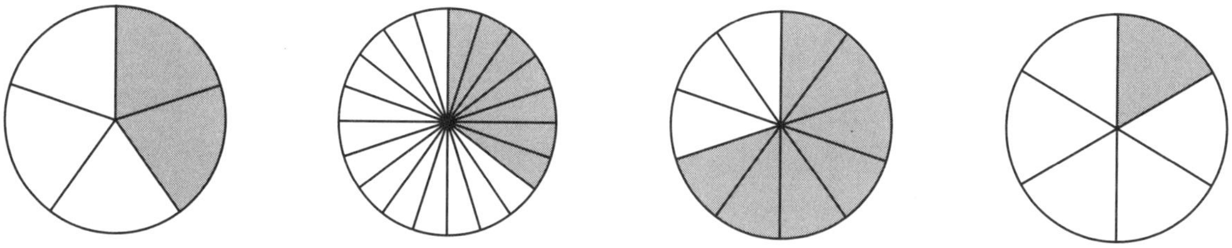

A B C D

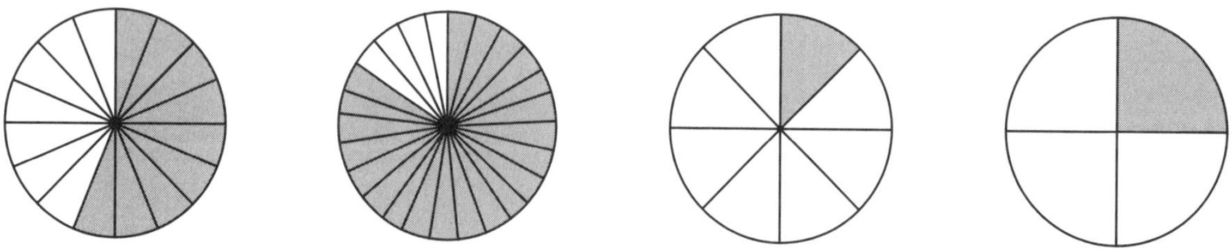

E F G H

Fraction, Decimal and Percent Equivalencies – Day 17

Name: ______________________________ Date: ______________

Problems 1 – 20: Insert an equal or inequality sign between in the blanks so the number sentence created is true. (Fractions based on the drawings should be formed such that the fraction represents the shaded part of the drawing.)

1.	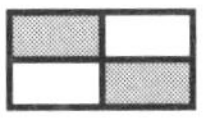		0.40
2.	$\frac{3}{5}$		$\frac{10}{25}$
3.	0.6		$\frac{75}{100}$
4.	$\frac{2}{5}$		0.05
5.	0.20		
6.	$\frac{3}{9}$		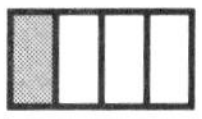
7.	$\frac{1}{50}$		2%
8.	5%		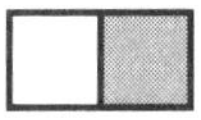
9.	20%		$\frac{3}{10}$
10.	2%		0.125
11.	$\frac{1}{4}$		40%
12.	0.5		$\frac{4}{20}$
13.	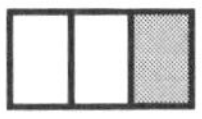		$\frac{2}{3}$
14.	.02		0.2%
15.	0.01		0.25%
16.	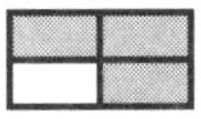		$\frac{5}{20}$
17.	0.2		$\frac{25}{100}$
18.	0.75		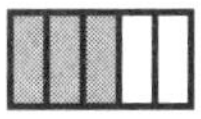
19.	$\frac{5}{8}$		$66\frac{2}{3}\%$
20.	62.5%		12.5%

Fraction, Decimal and Percent Equivalencies – Assessment – Day 18

Name: ______________________________ Date: ______________

1. Which of the following is a true statement?

Ⓐ $\frac{4}{5} < \frac{8}{9}$ Ⓑ $0.55 = \frac{1}{2}$ Ⓒ $\frac{1}{6} = 0.33$ Ⓓ $\frac{1}{3} \approx 0.66$

2. Which of the following is not the same as 0.05?

Ⓐ $\frac{1}{20}$ Ⓑ $\frac{5}{100}$ Ⓒ 50% Ⓓ 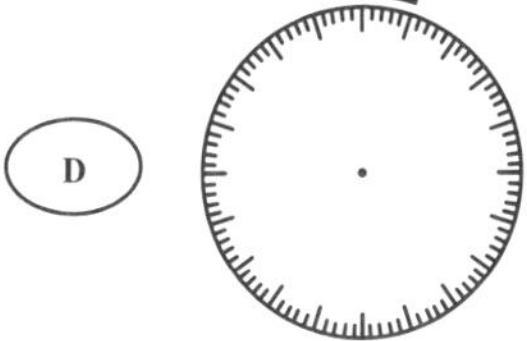

3. Which of the following is the best approximate fraction equivalent of 28%?

Ⓐ $\frac{2}{9}$ Ⓑ $\frac{2}{7}$ Ⓒ $\frac{2}{3}$ Ⓓ $\frac{3}{8}$

4. Which set of fractions is best represented by the shadings shown on this unit square?

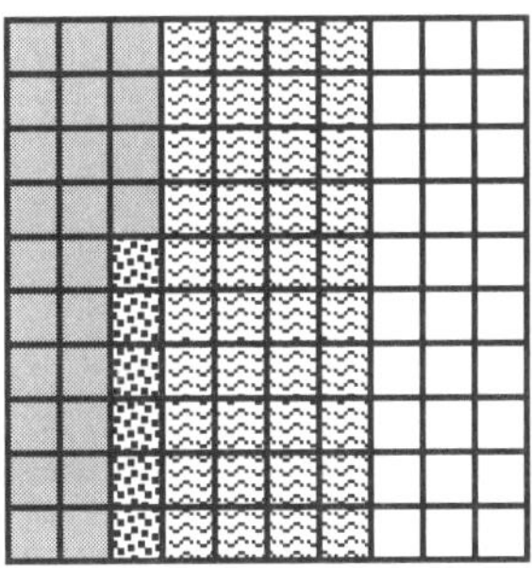

Ⓐ $\frac{6}{25}, \frac{1}{16}, \frac{9}{20}$ Ⓑ $\frac{1}{4}, \frac{1}{16}, \frac{2}{5}$ Ⓒ $\frac{6}{25}, \frac{1}{16}, \frac{2}{5}$ Ⓓ $\frac{1}{4}, \frac{1}{6}, \frac{2}{5}$

5. Which of the following does not show a complete set of equivalencies?

Ⓐ $0.3, \frac{30}{100}, 30\%, \frac{6}{20}$ Ⓑ $0.60, \frac{60}{100}, 60\%, \frac{12}{20}$

Ⓒ $0.45, \frac{9}{20}, 45\%, \frac{45}{100}$ Ⓓ $42\%, \frac{4}{7}, 0.42, \frac{42}{100}$

Estimating Square Roots – Day 19

Name: ______________________________ Date: ______________

1. List all perfect squares from 1 to 144. ______________________________

2. What square would you make on a geoboard to help estimate the $\sqrt{79}$? Tell why and give an estimate to the nearest hundredth.

3. What square would you make on a geoboard to help estimate $\sqrt{17}$? Tell why and provide an estimate to the closest hundredth.

4. What two perfect squares would you use to help you estimate the $\sqrt{42}$?

Think of perfect squares to help match the square roots with the estimates shown below.

5. $\sqrt{91}$ __________	A. 9.94
6. $\sqrt{99}$ __________	B. 3.61
7. $\sqrt{83}$ __________	C. 3.87
8. $\sqrt{15}$ __________	D. 9.54
9. $\sqrt{13}$ __________	E. 3.16
10. $\sqrt{10}$ __________	F. 9.11

Terminating, Repeating, and Non-terminating, Non-repeating Decimals
Day 20

Name: ______________________________ Date: ______________

The numbers in Column A were copied from the display of a calculator. Rewrite each of the irrational numbers in non-terminating notation and each of the repeating decimals in line segment notation.

	Column A	Column B
1. $\sqrt{6}$	2.449489743	
2. $\frac{2}{9}$	.222222222	
3. $\frac{11}{25}$	.44	
4. $\sqrt{398}$	19.94993734	
5. $\sqrt{156}$	12.489996	
6. $\frac{19}{20}$	.95	
7. $\frac{13}{22}$	.5909090909	
8. $\frac{9}{32}$	.28125	
9. $\frac{13}{30}$	.433333333	
10. $\sqrt{48}$	6.9282032302	
11. $\frac{17}{91}$	0.18681318681	
12. $\frac{3}{8}$	0.375	

Comparing and Ordering Integers – Day 21

Name: ______________________________ Date: ______________

Out of the 10 problems below, identify the ones that are incorrect by labeling them true or false. You may want to use the number line to help determine the answer.

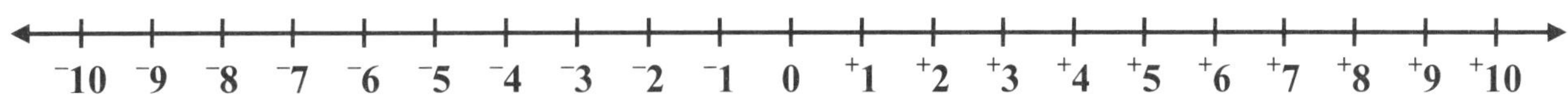

1. $^{-}5 > 4$ ____________ 2. $^{-}4 > {}^{-}8$ ____________

3. $3 < {}^{-}2$ ____________ 4. $^{-}8 < 0$ ____________

5. $8 > 5$ ____________ 6. $9 > 10$ ____________

7. $^{-}5 < {}^{-}3$ ____________ 8. $0 < {}^{-}3$ ____________

9. $^{-}8 > {}^{-}10$ ____________ 10. $4 > {}^{-}2$ ____________

Place the following sets of integers in order from least to greatest.

11. $^{-}4, 7, 10, {}^{-}3$ ____________

12. $0, {}^{-}2, {}^{-}1, 7$ ____________

13. $4, 8, 2, 0$ ____________

14. $^{-}3, {}^{-}5, {}^{-}7, {}^{-}1$ ____________

15. $^{-}2, 3, 6, 9$ ____________

16. $8, {}^{-}3, {}^{-}5, 10$ ____________

17. $^{-}4, 8, {}^{-}9, {}^{-}6$ ____________

18. $^{-}3, 4, 0, {}^{-}1$ ____________

19. $8, {}^{-}10, 3, 7$ ____________

20. $^{-}10, {}^{-}1, {}^{-}5, {}^{-}4$ ____________

Classify, Describe, Compare and Contrast Sets of Real Numbers – Day 22

Name: ______________________________ Date: ______________

Use Sets E – H of the Numbers, Numbers, Numbers Discovery Template (Page 172 to complete the following problems.

1. List all the irrational numbers in Set F. ______________

2. List all the terminating decimals in Set E. ______________

3. List all the repeating decimals in Set G. ______________

4. Which set(s) contain(s) only real numbers between 0 and $^{-}1$? ______________

5. Which set(s) contain(s) only real numbers between 0 and 1? ______________

6. List all the real numbers in Set F from the least value to the greatest value.

7. Which set of real numbers does the following graph represent?

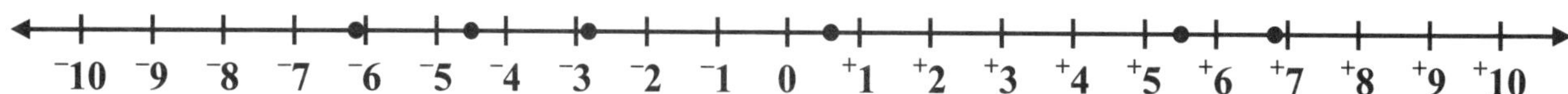

8. Plot and label all the rational numbers in Set F on the number line below.

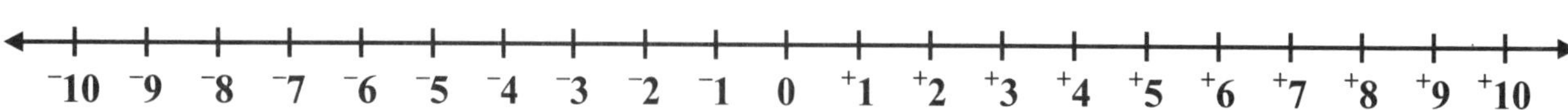

The "Get 4" Game – Day 23

Name: ______________________________ Date: ______________

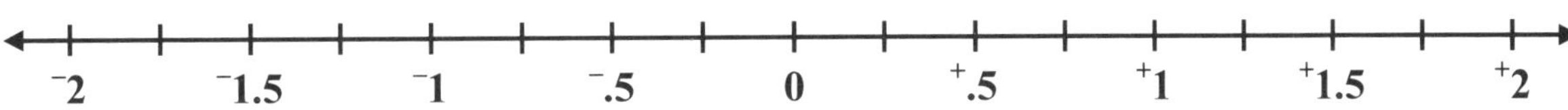

Create a deck of 16 cards by removing all the aces, 2s, 3s and 4s from a standard deck of playing cards. To generate a random number from the table, each player chooses two cards. The first card indicates the column; the second card indicates the row. Each player plots the point on the number line. The first player with four points that lie between $^-2$ and $^-1$, $^-1$ and 0, 0 and 1, or 1 and 2 wins the game. If a player plots the point, incorrectly the player loses the turn. When all the cards are played, the deck is reshuffled and play continues until someone wins.

Real Number Randomizer				
$^-0.42$	$^-\sqrt{2}$	0.15873...	1.0879	**Row 4**
$1\frac{1}{9}$	$-\frac{7}{8}$	$^-1\frac{7}{20}$	$0.\overline{9}$	**Row 3**
$^-0.\overline{25}$	$0.5\overline{34}$	$\sqrt{3}$	$^-1.7\overline{2}$	**Row 2**
$^-0.375$	$1.45\overline{11}$	$\frac{2}{3}$	$^-1.75915...$	**Row 1**
Column 1	**Column 2**	**Column 3**	**Column 4**	

Example:

Sally chooses a 4 of clubs and a 2 of diamonds. Her number is $^-1.7\overline{2}$. Boris chooses a 3 of hearts and an ace of hearts. His number is $\frac{2}{3}$.

Use the number lines below to graph the numbers in each of the rows.

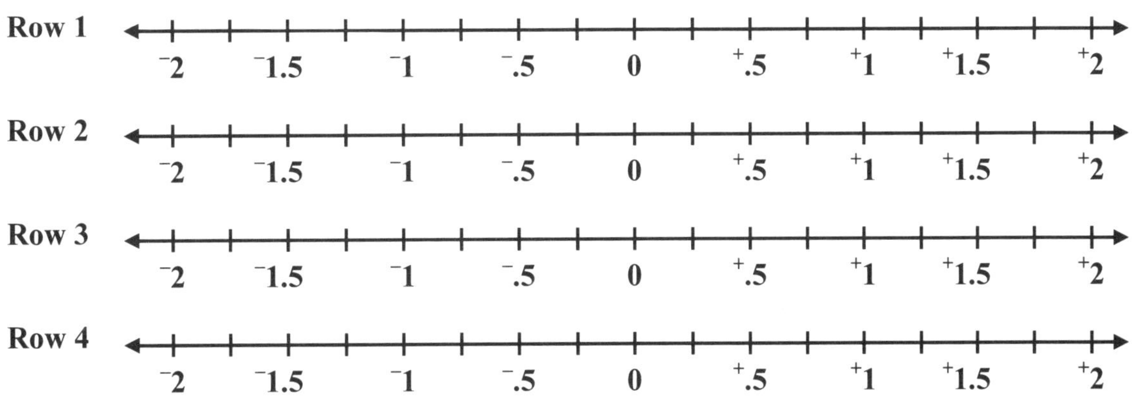

Working with Real Numbers – Assessment – Day 24

Name: ______________________________ Date: ______________

Choose the best answer for each question by filling in the correct oval. If you are using a separate answer sheet, be certain that you fill in the correct letter next to the appropriate question number.

1. Which of the following is equal to $0.\bar{1}$?

   (A) $\frac{1}{3}$ (B) $\frac{1}{4}$ (C) $\frac{1}{9}$ (D) $\frac{1}{10}$

2. Which of the following is the best approximation of $\sqrt{15}$?

   (A) 4.27… (B) 3.87… (C) 3.45 (D) 2.99…

3. In which of the following sets are the numbers ordered from greatest to least?

   (A) $^{-}51, ^{-}6, 7, 81$ (B) $^{-}0.0005, ^{-}0.005, ^{-}0.05, ^{-}0.5$

   (C) 3, 6, 9, 12 (D) $\frac{1}{10}, \frac{1}{6}, \frac{1}{3}, \frac{1}{2}$

4. Which of the sets below contains exactly two terminating decimals, two repeating decimals and two irrational numbers?

   (A) $\sqrt{112}, ^{-}0.\overline{285714}, \frac{4}{21}, \frac{3}{8}, 3\frac{7}{10}, ^{-}2.718231\ldots,$

   (B) $2\frac{7}{20}, \frac{5}{8}, 0.\overline{467}, -\frac{13}{25}, ^{-}1.0043413\ldots, ^{-}\sqrt{53}$

   (C) $^{-}15.87876657\ldots, 12.454\ldots, ^{-}0.\overline{8233}, \frac{17}{25}, 1\frac{14}{57}, \sqrt{13}$

   (D) $\frac{5}{16}, 0.443, ^{-}0.57834\ldots, ^{-}0.\overline{310489}, ^{-}2.0653, ^{-}\sqrt{89}$

5. Which of the following does not show the correct number for the plotted point on the number line?

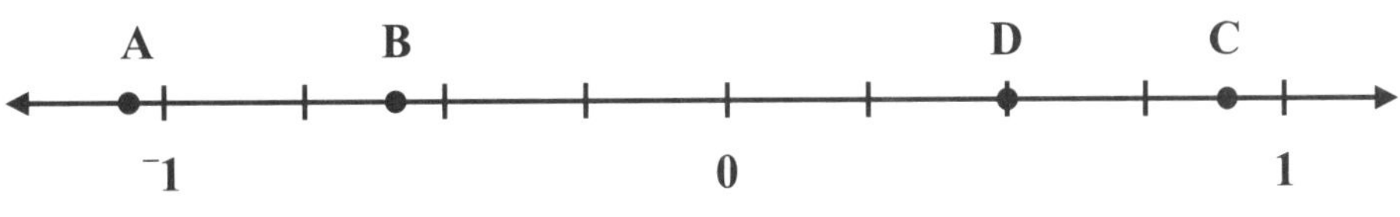

   (A) $^{-}0.88432$ (B) $-\frac{2}{3}$ (C) $0.8423432\ldots$ (D) 0.5

Four Digit Fun with Coordinates: Graphing Segments – Day 25

Name: ______________________________ Date: ______________

Write all the ordered pairs that can be created from the digits 3, 5, 7, and 9. Select pairs of points that will form four of the longest vertical segments that are possible, and plot them on the grid provided. Label them $\overline{AB}$, $\overline{CD}$, $\overline{EF}$, and $\overline{GH}$, from left to right.

____

____

____

____

Tell how many units are in the length of each segment.

$\overline{AB}$ ____________ $\overline{CD}$ ____________ $\overline{EF}$ ____________ $\overline{GH}$ ____________

Graph the pairs of coordinates that will form horizontal line segments that are 6 units in length.

A (0,8) B (6,8)
C (2,1) D (2,7)
E (1,6) F (7,6)
G (2,4) H (8,4)
I (4,2) J (4,8)
K (6,3) L (6,9)
M (3,2) N (9,2)

What do you notice about the coordinates that form horizontal line segments?

____

Four Digit Fun with Coordinates: Creating Rectangles – Day 26

Name: ______________________________ Date: ______________

Select and then plot four ordered pairs from the nine listed below that will form a rectangle that has a height of 4 units and a base with a length of 7 units.

(1,3), (1,4), (1,7)

(7,3), (7,4), (7,7)

(8,3), (8,4), (8,7)

Selected points: ____________________

What is the area of this rectangle? __________

What is the perimeter of this rectangle? ________

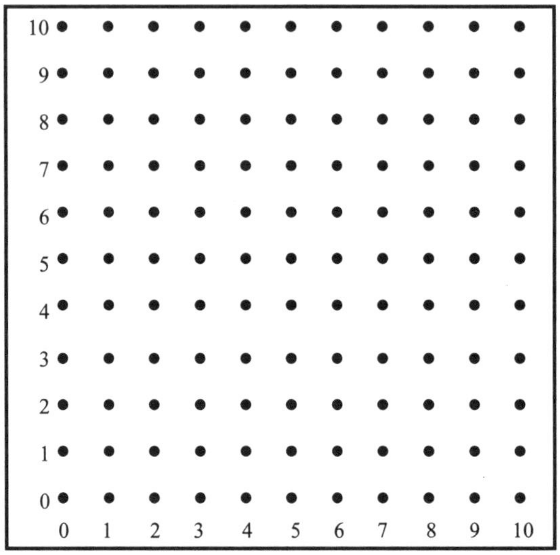

Create a rectangle whose area is 35 square units such that one of the vertices is located at (2,4). Then list the coordinates of the endpoints that form the sides of the rectangle.

____

____

____

____

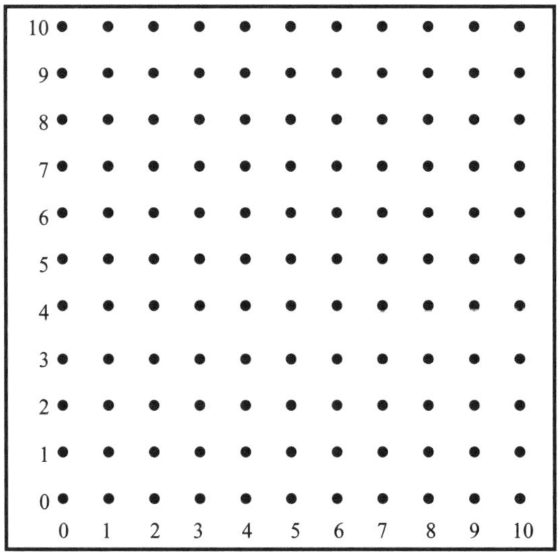

What is the perimeter of this rectangle? __________

Four Digit Fun with Coordinates: Area and Perimeter 1 – Day 27

Name: ______________________________ Date: ______________

1. List all the ordered pairs that can created from the digits 2, 6, 7, and 10.

____

____

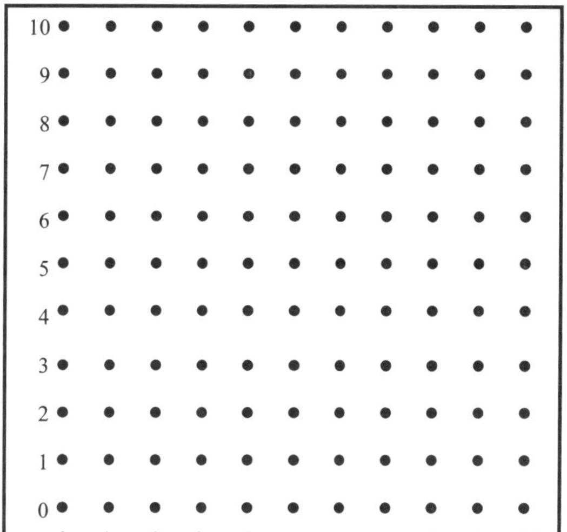

2. List and then plot the ordered pairs that can be used to create a rectangle whose area is 12 square unit and perimeter is 14 units.

____

____

3. Which of the following sets of ordered pairs form a rectangle whose area is 40 square units and whose perimeter is 26 units? Plot the set to verify results.

   Set A: (0,2), (0,4), (10,2), (10,4)

   Set B: (1,3), (1,8), (9,3), (9,8)

   Set C: (0,0), (0,10), (4,0), (4,10)

   Set D: (2,1), (2,6), (7,1), (7,6)

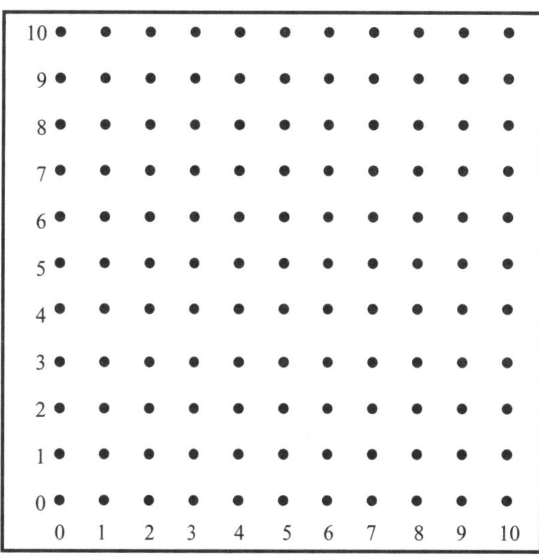

4. Create a set of ordered pairs that will make a rectangle whose area is 42 square units and whose perimeter is 26 units and that has one vertex at (4,2).

____

Four Digit Fun with Coordinates: Area and Perimeter 2 – Day 28

Name: ______________________________ Date: ______________

1. All three of the sets of ordered pairs shown below form rectangles whose areas are 36 square units. Determine the set that has the smallest perimeter and graph the figure.

   Set A: (1,2), (1,6), (10,2), (10,6)

   Set B: (0,1), (0,10), (4,1), (4,10)

   Set C: (0,3), (0,9), (6,3), (6,9)

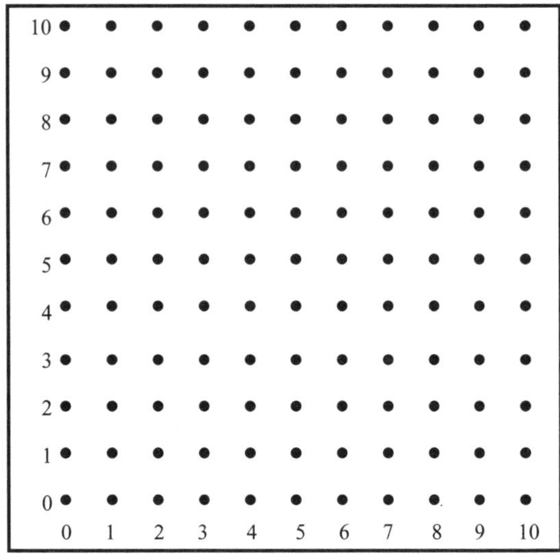

2. List all the ordered pairs that can created from the digits 1, 0, 4, 9.

   ____

   ____

3. List and then plot the ordered pairs that can be used to create a rectangle with the largest possible area.

   ____

   ____

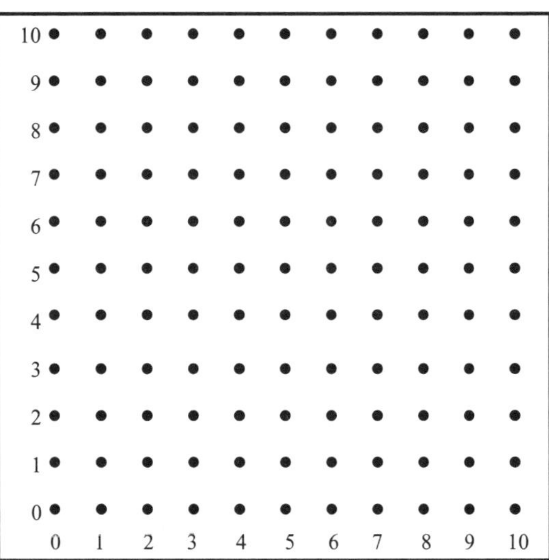

4. What is the perimeter of the figure that has the largest area? ______________

Four Digit Fun with Coordinates: Assessment – Day 29

Name: ______________________________ Date: ______________

1. Which of the following sets of ordered pairs form a pair of vertical parallel line segments that are 5 units apart?

(A) (3,1), (3,6) and (5,1), (5,6)
(B) (4,2), (8,2) and (4,7), (8,7)
(C) (1,3), (1,10) and (6,3), (6,10)
(D) (3,1), (8,1) and (3,6), (8, 6)

2. Which set of ordered pairs forms a rectangle whose base has a length of 4 units and whose height is 6 units?

(A) (2,1), (2,7), (6,1), (6,7)
(B) (2,1), (8,1), (2,5), (8,5)
(C) (0,0), (0,4), (6,0), (6,4)
(D) (0,0), (2,6), (4,0), (6,6)

3. The coordinates of the endpoints that form a horizontal line segment must:

(A) have the same x-coordinates
(B) have the same y-coordinates
(C) include the point (0,0).
(D) form a segment that is 5 units in length.

4. List all the ordered pairs that can be formed from the digits 4, 2, 8, 5.

5. List the ordered pairs from Problem #4 that will create a rectangle whose area is 12 square units. Then plot the ordered pairs and draw the rectangle.

Four Digit Fun with Coordinates – Computation in Context – Day 30

Name: ______________________________ Date: ______________

Study the twelve problems below, and decide whether to use mental math, paper and pencil, or estimation and a calculator to complete each by circling the method. Write answers or estimates in the blanks at the right.

			Estimate / Exact Answer
1. $\begin{array}{r} 35 \\ +68 \\ \hline \end{array}$ PP MM EC	2. $456 + 341 + 702 =$ PP MM EC	3. $14{,}235 + 2986 + 75 + 634 =$ PP MM EC	1. ____ ____ 2. ____ ____ 3. ____ ____
4. $\begin{array}{r} 8502 \\ -\ \ 387 \\ \hline \end{array}$ PP MM EC	5. $325 \div 25 =$ PP MM EC	6. $456 \times 873 =$ PP MM EC	4. ____ ____ 5. ____ ____ 6. ____ ____
7. $101 - 76 =$ PP MM EC	8. $3654 \div 63 =$ PP MM EC	9. $\begin{array}{r} 29 \\ \times 32 \\ \hline \end{array}$ PP MM EC	7. ____ ____ 8. ____ ____ 9. ____ ____
10. $2811 - 294 =$ PP MM EC	11. $43\overline{)4214}$ PP MM EC	12. $\begin{array}{r} 78 \\ -43 \\ \hline \end{array}$ PP MM EC	10. ____ ____ 11. ____ ____ 12. ____ ____

Angles and Polygons: Classifying Angles – Day 31

Name: ______________________________ Date: ______________

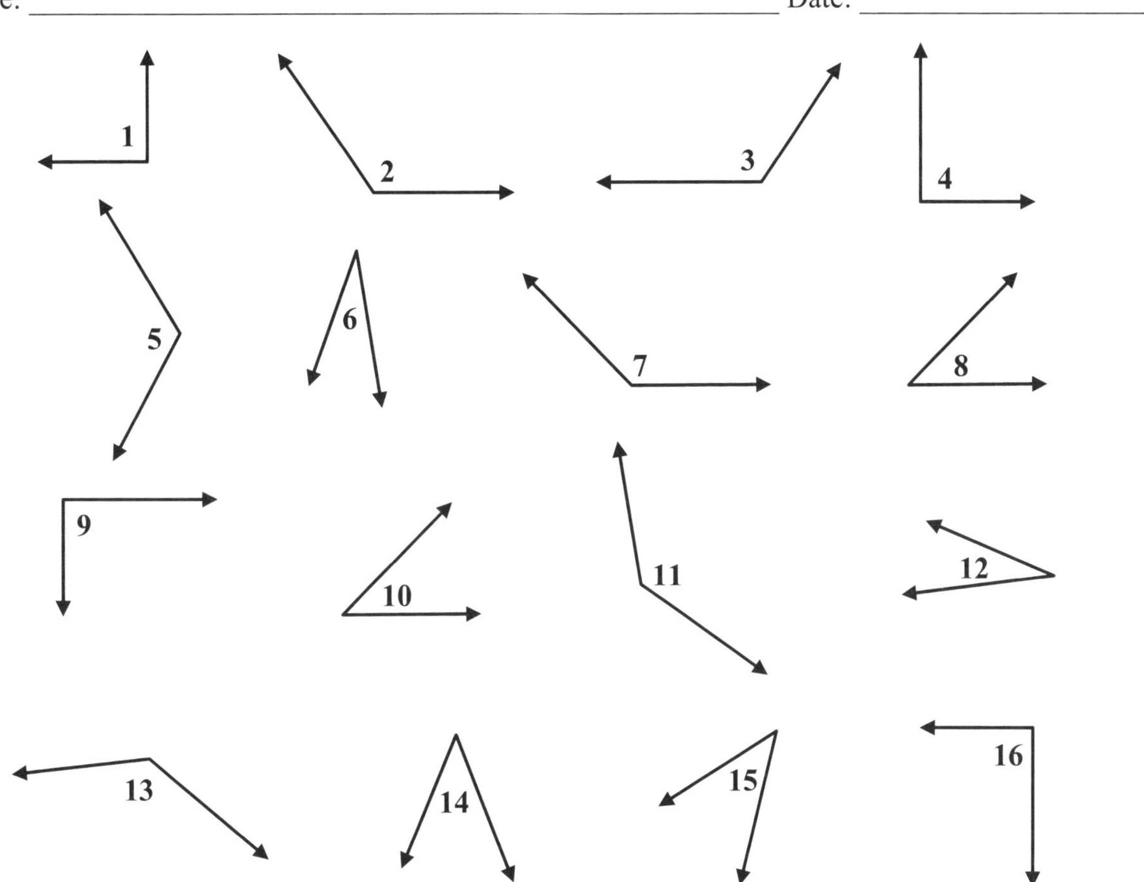

1. List the angles that appear to be right angles. ______________________
2. List the angles that appear to be acute angles. ______________________
3. Which angles appear to be congruent to ∠ 2? ______________________
4. Based on the pattern above what kind of angle would be ∠17? ______________________
5. Based on the pattern above, in which place would the next right angle occur?

6. Based on the pattern of angles below, what kind of angle would be in the 100th position?

Applying Straight, Complementary and Supplementary Angles – Day 32

Name: ______________________________ Date: ______________

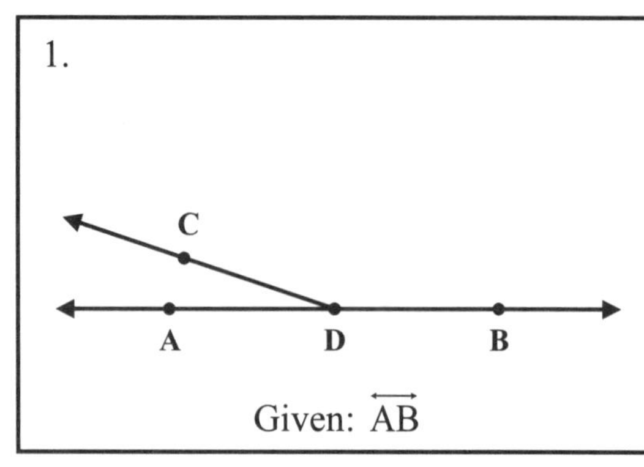

Given: $\overleftrightarrow{AB}$

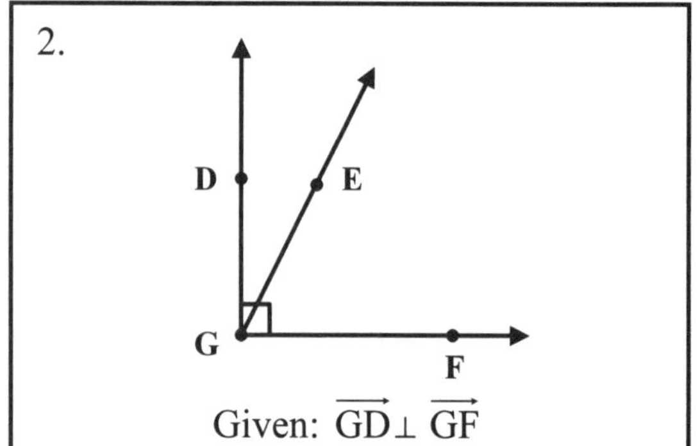

Given: $\overrightarrow{GD} \perp \overrightarrow{GF}$

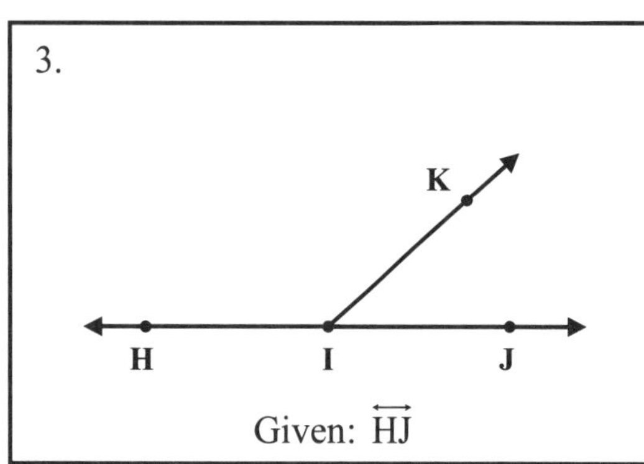

Given: $\overleftrightarrow{HJ}$

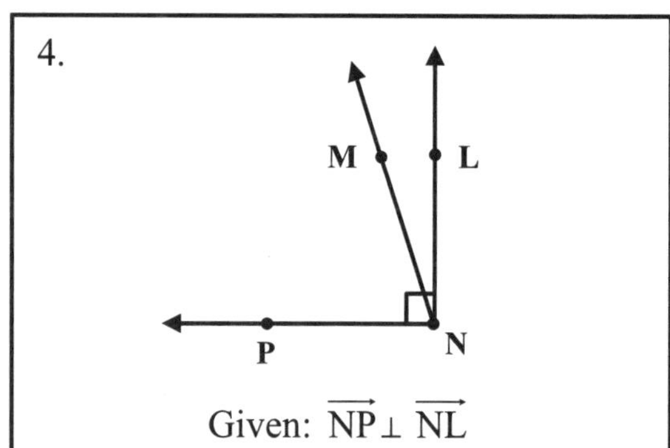

Given: $\overrightarrow{NP} \perp \overrightarrow{NL}$

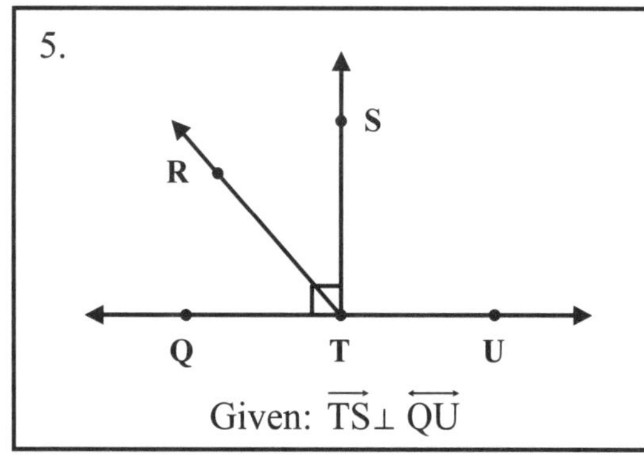

Given: $\overrightarrow{TS} \perp \overleftrightarrow{QU}$

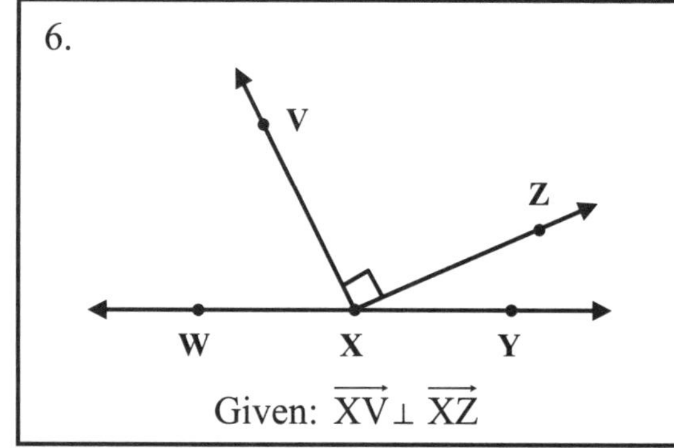

Given: $\overrightarrow{XV} \perp \overrightarrow{XZ}$

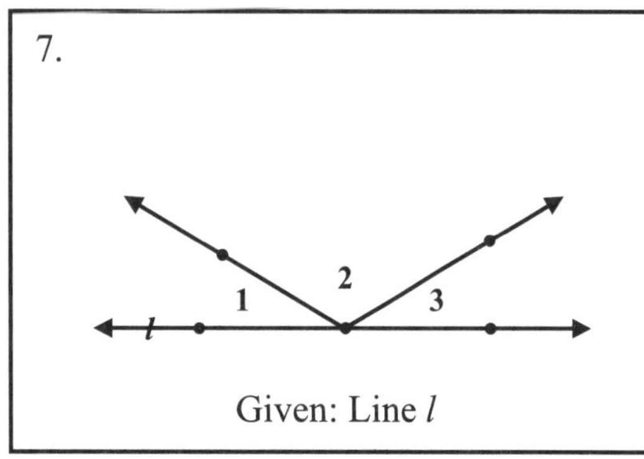

Given: Line *l*

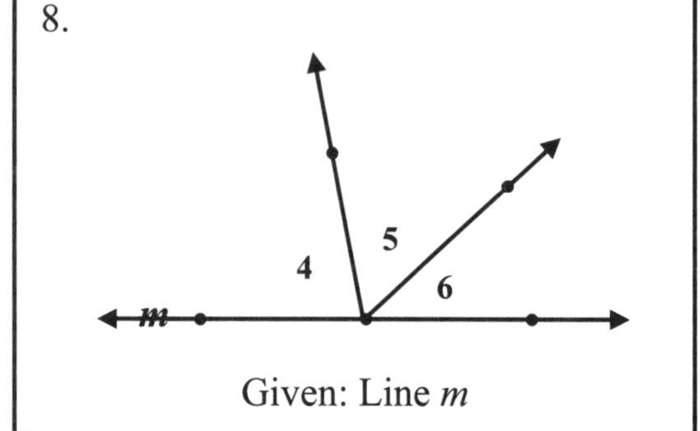

Given: Line *m*

Use the angles on the previous page to answer the questions below.

1. What is the measure of ∠ ADC if ∠ CDB measures 158°? ________________

2. What is the measure of ∠ EGF if ∠ DGE measures 15°? ________________

3. What is the measure of ∠ KIJ if ∠ KIH measures 138°? ________________

4. What is the measure of ∠ MNP if ∠ MNL measures 20°? ________________

5. What is the measure of ∠ RTS if ∠ STU measures 90° and ∠ RTQ measures 45°? ________________

6. What is the measure of ∠ VXW if ∠ VXZ is a right angle and ∠ ZXY measures 22°? ________________

7. If ∠ 1 = ∠ 3 and each measures 32°, what is the measure of ∠ 2? ________________

8. What is the measure of ∠ 4 and ∠ 5 if ∠ 6 = 45° and ∠ 5 is 10° more than ∠ 6.

Working with Angles and Parallel Lines – Day 33

Name: ______________________________ Date: ______________

Given: $r \parallel s$

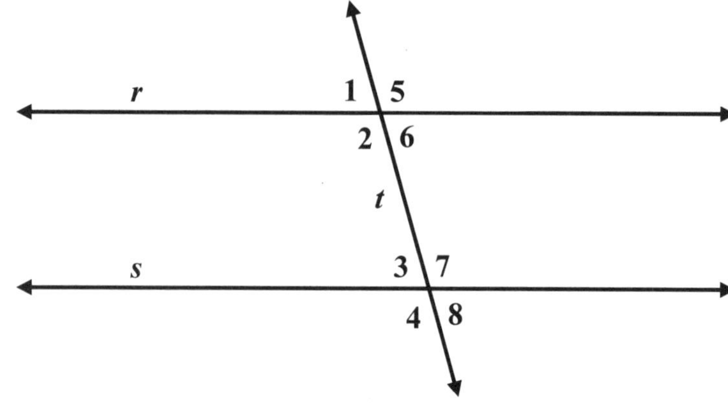

Use the diagram above to answer Questions 1 – 7. When describing angles, use as many terms as appropriate.

1. Highlight $\angle 1$. List all the angles that are equal in measure to $\angle 1$. ______________

2. What kind of angles are $\angle 3$ and $\angle 8$?

3. What kind of angles are $\angle 2$ and $\angle 6$?

4. What kind of angles are $\angle 2$ and $\angle 7$?

5. What kind of angles are $\angle 7$ and $\angle 8$?

6. What kind of angles are $\angle 6$ and $\angle 7$?

7. Determine the measures of angles 1 – 2 and 4 – 8 if the measure of $\angle 3 = 56°$

$\angle 1$ ________ $\angle 2$ ________ $\angle 3$ ________ $\angle 4$ ________

$\angle 5$ ________ $\angle 6$ ________ $\angle 7$ ________ $\angle 8$ ________

Sum of the Angles in a Triangle – Day 34

Name: ______________________________ Date: ______________

1. How do you know that a triangle cannot have both a right angle and an obtuse angle?

____

____

2. How do you know that a triangle cannot have two obtuse angles?

____

____

Of the nine angles below, three will form a right triangle, three will form an obtuse triangle, and three will form an acute triangle. Name the angles that will form each of the triangles.

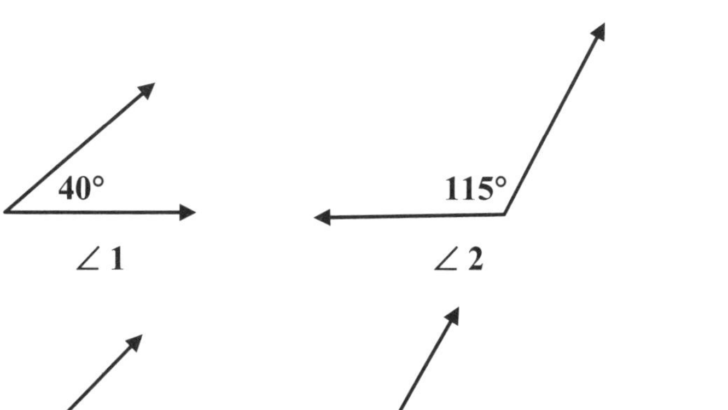

90°
∠3

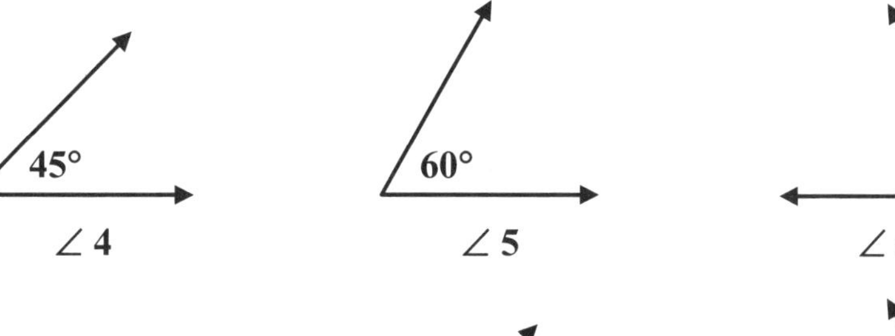

60°
∠6

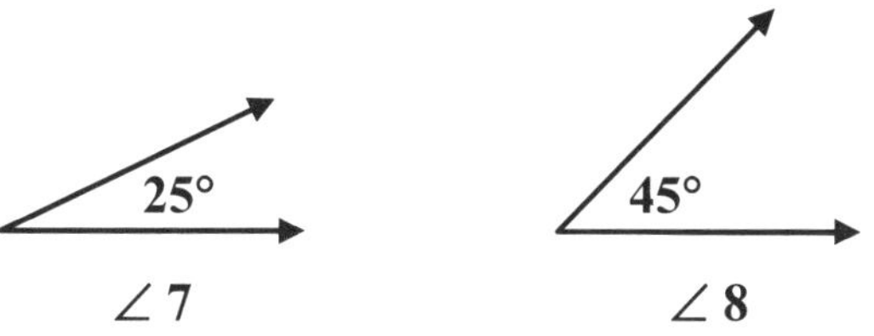

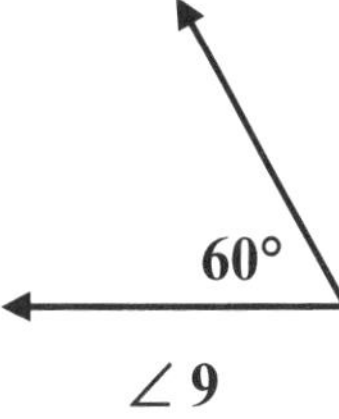

3. Right triangle: ____________________

4. Obtuse triangle: ____________________

5. Acute triangle: ____________________

Sum of the Angles in a Polygon – Day 35

Name: ______________________________ Date: ______________

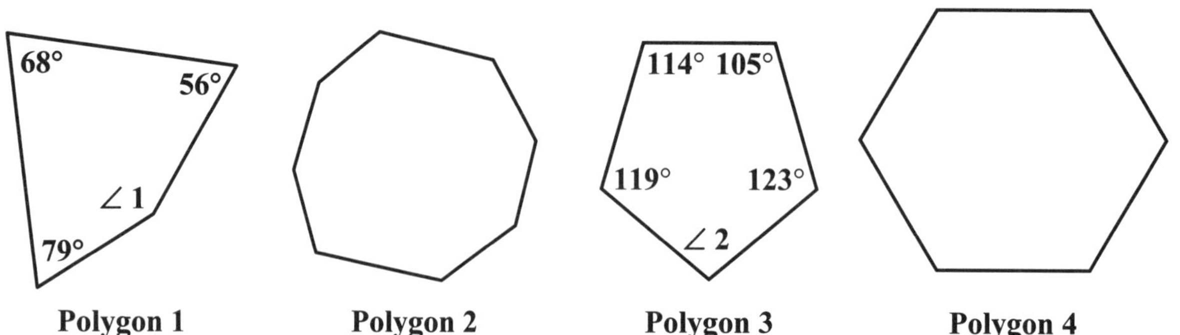

Polygon 1 Polygon 2 Polygon 3 Polygon 4

1. How many degrees are in ∠ 1? ____________

2. How many degrees are in all the angles in Polygon 2? ____________

3. How many degrees are in ∠2? ____________

4. If all the angles in Polygon 4 have the same measure, what is the measure of one of the angles?

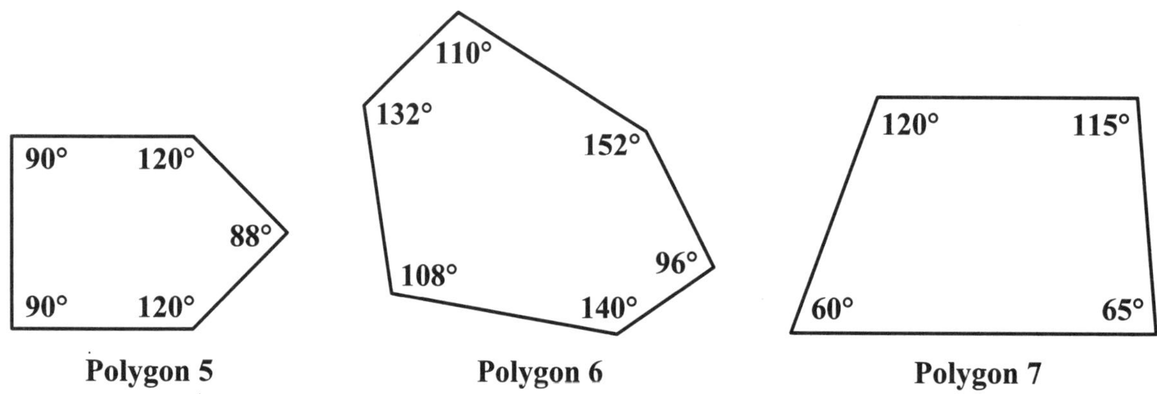

Polygon 5 Polygon 6 Polygon 7

Two of the polygons above have mistakes because the sum of the angles is incorrect. Which two are they?

Angles and Polygons – Assessment – Day 36

Name: ______________________________ Date: ______________

Given: $m \parallel n$

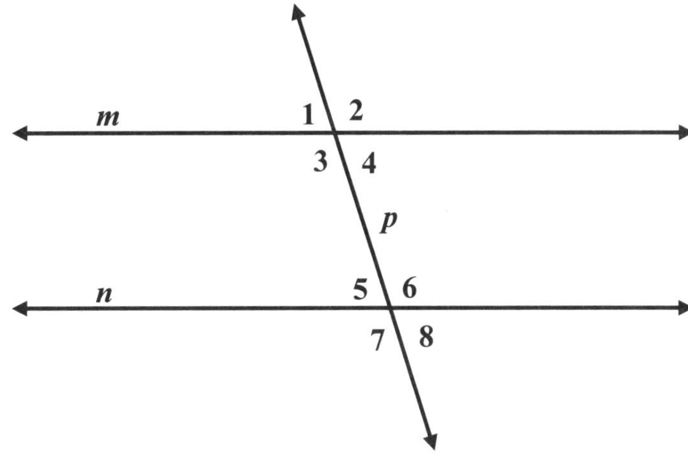

1. If $\angle 6 = 105°$, then which of the choices below is true?

   (A) $\angle 4 = 105°$ (B) $\angle 2 = 75°$ (C) $\angle 1 = 105°$ (D) $\angle 5 = 75°$

2. Which of the following angles sum to 180°?

   (A) $\angle 4$ and $\angle 6$ (B) $\angle 3$ and $\angle 6$ (C) $\angle 6$ and $\angle 7$ (D) $\angle 2$ and $\angle 6$

3. Which of the following is NOT a true statement?

   (A) Supplementary angles must be adjacent angles.

   (B) Corresponding angles are equal in measure.

   (C) Vertical angles are equal in measure.

   (D) Vertical angles cannot have a common side.

4. By connecting one vertex to all of the other vertices in a polygon, Jedeiah created two non-overlapping triangles. Based on this information, what type of polygon is this?

   (A) heptagon (B) hexagon (C) pentagon (D) quadrilateral

5. What is the measure of each interior angle in a regular octagon?

   (A) 108° (B) 120° (C) 135° (D) 1040°

Use the angles below to answer Questions 6 and 7. You may want to use your Communicator® clearboard to help determine the answers.

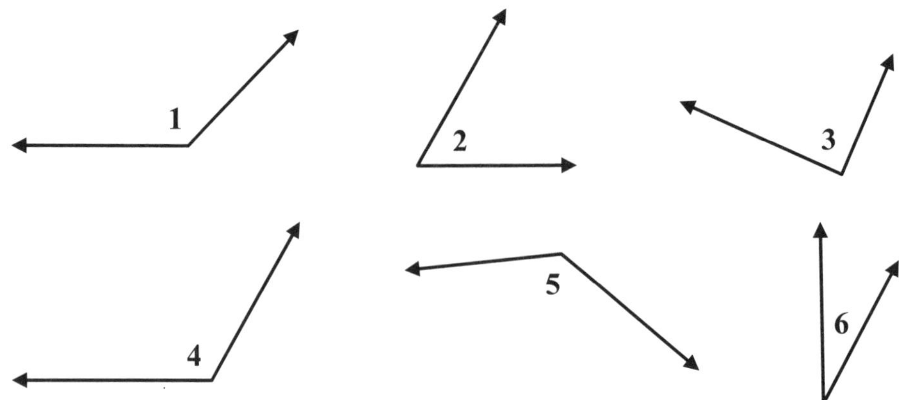

6. Which two angles best represent supplementary angles?

   (A) ∠ 1 and ∠ 3 (B) ∠ 2 and ∠ 6 (C) ∠ 2 and ∠ 5 (D) ∠ 2 and ∠ 4

7. Angle 6 and ∠ 2 form complementary angles. If ∠ 6 measures 30°, what is the measure of ∠ 2?

   (A) 20° (B) 60° (C) 90° (D) 150°

Regular and Irregular Polygons – Day 37

Name: ______________________________________ Date: ________________

Study the figures in the table below. Then answer the questions on this and the next page.

1. 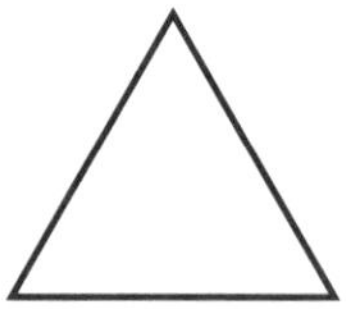	**2.**	**3.** 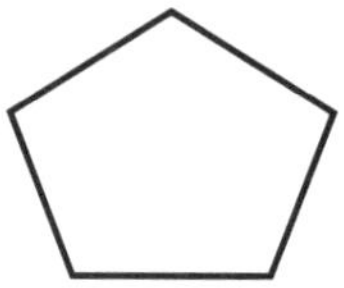	**4.** 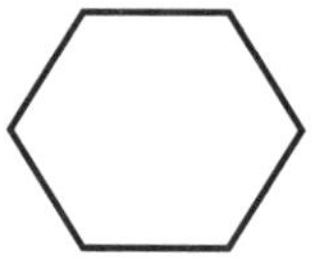
5. 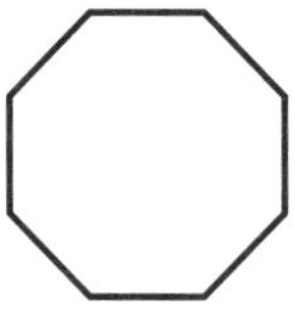	**6.** 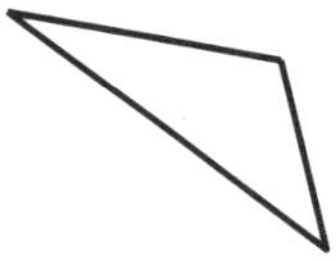	**7.** 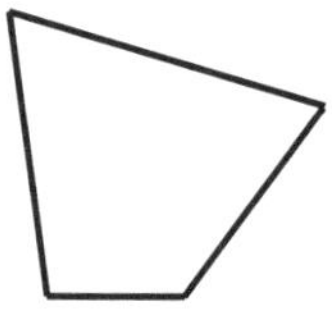	**8.** 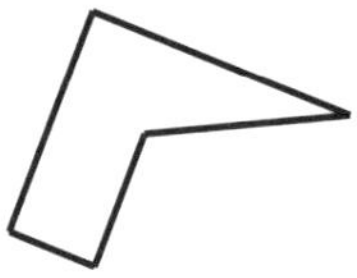
9. 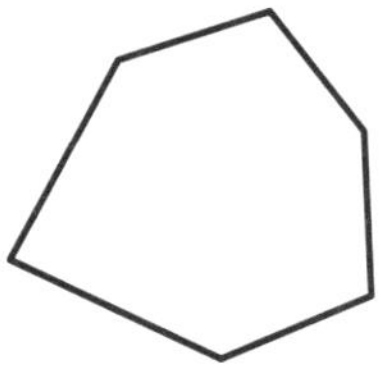	**10.** 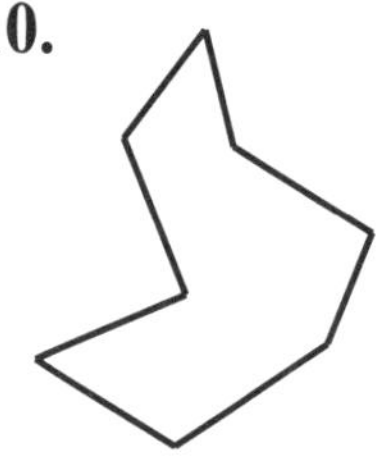	**11.** 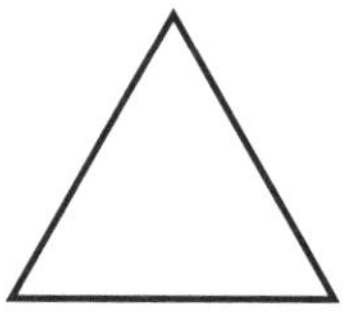	**12.**
13. 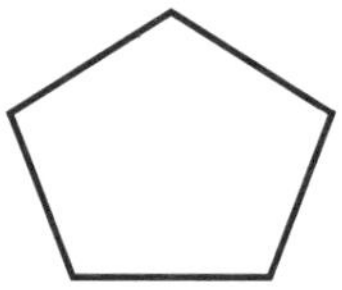	**14.** 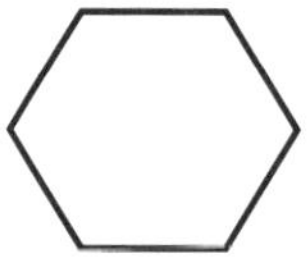	**15.** 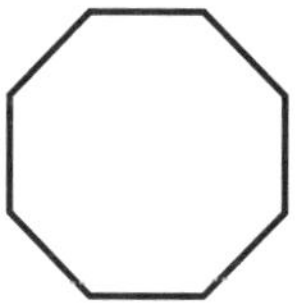	**16.** 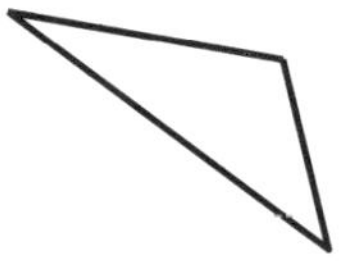

1. Which boxes appear to contain equilateral triangles? ____________________

2. Which boxes appear to contain regular polygons? ____________________

3. Which boxes appear to contain octagons? ____________________

4. What kind of figures are in Boxes 2, 7, and 12? ____________________

5. Which boxes show regular hexagons? ____________________

6. If the pattern of the boxes continues, what figure will be in Box 17? ____________________

7. If the pattern were to continue, after Box 16, what would be the next box to contain an irregular pentagon?

8. The length of a side of the figure in Box 4 is 8 units. What is its perimeter?

9. The length of a side of the figure in Box 12 is 5 units. What is its area? ____________________

10. List the boxes that appear to contain figures that are congruent to the shape in Box 15?

11. If the pattern below were to continue, what would the next two figures be?

△ □ ⬠ △ □ ⬠ △ ____________ ____________

12. If the pattern above were to continue, what figure would be in the 27th place?

Identifying and Classifying Triangles – Day 38

Name: ______________________________ Date: ______________

Study the figures in the table below. Then answer the questions on the next page.

1. 	2. 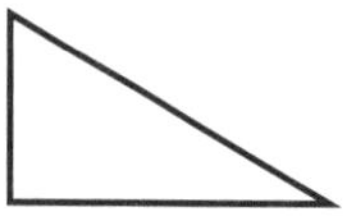	3. 	4. 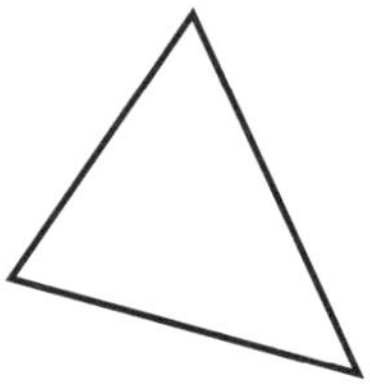
5. 	6. 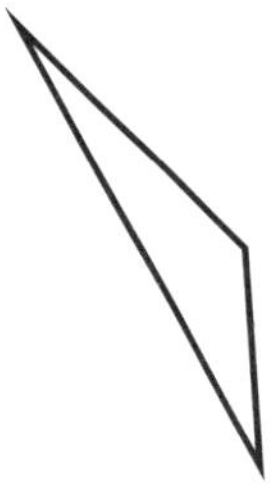	7. 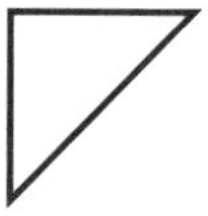	8. 
9. 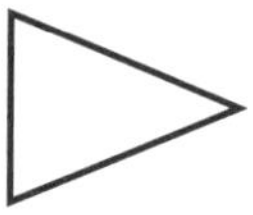	10. 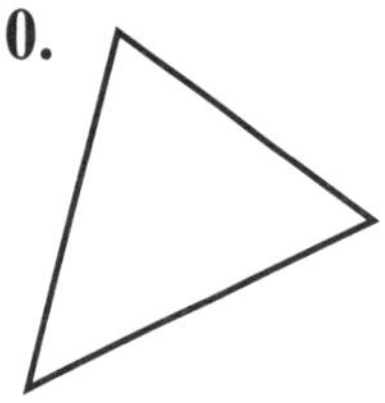	11. 	12. 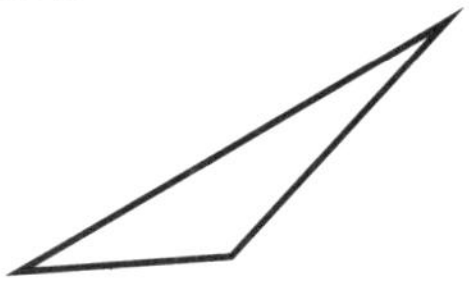
13. 	14. 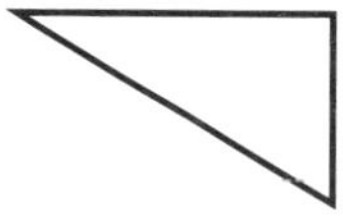	15. 	16. 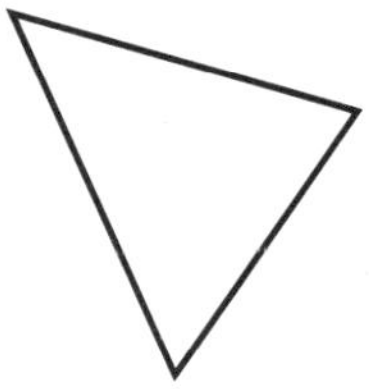

1. Which boxes appear to contain isosceles right triangles? ____________

2. What kind of triangle appears to be in Box 5? ____________

3. Which boxes appear to contain scalene obtuse triangles? ____________

4. Which boxes contain figures that appear to be congruent to the figure in Box 3?

5. Which boxes appear to contain scalene acute triangles? ____________

6. If the pattern of the boxes continues, what figure will be in Box 17?

7. In which box will the figure in Box 7 be shown in exactly the same position?

8. After Box 16, in which box will the next acute scalene triangle appear? ____________

9. Describe the relationship between each consecutive pair of triangles.

____

____

____

____

10. If the pattern below were to continue, what would the next two figures be?

△ ▷ ▽ ◁ △ ▷ ▽ ◁ △ ▷ ____________ ____________

Identifying and Classifying Quadrilaterals – Day 39

Name: ______________________________ Date: ______________

Study the figures in the table below. Then answer the questions on the next page.

1. 	2. 	3. 	4. 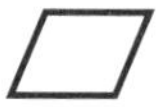
5. 	6. 	7. 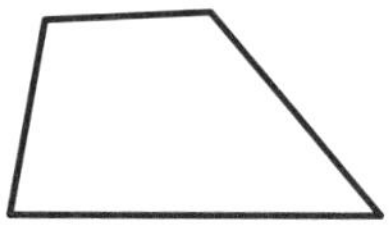	8. 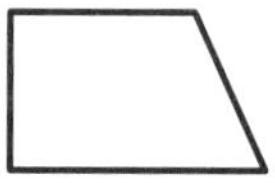
9. 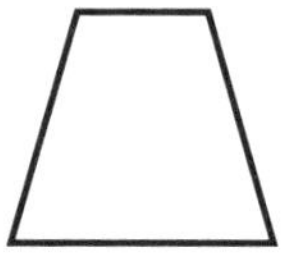	10. 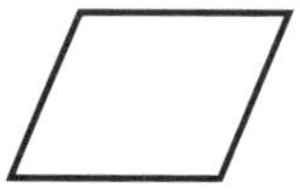	11. 	12.
13. 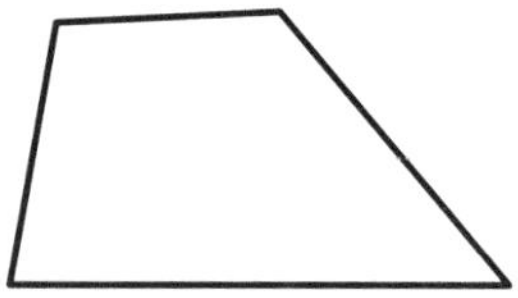	14. 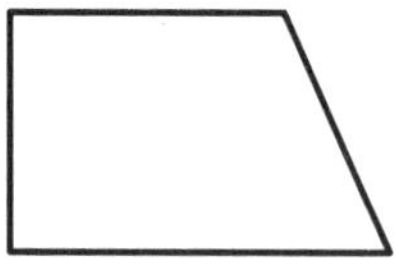	15. 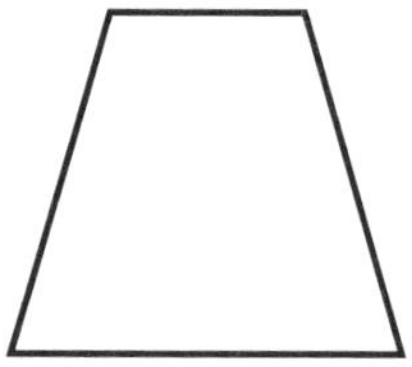	16. 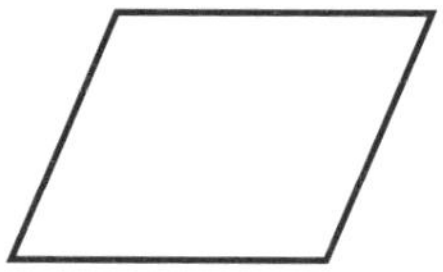

1. What one name can be used to describe all of the figures in Boxes 1 – 16? ________________

2. What is the most specific name for the figure that appears to be in Box 2? ________________

3. Which boxes appear to contain rectangles? ________________

4. Which boxes appear to contain figures that are similar to the figure in Box 1? ____________

5. What one term describes the figures that appear to be in Boxes 4, 5 and 6? ________________

6. If the pattern of boxes continues, what figure would be in Box 17?

7. After Box 16, in which box will the next square appear? ________________

8. After Box 16, in which box will the next isosceles trapezoid appear? ________________

9. How many times larger than the original will the figures in Boxes 19 – 24 be?

10. If the pattern below were to continue, what would the next two figures be? Sketch your answer in the two blanks below.

________________ ________________

11. If the pattern above were to continue, what would be the 24th figure?

Identifying and Classifying Solids – Day 40

Name: ______________________________ Date: ______________

Study the figures in the table below. Then answer the questions on the next page.

1.	2.	3.	4.
5.	6.	7.	8.
9.	10.	11.	12.
13.	14.	15.	16.

1. What name or description can be applied to all of the figures in the table?

2. What kind of figure appears to be in Box 15? ____________________

3. Which boxes appear to contain prisms? ____________________

4. What kind of figures are in the boxes that have prime numbers? ____________________

5. What kind of figures appear to be in the boxes whose numbers are perfect squares?

6. If the pattern were to continue, what figure would be in Box 17? ____________________

7. What name would best describe the figure that will appear in Box 25? ____________________

8. After Box 19, in which box will the next rectangular prism occur?____________________

9. What kind of faces are on a cube?____________________

10. If the pattern below were to continue, what would the next two figures be?

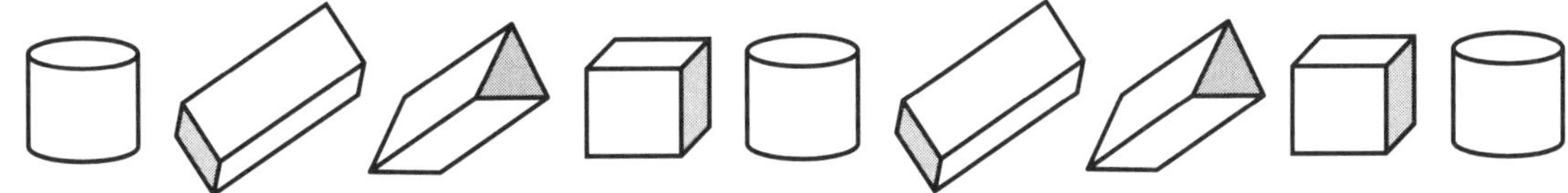

- What figure would be in the 85th place? ____________________

Identifying and Classifying Nets and Solids – Day 41

Name: ______________________________ Date: ______________

Study the figures in the table below. Then answer the questions on the next page.

1. 	2. 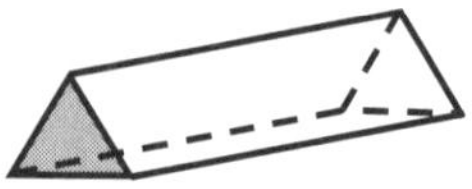	3. 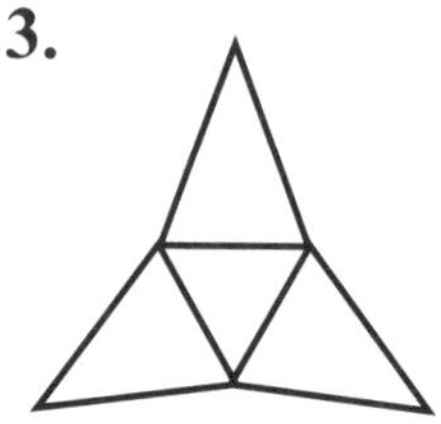	4. 
5. 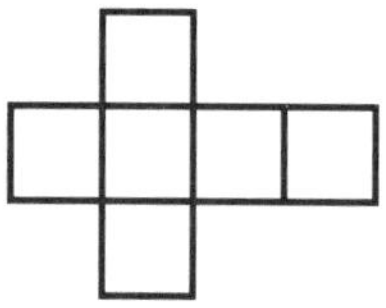	6. 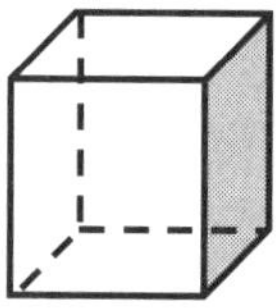	7. 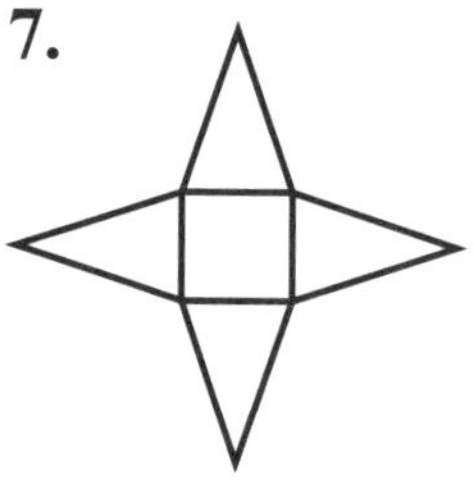	8. 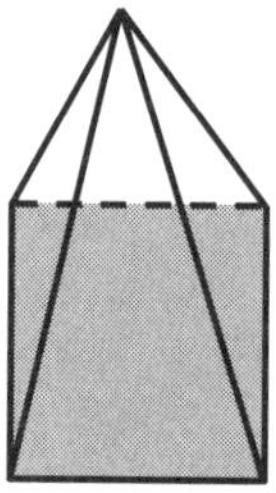
9. 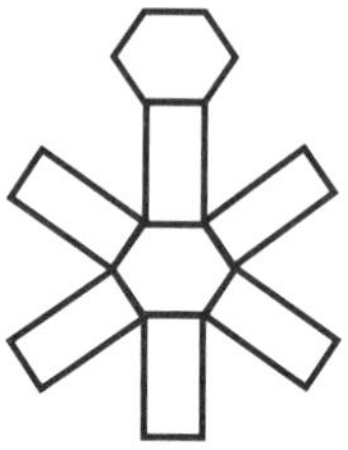	10. 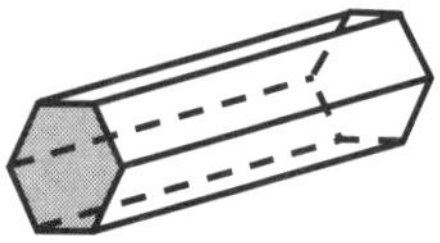	11. 	12. 
13. 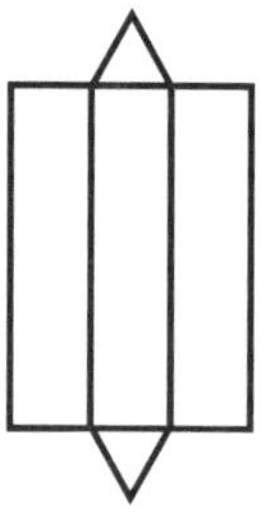	14. 	15. 	16. 

1. Which boxes contain nets? ___________________________

2. What name or description can be applied to all of the shapes in the even-numbered boxes?

3. Which boxes appear to contain prisms? ___________________________

4. Which boxes appear to contain pyramids? ___________________________

5. What kind of shape has exactly two bases? ___________________________

6. If the pattern were to continue, which figure would be in Box 17? ___________________________

7. What name best describes the shape that will appear in Box 20? ___________________________

8. After Box 16, in which box will the next cube appear? ___________________________

9. Which shape will appear in Box 27? ___________________________

10. If the pattern below were to continue, what would the 11th shape be?

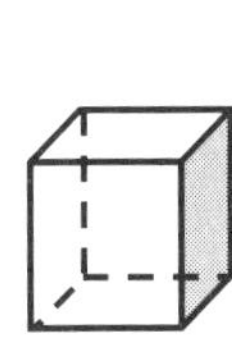  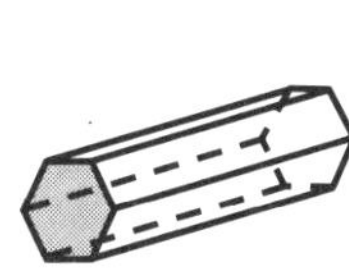  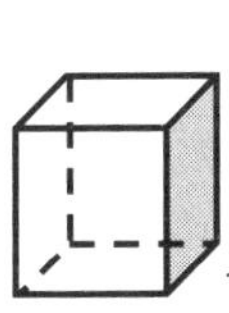 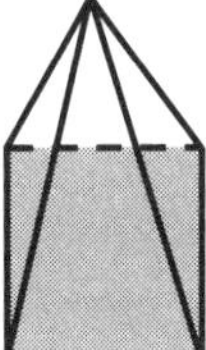 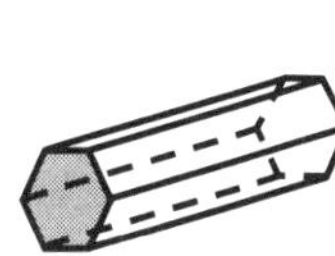 

11. What would the 17th shape be?

Patterns and Shapes – Day 42

Name: ______________________________ Date: ______________

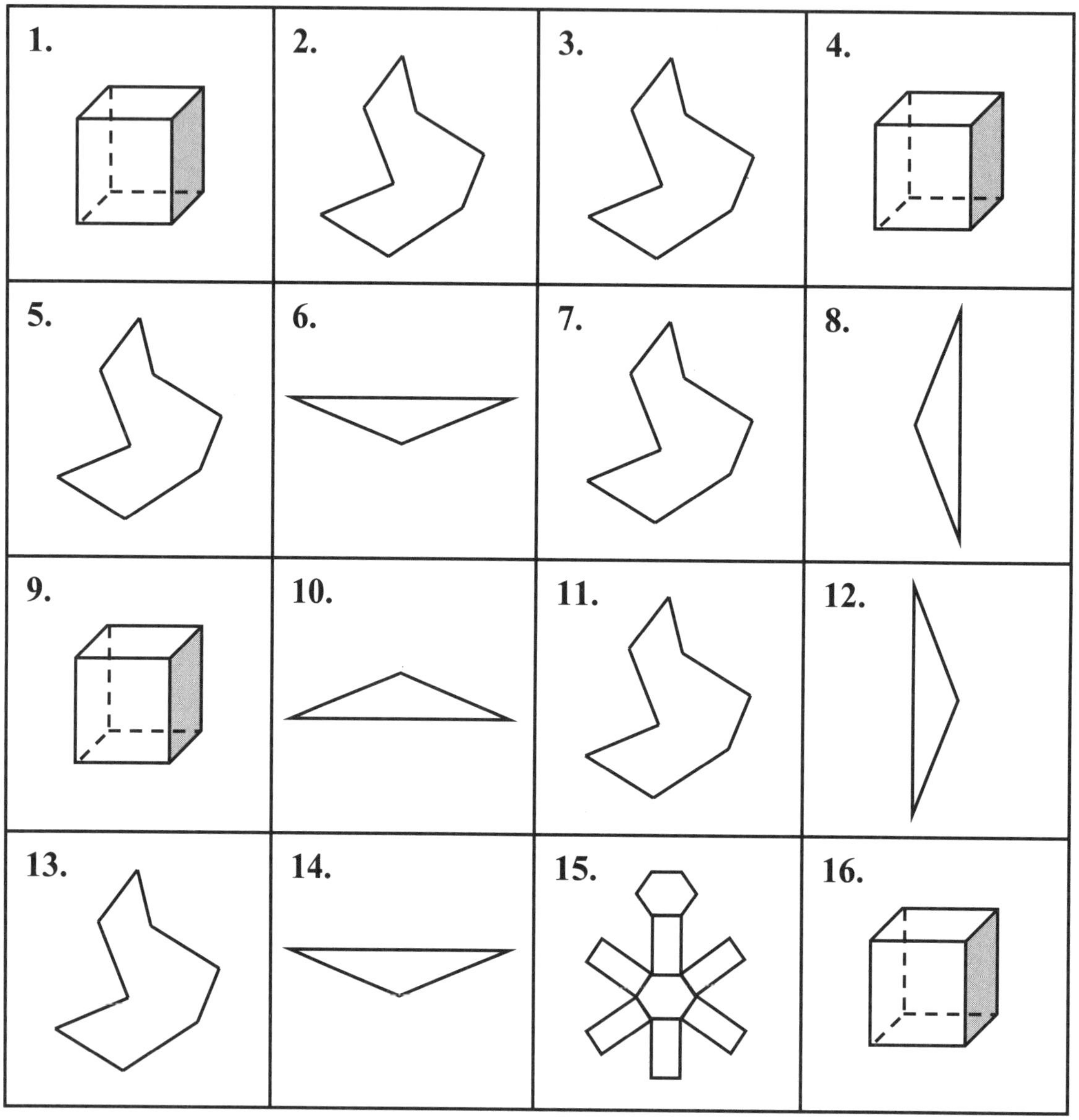

1.	2.	3.	4.
5.	6.	7.	8.
9.	10.	11.	12.
13.	14.	15.	16.

Patterns and Shapes – Assessment – Day 42

Name: ____ Date: ______________

1. If the pattern below were to continue, what would be the most descriptive name for the next figure to appear?

   (A) rhombus (B) square (C) rectangle (D) trapezoid

2. If the pattern below were to continue, what would be the most descriptive name for the 22nd figure in the pattern? (Opposite sides in all figures are parallel and equal in measure.)

   (A) equilateral triangle (B) regular hexagon (C) regular pentagon (D) square

3. Which of following is NOT a true statement about the figures below?

   A B C D

   (A) All of the figures appear to be parallelograms.

   (B) All of the figures are polygons.

   (C) Figures C and D have 4 right angles.

   (D) Figures A and C are regular polygons.

4. Which of the following is a net that will form a rectangular prism?

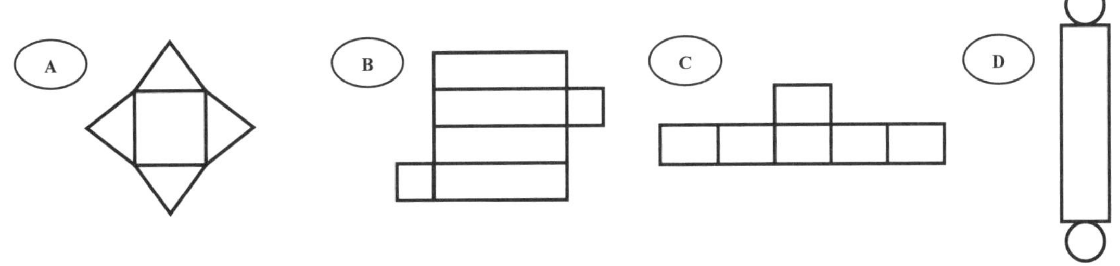

5. If a plane passes through a triangular pyramid parallel to its base, what figure would be formed in the cross section?

   (A) trapezoid (B) rectangle (C) triangle (D) square

6. Which kind of figure has 7 faces, 15 edges, and 10 vertices?

   (A) pentagonal pyramid (B) pentagonal prism
   (C) hexagonal pyramid (D) hexagonal prism

Perimeter and Area of Rectangles and Triangles – Day 43

Name: ______________________________ Date: ______________

Use the columns in the table below to indicate the figures whose areas or perimeters match the dimensions shown.

Area	Perimeter	Length of Base (Units)	Height (Units)
		4	8
		5	9
		3	6
		7	2
		4	2
		4	4

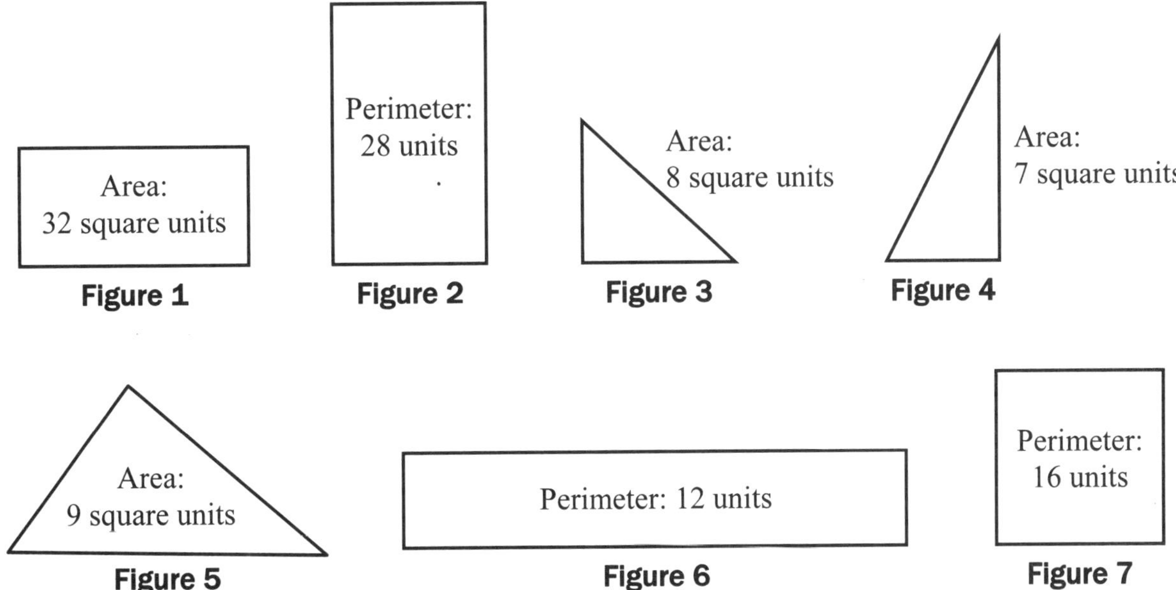

Area of Trapezoids and Parallelograms – Day 44

Name: ______________________________ Date: ______________

Plot the coordinates below and connect them to form a polygon. Determine the area of each of the polygons by partitioning.

1. (1,1), (3,8), (9,8), (7,1)

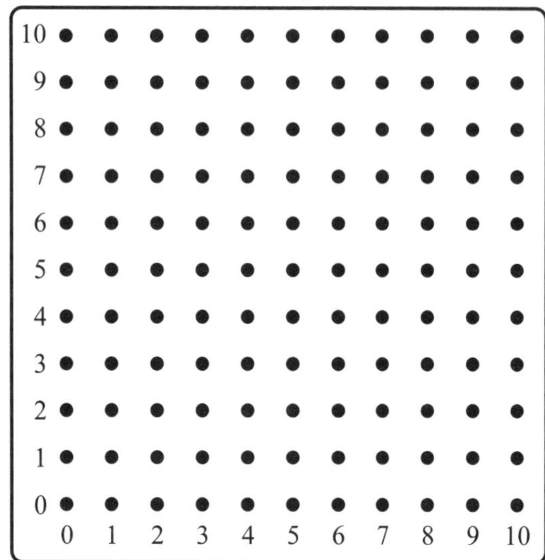

2. (1,2), (2,8), (6,8), (10,2)

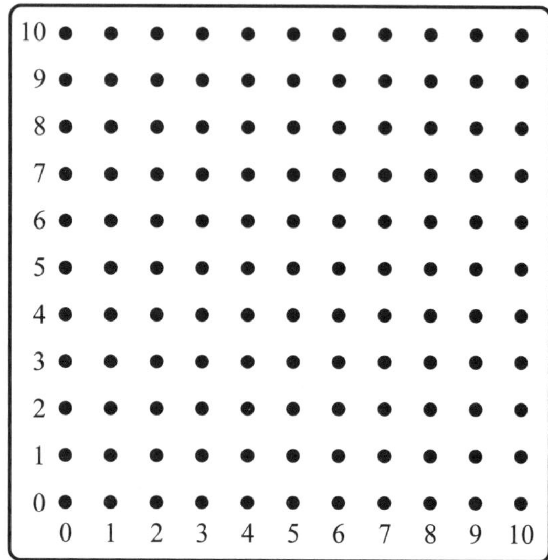

3. (1,8), (6,8), (6,3), (1,0)

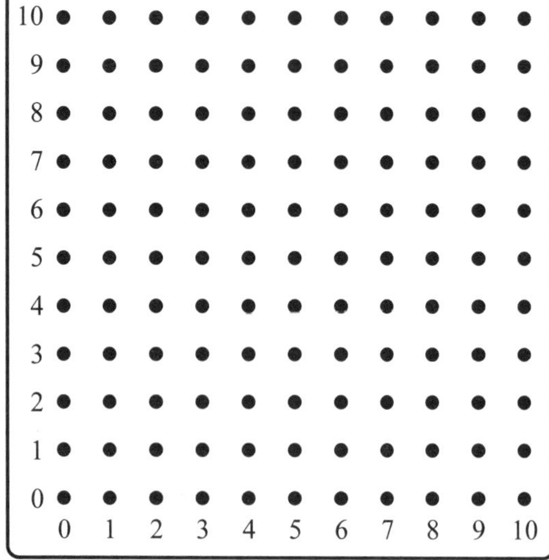

4. The formula for the area of a parallelogram is $A = bh$. The formula for the area of a trapezoid is $A = \frac{1}{2}(b_1 + b_2)h$. For Problems 1 – 3 on the previous page, indicate the length of b, b_1 or b_2, and h. Then use the formula to determine the areas of the figures.

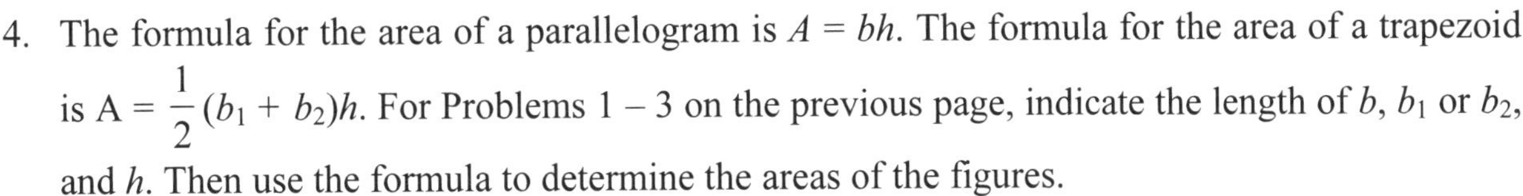

Problem 1: $b =$ __________ $h =$ __________ $A =$ ____________

Problem 2: $b_1 =$ __________ $b_2 =$ __________ $h =$ __________ $A =$ ____________

Problem 3: $b_1 =$ __________ $b_2 =$ __________ $h =$ __________ $A =$ ____________

5. Draw a parallelogram whose area is 35 square units on the geoboard on the left. Then change it into an isosceles trapezoid that has the same area, and draw it on the geoboard on the right. Give the length of each base and the height.

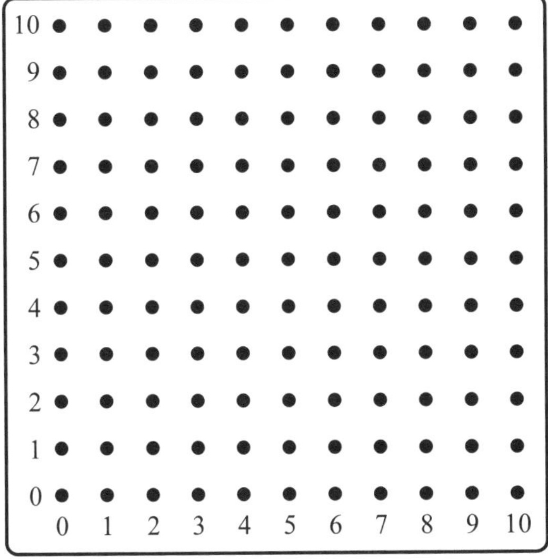

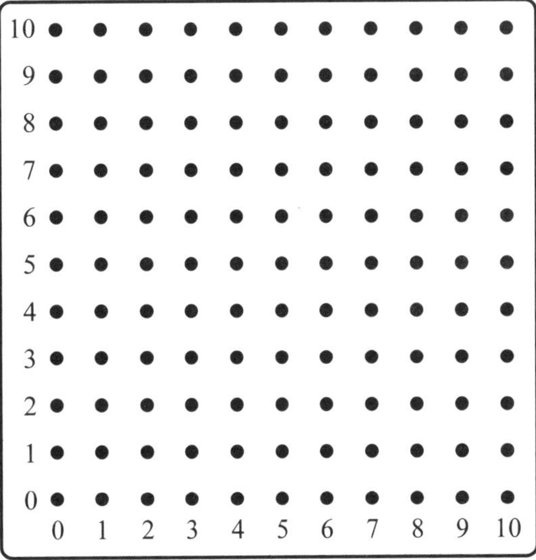

Area and Perimeter of Irregular Figures – Day 45

Name: ______________________________ Date: ______________

Determine the areas of Figures 1 – 3 and the perimeter of Figure 1.

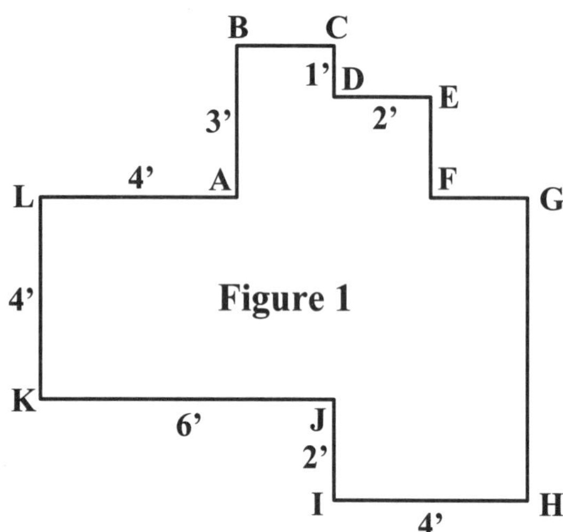

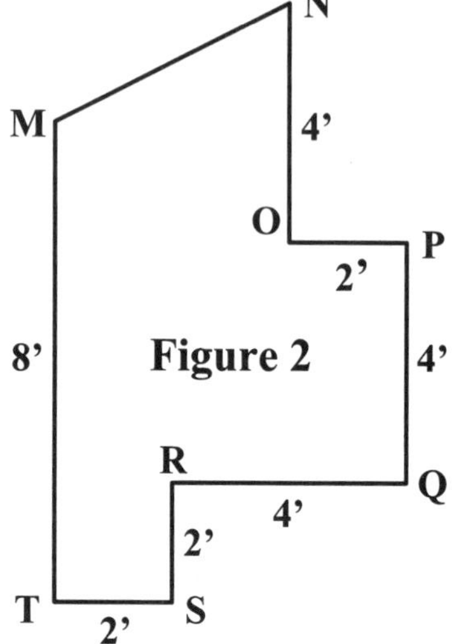

Area: ______________________ Area: ______________________

Perimeter: ______________________

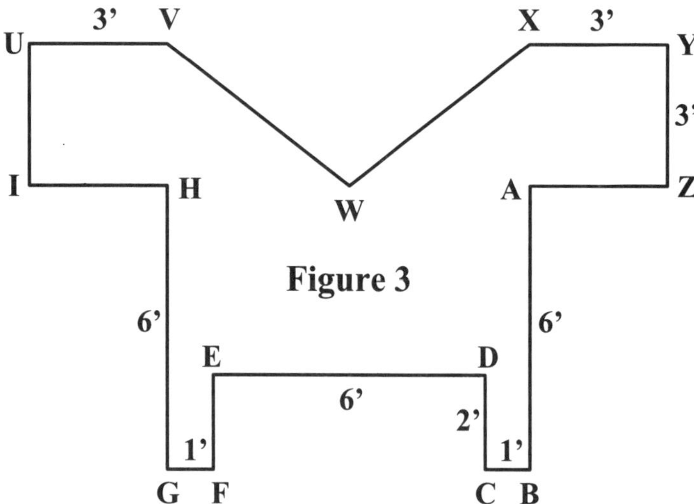

Area: ______________________

Volume of Prisms and Cylinders - Day 46

Name: ______________________________ Date: ____________

Determine the remaining dimensions for each of the figures based on the volume given. The height (H) of all figures is 7 units, and none of the dimensions have a value of 1 unit.

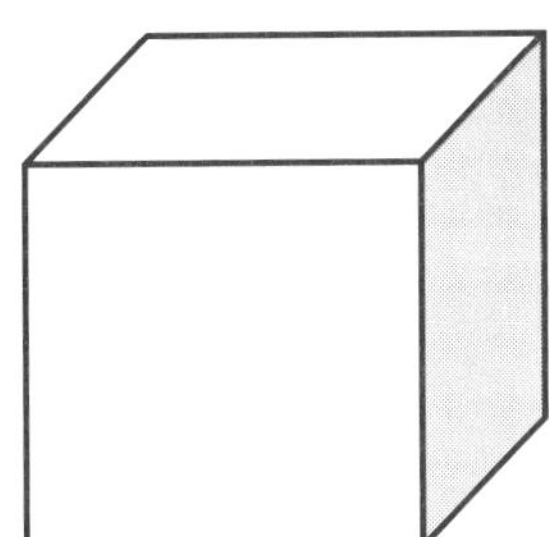

$V = b^2H$

Volume = 343 cubic units.

b = __________

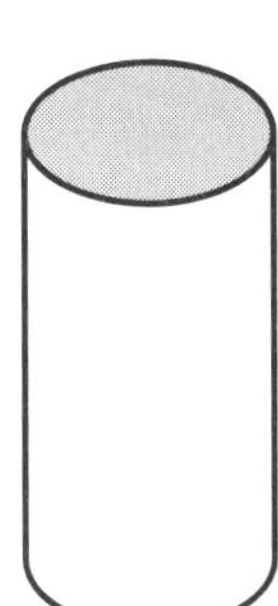

$V = \pi r^2H$

Volume = 87.92 cubic units.

r = __________

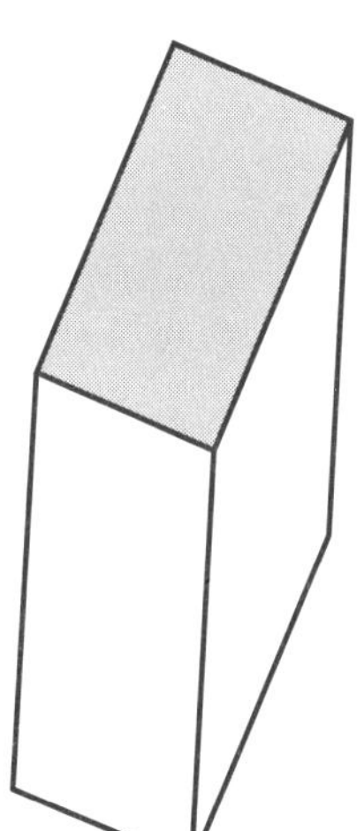

$V = bhH$

Volume = 105 cubic units.

b = __________

h = __________

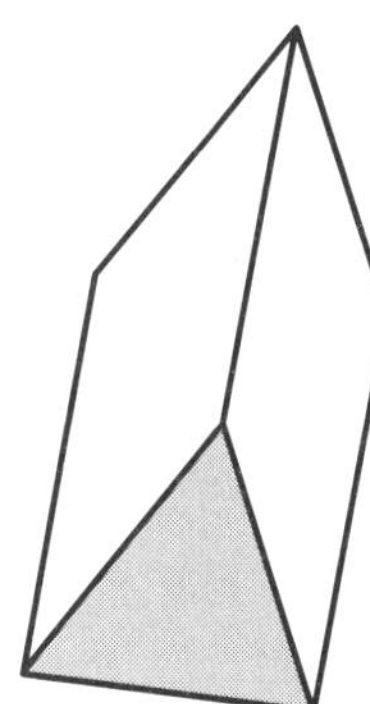

$V = \frac{1}{2}bhH$

Volume = 42 cubic units.

b = __________

h = __________

Volume of Pyramids and Cones – Day 47

Name: ______________________________ Date: ______________

Determine the volume of each of the figures below.

1.

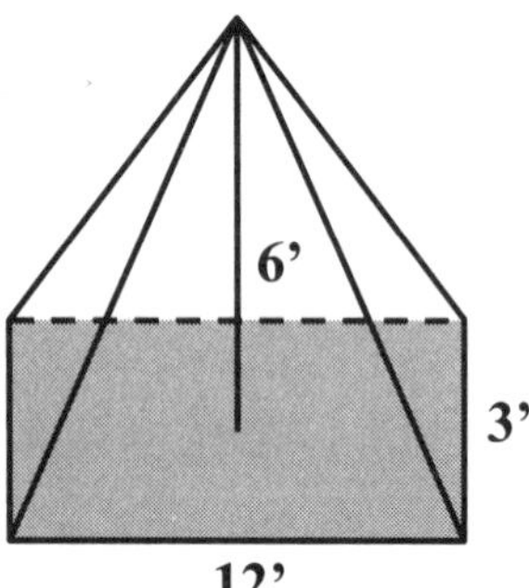

Volume = ____________

2.

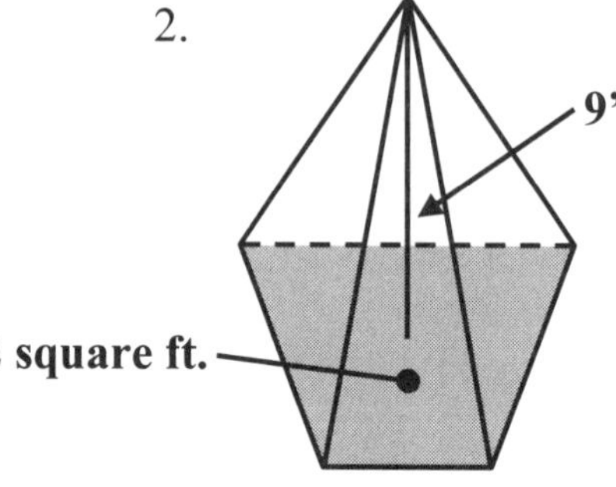

Volume = ____________

3.

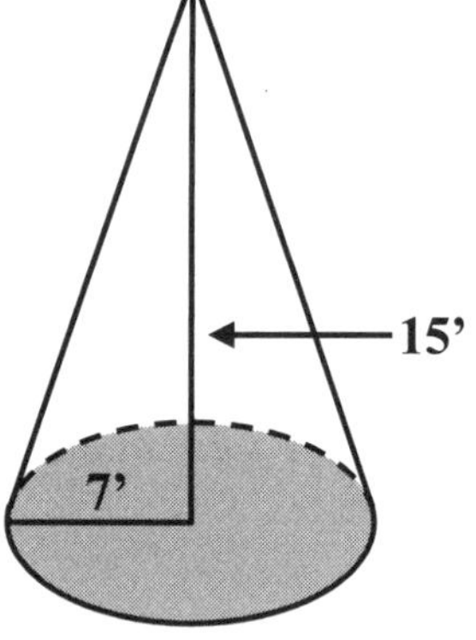

Volume = ____________

4.

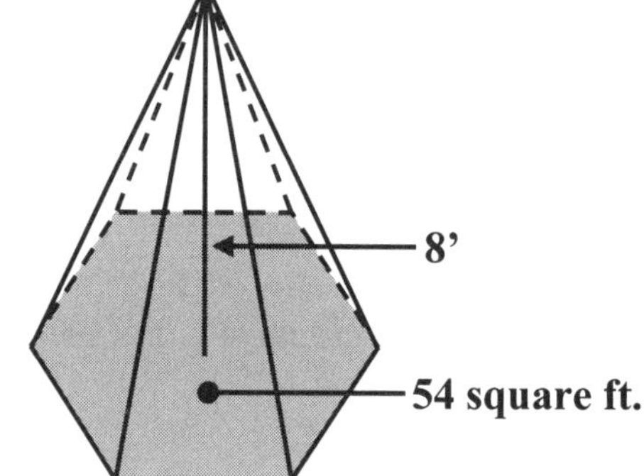

Volume = ____________

Perimeter, Area and Volume – Assessment – Day 48

Name: ____ Date: ________________

1. What is the area of the figure at the right? Show how you found the answer.

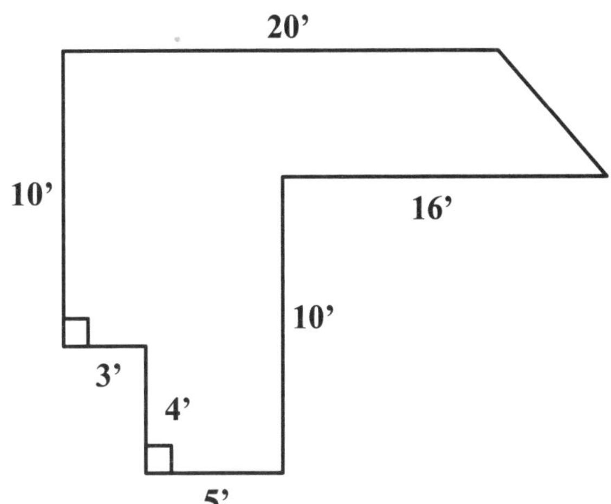

(A) 120 sq. ft

(B) 132 sq. ft

(C) 156 sq. ft

(D) 172 sq. ft

2. Which could be the length and height of the triangular bases of a triangular prism whose height is 5 inches and whose volume is 60 cubic inches?

(A) $b = 3$ inches, $h = 4$ inches (B) $b = 6$ inches, $h = 4$ inches (C) $b = 6$ inches, $h = 2$ inches (D) $b = 6$ inches, $h = 5$ inches

3. What is the volume of a pyramid with a height of 4 units and a rectangular base with dimensions of 3 units by 4 units?

(A) 16 cubic units (B) 32 cubic units (C) 44 cubic units (D) 48 cubic units

4. Which of the following are the length of the base and height of a triangle whose area is 12 square units?

(A) $b = 4$ units, $h = 3$ units (B) $b = 2$ units, $h = 6$ units (C) $b = 1$ units, $h = 12$ units (D) $b = 2$ units, $h = 12$ units

5. Determine the perimeter of the figure at the right.

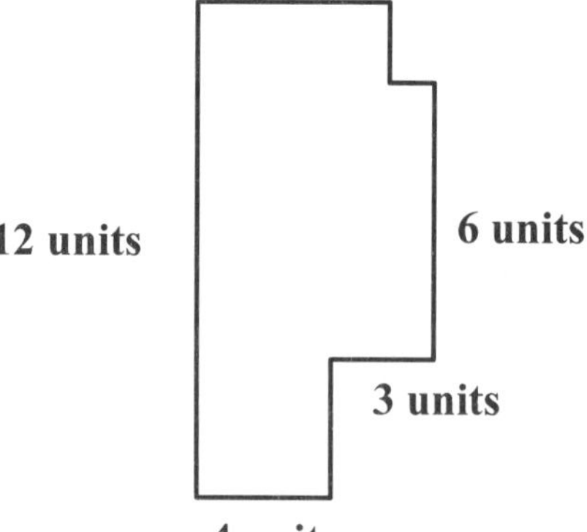

(A) 22 units

(B) 27 units

(C) 38 units

(D) 39 units

6. Which of the following are the radius and height of a cone whose volume is 37.58 cubic units?

(A) $r = 4$ units, $h = 3$ units

(B) $r = 3$ units, $h = 4$ units

(C) $r = 2$ units, $h = 3$ units

(D) $r = 3$ units, $h = 2$ units

Tessellations 1– Day 49

Name: ______________________________ Date: ______________

1. Determine the measure of each of the three congruent obtuse angles in the pentagons at the right, given that the each of the remaining two are right angles.

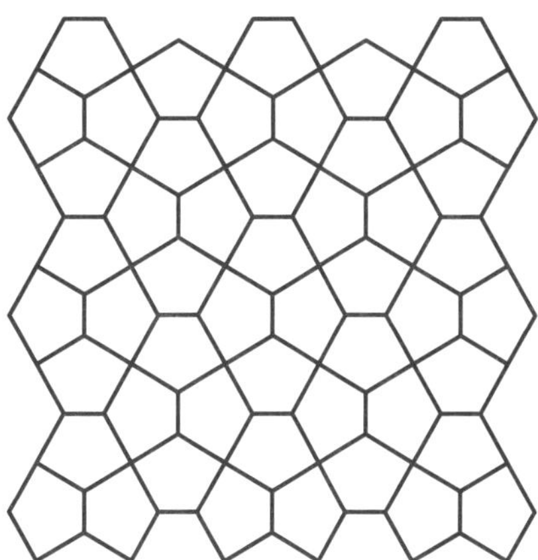

2. Determine the measure of each of the obtuse angles and acute angles in the pentagons at the left if all the obtuse angles in the figure are congruent.

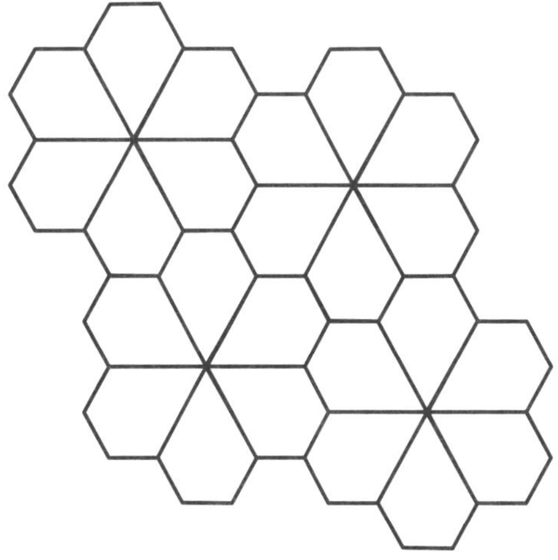

3. Determine the measure of each of the three congruent obtuse angles, and the acute and reflex angles in the octagon at the right, given the two right angles shown and that the acute angle is half the measure of the obtuse angle.

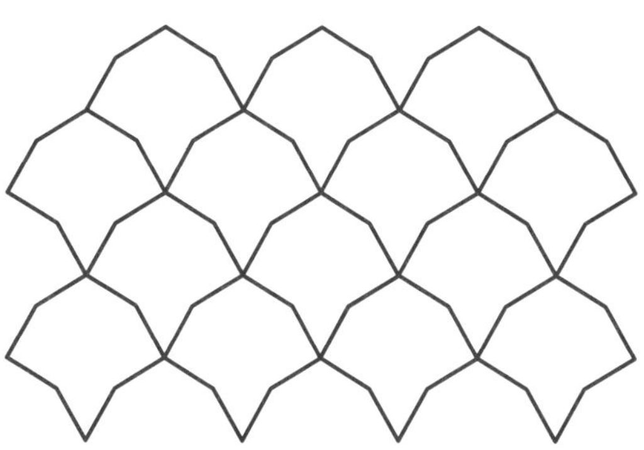

Tessellations 2– Day 50

Name: ______________________________ Date: ______________

1. Determine the measure of the acute and obtuse angle in the nonagon if the hexagon and pentagon are regular polygons.

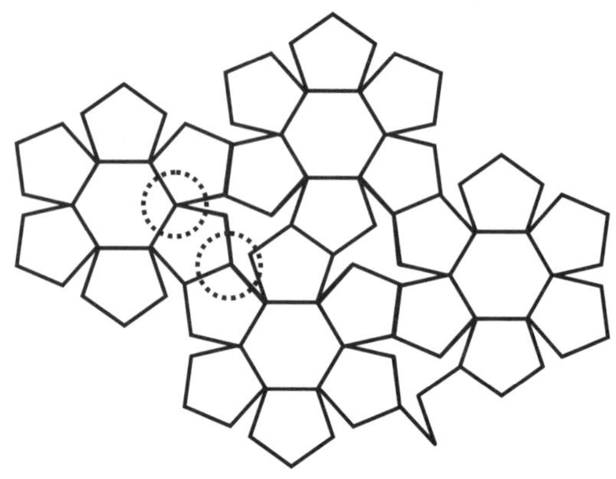

2. Given the right angle in the octagon, determine the measure of the obtuse angle in the octagon if the rhombus has angle measures of 120° and 60°.

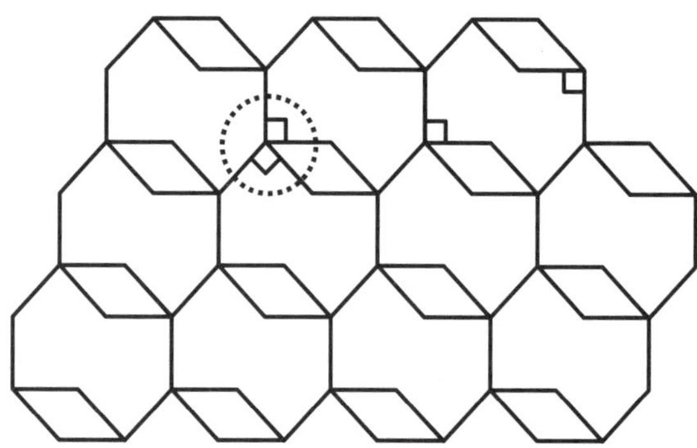

3. Given that the rhombus has angle measures of 120° and 60°, determine the measure of each angle in the octagon.

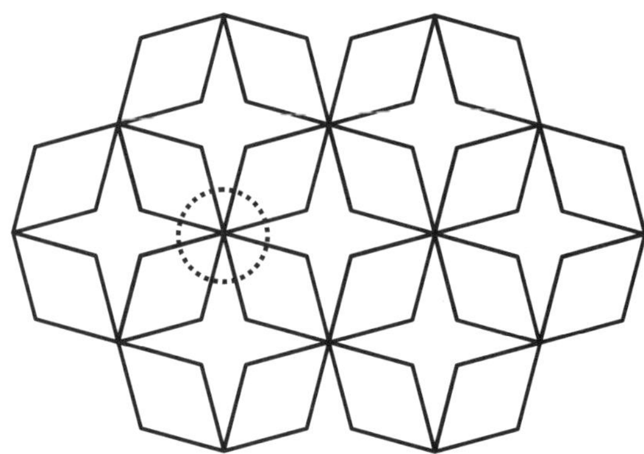

Symmetry – Day 51

Name: ______________________________ Date: ____________

Design 1

Design 2

Design 3

Design 4

Design 5

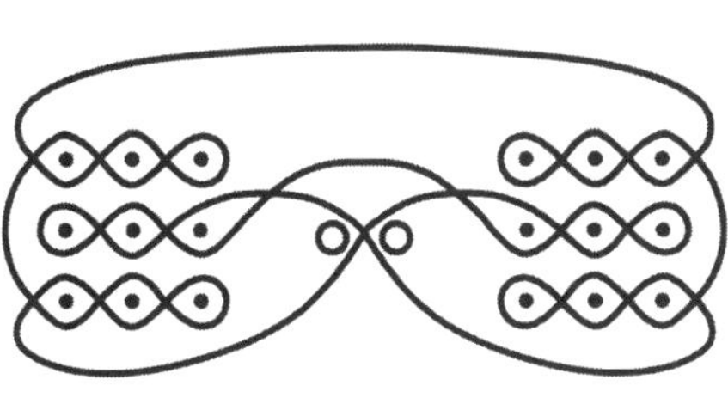
Design 6

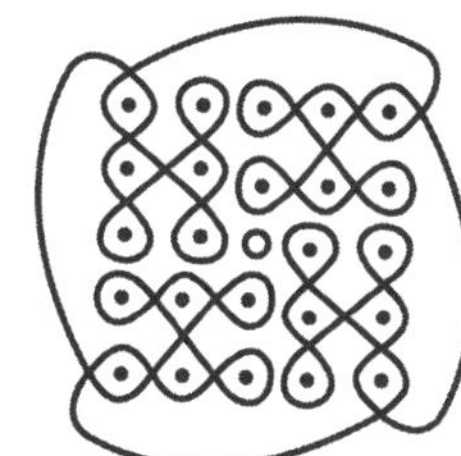
Design 7

1. Which designs have eight lines of symmetry and 45° rotational symmetry? ____________
2. Which designs have no line symmetry but have rotational symmetry? ____________
3. Which designs have six lines of symmetry and 60° rotational symmetry? ____________
4. Which designs have four lines of symmetry and 90° rotational symmetry? ____________
5. Which designs have line symmetry but no rotational symmetry? ____________

Transformations – Day 52

Name: ____ Date: ____________________

Use the figures below to answer the questions on the next page

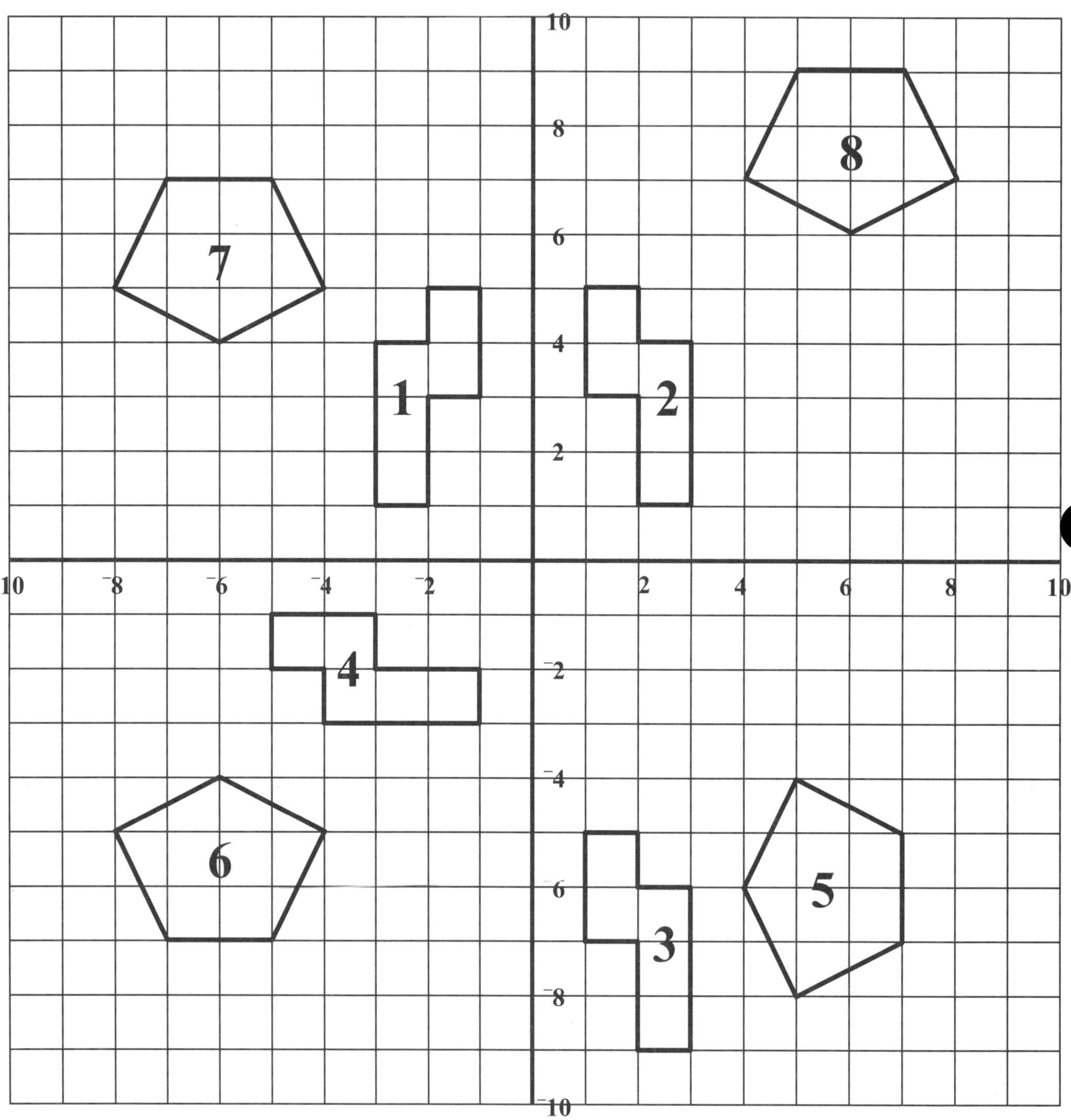

1. Which two pentagons show a reflection over the x-axis?

2. Describe the transformation to move Pentagon 5 to Pentagon 6's position.

3. Describe the transformation to move Heptagon 2 to Heptagon 3's position.

4. Name two shapes that show a reflection over the y-axis.

5. Describe the transformation between Heptagon 1 and Heptagon 4.

6. Which two pentagons show a translation? Describe this translation.

Tessellations, Transformations and Symmetry – Assessment – Day 53

Name: ______________________________ Date: ______________

Use the figures below to answer Questions 1 – 3.

Figure 1 **Figure 2** **Figure 3** **Figure 4** **Figure 5** **Figure 6** **Figure 7** **Figure 8**

1. Figure 3 has exactly:

   (A) no lines of symmetry and no rotational symmetry.

   (B) one line of symmetry and no rotational symmetry.

   (C) two lines of symmetry and no rotational symmetry.

   (D) two lines of symmetry and 180° rotational symmetry.

2. Which figure(s) has/have exactly one line of symmetry and no rotational symmetry?

   (A) Only Figure 1

   (B) Only Figure 2

   (C) Figures 1, 2 and 6

   (D) None of the figures

3. Which of the figures below could be added to the existing figure so that the dashed line becomes a horizontal line of symmetry for the entire figure?

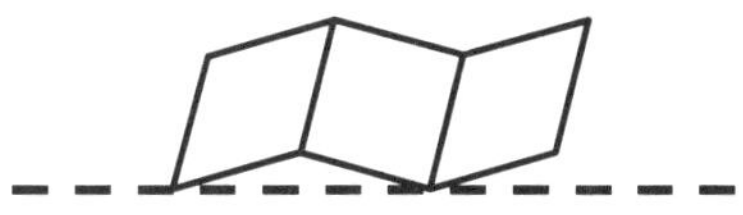

(A) 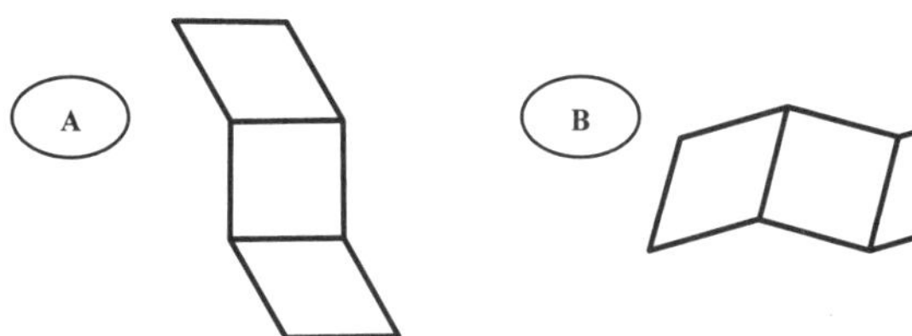 (B) (C) (D) 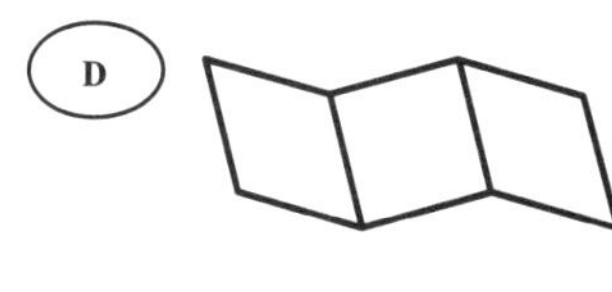

4. Which of the following figures does not tessellate the plane?

(A) 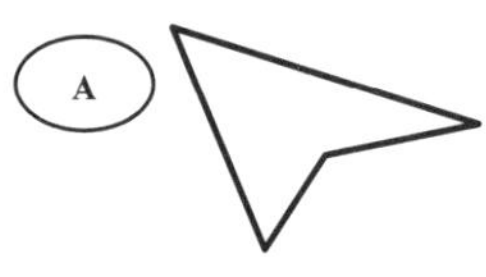

(B) 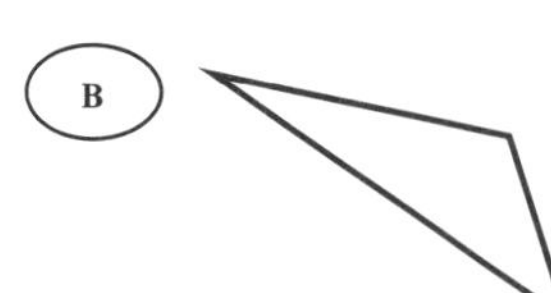

(C) 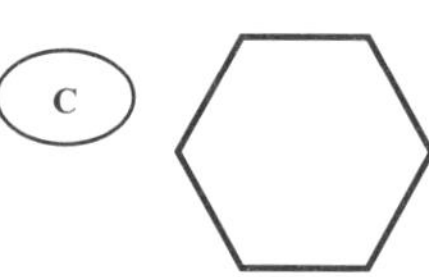

(D) 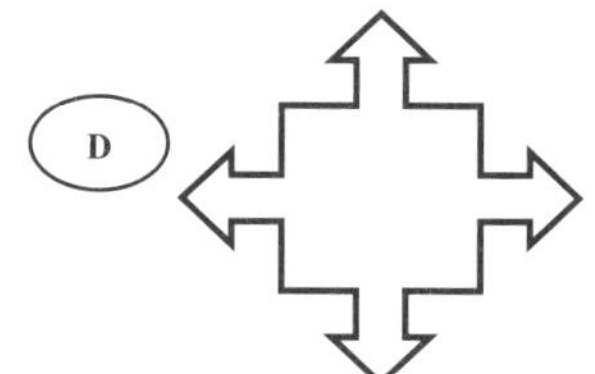

5. Which of the shapes below tessellates?

(A) 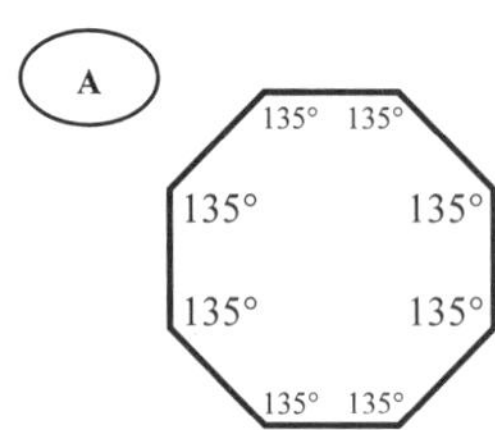

(B) 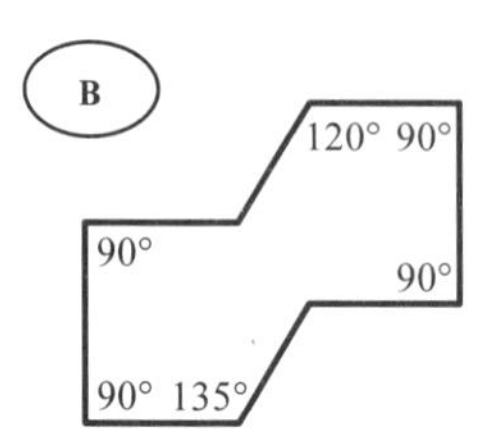

(C) 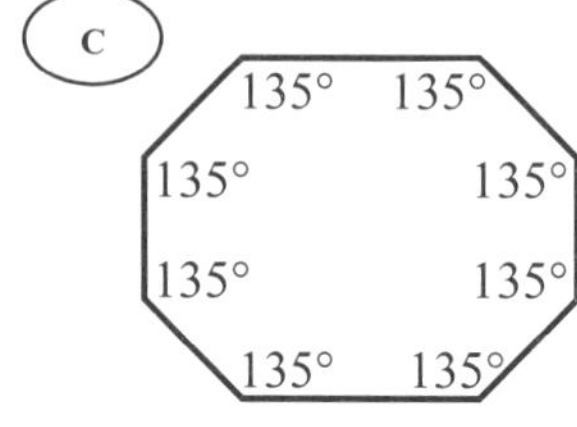

(D) 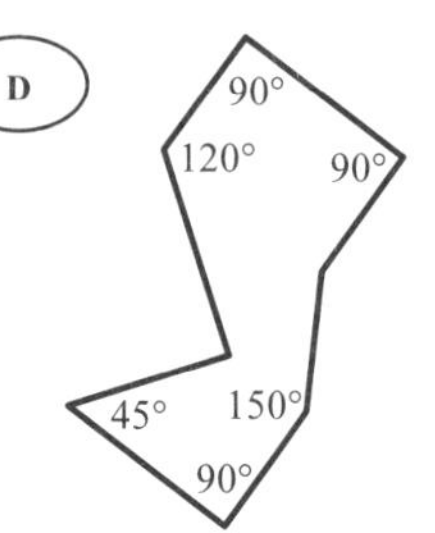

Use the diagram below to answer Questions 6 and 7.

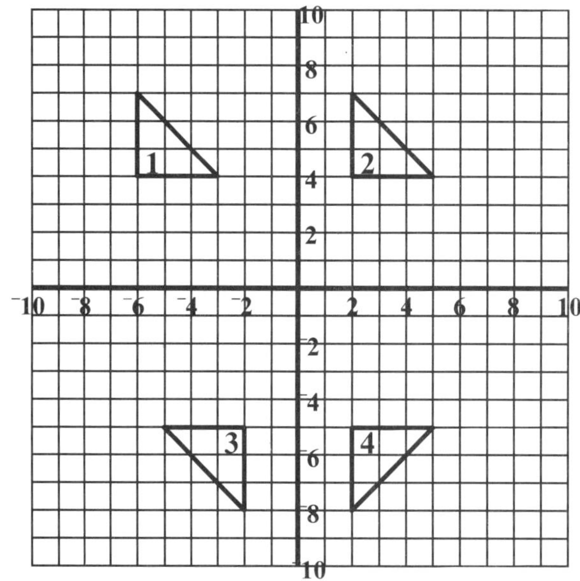

6. Which of the following shows a reflection of the two figures over the *y*-axis?

(A) Triangles 1 and 3

(B) Triangles 1 and 2

(C) Triangles 3 and 4

(D) Triangles 2 and 4

7. How can the relationship between Triangle 1 and Triangle 2 be described?

(A) A reflection over the *y*-axis.

(B) A translation of 5 units on the *x*-axis.

(C) A 90° clockwise rotation.

(D) A translation of 8 units on the *x*-axis.

Computation in Context – Day 54

Name: ______________________________ Date: ______________

Study the eight problems below, and decide whether to use mental math, paper and pencil, or estimation and a calculator to complete each by circling the method. Write answers or estimates in the blanks at the right.

		Estimate / Exact Answer
1. $\frac{8}{9} \div \frac{2}{9}$ MM PP EC	2. $3\frac{4}{15} + 2\frac{2}{9}$ MM PP EC	1. ______ ______ 2. ______ ______
3. $10\frac{2}{7} \times 2\frac{4}{9}$ MM PP EC	4. $9\frac{1}{4} - 6\frac{1}{12}$ MM PP EC	3. ______ ______ 4. ______ ______
5. $2\frac{1}{2} + 6\frac{3}{10}$ MM PP EC	6. $5\frac{3}{4} \div 1\frac{6}{7}$ MM PP EC	5. ______ ______ 6. ______ ______
7. $\frac{3}{8} \times \frac{4}{5}$ MM PP EC	8. $14\frac{9}{11} - \frac{2}{3}$ MM PP EC	7. ______ ______ 8. ______ ______

Mean, Median and Mode – Day 55

Name: ____ Date: ________________

Determine the mean, median, mode, and range of this data.

28, 71, 72, 56, 84, 100, 85, 77, 63, 90, 66, 71, 79, 78, 71, 84, 92, 80, 81, 70, 93, 83, 64, 95, 67

Note: The last entry in the table is the sum of the grades.

Mean: ____________

Median: ____________

Mode: ____________

Range: ____________

Grades in Ascending Order
1900

Applying Mean – Day 56

Name: ______________________________ Date: ____________

1. Use the points on the sides of the square to create eight congruent rectangles within the square. Count the number of shapes in one of the rectangles and use the data to calculate a reasonable estimate for the total number of shapes.

   Number of shape in sample: ____________

   Total based on the sample: ____________

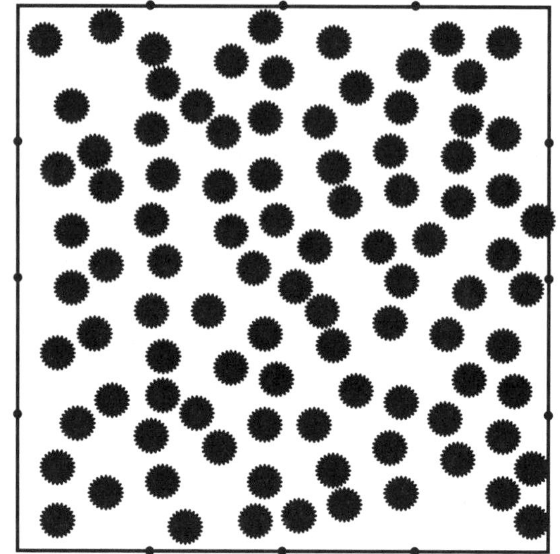

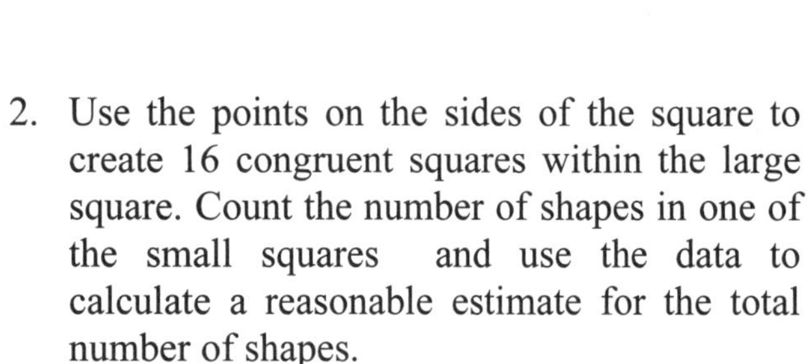

2. Use the points on the sides of the square to create 16 congruent squares within the large square. Count the number of shapes in one of the small squares and use the data to calculate a reasonable estimate for the total number of shapes.

   Number of shape in sample: ____________

   Number of shape in sample: ____________

3. The average number of points scored by each of the five players on the High Top basketball team was 13.4 points. Based on this average, how many points were scored by High Top for the game?

4. During the last four weekends, Barney worked as a waiter and made the amount shown in the table at the right. Based on the amounts shown, how much money in tips should he make during the next 20 weekends?

Weekend	Total Tips
1	$120.00
2	$70.00
3	$90.00
4	$80.00

Box-and-Whisker Plots – Day 57

Name: ______________________________ Date: ______________

Use the table and number line below to create a box-and-whisker plot for the following data:

88, 61, 76, 36 100, 82, 74, 68, 91, 63, 75, 77, 58, 41, 85, 91, 82, 83, 76, 90, 81, 65, 94, 63

Grades in Descending Order
1800

Representing Data – Day 58

Name: ______________________________ Date: ______________

Indicate the type of graph that would best represent the descriptions below. Use the following terms: bar graph, box-and-whisker plot, circle graph, histogram, line plot, stem-and-leaf plot, scatter plot, and multi-line graph.

1. The school board wants to show how the entire yearly budget is allocated to various expenses such as salaries, supplies, building maintenance and operational expenses. ______________

2. Mr. Thompson wants to show how much different types of tomato plants grow over a two-month period. ______________

3. Mrs. Variable wants to display the recent test results for each of three algebra classes so that the range and median score can easily be compared. ______________

4. Mrs. Cooper wants to show individual scores and their distribution. ______________

5. Sally Ann wants to display traffic accidents by age group. ______________

6. Jorge wants to display the top 10 scoring basketball players of all time. ______________

7. Harry wants to show the relationship between hours biked and miles ridden. ______________

8. Aiden wants to show the number of bags of candy that contain a specified quantity of candy. ______________

9. Mr. Spielberg wants to display the top 10 grossing movies of all time by movie, and by gross revenue. ______________

10. Lee Ann wants to represent the total cost for 0 to 1000 minutes at four different phone companies. ______________

Interpreting Data - Day 59

Name: ______________________________ Date: ______________

Use the "Graphs, Graphs, Graphs" Discovery Templates (Pages 187 – 189) to answer the questions below.

1. Which airline's stock had the greatest range of prices? ______________

2. Which two airlines account for 25% of late arrivals? ______________

3. Which airline serves about a million passengers in both domestic and international flights? ______________

4. Represent the data in Graph 6 with a box-and-whisker plot.

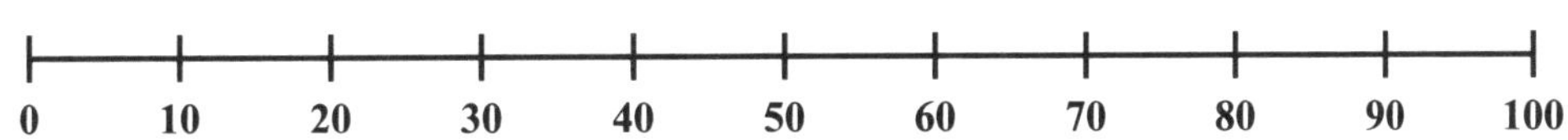

5. About how many people fly on Saturday and Sunday on the five largest airlines? ______________

6. Which airline has the greatest range of fares? ______________

7. Which two airlines have exactly the same range of fares? ______________

True or False Headlines

8. Out of the five major airlines, First Class Only has the fewest late arrivals. ______________

9. On Time Airlines accounts for half the domestic flights of the five largest airlines. ______________

10. Four out of Five of the airlines' stock prices increased from January to December. ______________

11. Half the fares at On Time and Frugal Airways are $700 or less. ______________

Data Analysis – Assessment – Day 60

Name: ______________________________ Date: ______________

1. Vanita has earned scores of 80, 75, 60 and 90 on the first four 100-point tests in her math class. What is the minimum score Vanita can get on the fifth test and have an average of 80 for the five tests?

(A) 76 (B) 80 (C) 90 (D) 95

2. Which of the data sets below has the same mean, median and mode?

(A) 5, 5, 5, 5, 10

(B) 1, 1, 2, 3, 4, 5, 6, 7, 8, 8

(C) 1, 3, 7, 8, 9, 10, 10, 11, 12, 13, 17, 19

(D) 2, 5, 5, 8, 10, 15, 15, 15, 20, 25

3. Based on the chart below, what was the average number of points earned by a player on Team A?

Team A	
Player Number	**Points Earned**
1	13
2	12
3	24
4	10
5	31

(A) 18 (B) 19 (C) 21 (D) 63.2

4. Team B scored 109 points and won the game against Team A, whose points are shown in the table above. What is the average number of points that each player on Team A would have to score in order to beat Team B by 1 point?

(A) 1 (B) 3 (C) 4 (D) 15

5. Which of the following would be the best type of graph to use to show the relationship between the gallons of gas used and number of miles traveled?

(A) box and whisker (B) line plot (C) scatter plot (D) stem-and-leaf plot

6. Which of the following graphs is most likely to show individual data elements?

(A) circle graph (B) scatter plot (C) box and whisker (D) histogram

7. What would a double bar graph best be used for?

(A) To compare the distribution of grades earned by students in two classes.

(B) To compare the median age of men and women at their first marriage during 2006.

(C) To display the 10 highest grossing animated films of all times.

(D) To show the change in temperature each hour for a 24-hour period.

8. The graph at the right shows the results for a test Ms. Sundar gave in her four Algebra classes. Based on this data, which class had the highest median score?

(A) Period 1

(B) Period 3

(C) Period 5

(D) Period 7

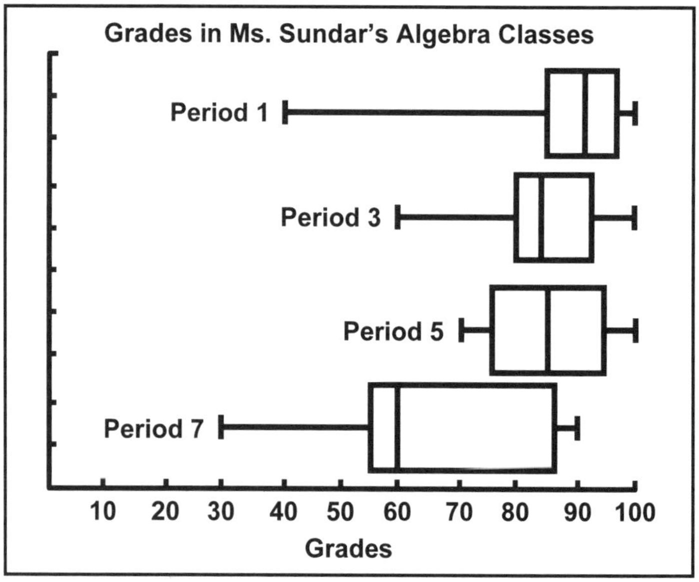

9. Based on the box-and-whisker plot above, which class had the smallest range of grades?

(A) Period 1 (B) Period 3 (C) Period 5 (D) Period 7

10. Which type of graph would BEST show what part of all licensed drivers each age group represented?

Age	Percent of All Licensed Drivers
16-19	4.7
20-29	17.2
30-39	19.6
40-49	21.2
50-59	16.7
60-69	10.3
70-79	6.9
80 and older	3.2

(A) box-and-whisker plot

(B) circle graph

(C) line graph

(D) stem-and-leaf plot

What Went Wrong?– Day 61

Name: ______________________________ Date: ______________

Each problem below has been calculated incorrectly. Describe the error that you think caused the incorrect answer. Then provide the correct answer.

1. $5^3 = 15$

____

____

____

2. $2^6 = 12$

____

____

____

3. $3 \cdot 4^2 = 144$ ______________________________

____

____

____

4. $(2 \cdot 3)^4 = 625$

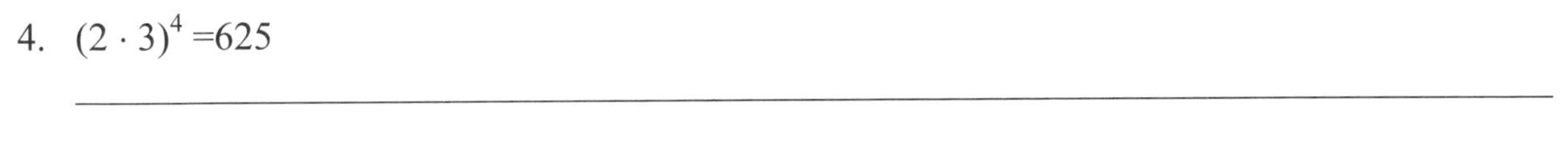

____

____

____

5. $(1 + 2)^3 = 9$

____

____

____

6. $10^3 = 30$

7. $-3^4 = 81$

8. $5^2 \cdot 2^5 = 100$

9. $-8^4 = {}^{-}32$

Applying Order of Operations– Day 62

Name: ______________________________ Date: ______________

Use the order of operations to complete the problems below.

1. $2 + 3 \cdot 5 =$ __________

2. $3 + 4 \cdot 6 =$ __________

3. $8 + 6 \div 2 =$ __________

4. $5 + 10 \div 2 =$ __________

5. $9 + 6 \div 3 =$ __________

6. $8 + 12 \cdot 4 =$ __________

7. $8 + 12 \div 4 =$ __________

8. $12 - 6 \div 2 =$ __________

9. $8 - 2 \cdot 4 =$ __________

10. $16 + 8 \div 4 =$ __________

11. $16 + 8 \cdot 4 =$ __________

12. $16 - 8 \div 4 =$ __________

13. $1 + 2^3 \div 4 =$ __________

14. $1 + 3^2 \div 3 =$ __________

15. $3^2 + 4^3 \div 8 =$ __________

16. $4 + 4^2 \div 2 =$ __________

17. $15 + 9 \div 3 =$ __________

18. $15 - 3^2 \div 3 =$ __________

19. $18 + 6 \div 2 \cdot 3 =$ __________

20. $18 + (6 \div 2) \cdot 3 =$ __________

21. $(18 + 6) \div 2 \cdot 3 =$ __________

22. $(18 + 6) \div (2 \cdot 3) =$ __________

23. $(15 + 5^2) \div 5 + 5 =$ __________

24. $(15 + 5^2) \div (5 + 5) =$ __________

Applying Order of Operations – Day 63

Name: ______________________________ Date: ______________

Use the order of operations to complete the problems below.

1. $12 + 18 \div 2 \cdot 3 =$ ____________________

2. $12 + 18 \div (2 \cdot 3) =$ ____________________

3. $(6 + 18) \div 2 \cdot 3 =$ ____________________

4. $(6 + 18) \div (2 \cdot 3) =$ ____________________

5. $10 + 8 \div 2 =$ ____________________

6. $(10 + 8) \div 2 =$ ____________________

7. $16 + 2^3 \div 4 =$ ____________________

8. $(16 + 2^3) \div 4 =$ ____________________

9. $15 + 25 \div 5 =$ ____________________

10. $(15 + 5^2) \div 5 =$ ____________________

11. Insert parentheses to make the problem below yield an answer of 18.

$$4 + 2^3 \div 2 \cdot 3$$

12. Use the order of operations and each of the digits 2, 3, 4 and 5 to create a problem whose answer is 54.

Creating Expressions – Day 64

Name: ______________________________ Date: ______________

Study each of the patterns below, and then write an expression that represents the relationship between the term number n and the number of toothpicks used to create that term. Then use the expression to determine the number of toothpicks needed to make the 100th term. You may want to make a table to help determine the pattern.

1.

Expression: ______________ 100th term: ______________

2.

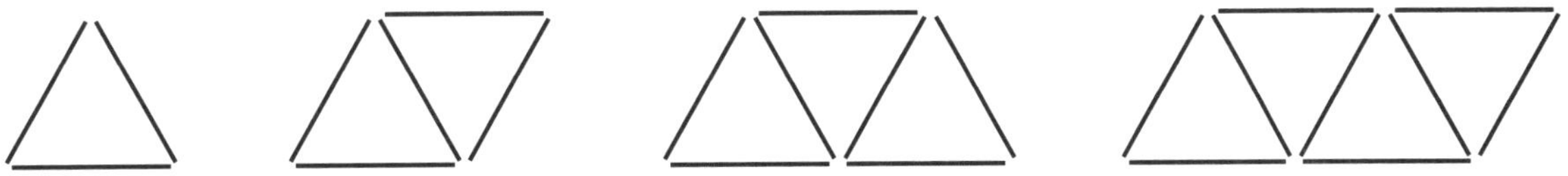

Expression: ______________ 100th term: ______________

3.

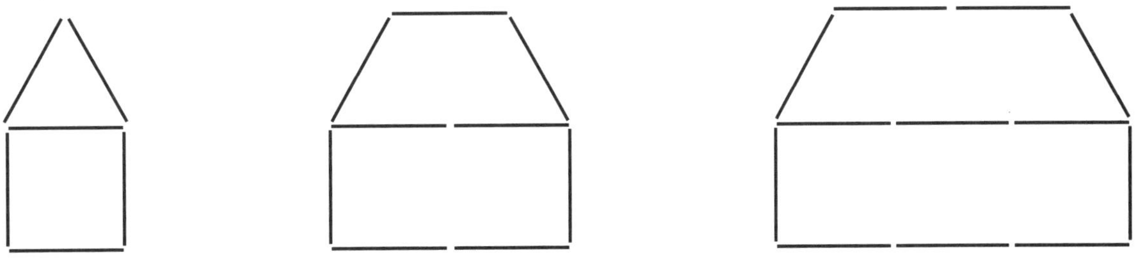

Expression: ______________ 100th term: ______________

4.

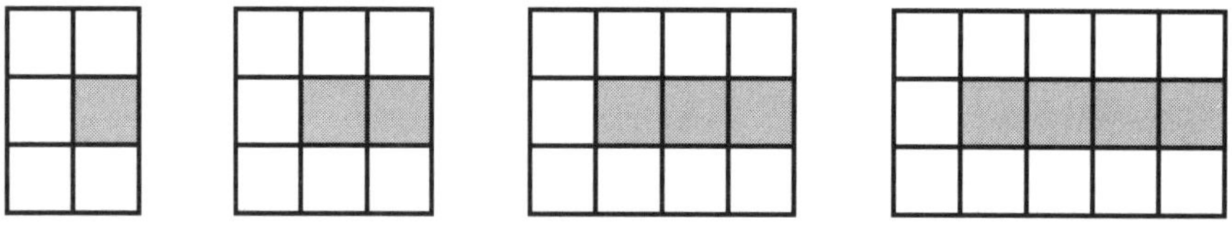

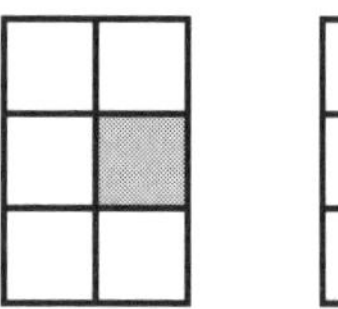

Figure 1

Figure 2

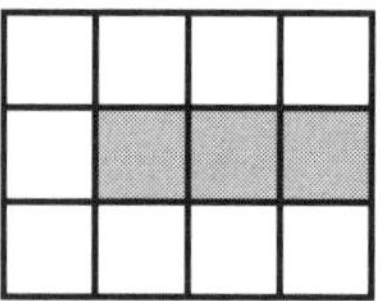

Figure 3

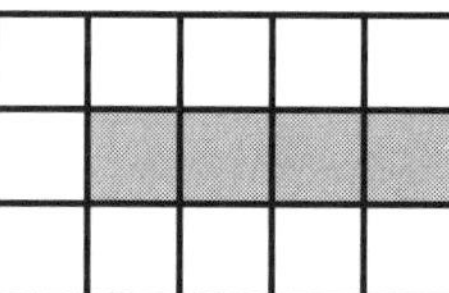

Figure 4

a. If n represents the position number of the figures in the pattern above, write an algebraic expression to describe the pattern for the number of shaded squares in each figure.

b. If n represents the position number of the figures in the pattern, write an algebraic expression to describe the pattern for the number of squares in each figure.

c. If n represents the position number of the figures in the pattern, write an algebraic expression to describe the pattern for the number of unshaded squares in each figure.

d. Based on these patterns, how many shaded and unshaded squares would be in the 100th figure?

Evaluation Game - Day 65

Name: ______________________________ Date: ______________

Objective:

Win five rounds by correctly evaluating randomly-generated variables and expressions.

Materials:

"The Evaluation Game" Variable and Expression Generator, a set of regular playing cards separated into a deck of face cards, a deck of spades and clubs from ace to 10 (aces will equal 1), and a deck of diamonds and hearts from ace to 10 (aces will equal 1).

Rules:

Single Variable Game

Players choose the variable column that will be used during the game. The deck of cards is separated into a deck of all black cards and a deck of all red cards. Each player chooses a card from the black deck and a card from the red deck. The black card will determine the value of the variable, and the red card will determine the expression. Each player evaluates the expression based on the value of the variable. Once the value of the expressions are determined and validated (a calculator may be used to settle disagreements), another card is chosen, this time from the deck of face cards. If the card is black, the player with the greatest (or bigger, remember B for black) value wins the round. If the card is red, the player with the least value wins the round. The first player to win five rounds wins the game.

Example:

using the x-column as the variable:

Player 1 chooses an ace of clubs and a 5 of hearts, which generates $x = 4$ and $3x - 1$. The value of the expression is $3(4) - 1 = 11$.

Player 2 chooses a 4 of spades and a 2 of diamonds, which generates $x = {}^{-}7$ and x^2. The value of the expression is 49. (Note: If students check this problem with a TI-83 or TI-73, they must input the data, including grouping symbols: [(] [(-)] [7] [)] [x^2]. If the parentheses are omitted, the calculator will display an answer of $^{-}49$.)

A card is then chosen from the shuffled deck of face cards. A king of clubs is chosen. Since it is a black card, the player with the greatest value wins the round. So Player 2 gets one point.

Play continues until one player earns five points.

Black Card Double Variable Game

Each player chooses three cards from a shuffled deck of all black cards consisting of aces to 10. The first card indicates the value of the x-variable, the second card indicates the value of the y-variable, and the third card indicates the expression in the third column, which contains both x- and y-values. Each player evaluates the expression based on the value of the variables. Once the value of the expressions are determined and validated (a calculator may be used to settle disagreements), a card is chosen from the shuffled deck of face cards. If the card is black, the player with the greatest (or bigger, remember B for black) value wins the round. If the card is red, the player with the least value wins the round. The first player to win five rounds wins the game.

Example:

Player 1 chooses a 4 of clubs, a 4 of spades, and a 9 of clubs, which generates $x = 1$, $y = {}^{-}7$ and $5y - 9x = 5({}^{-}7) - 9(1) = {}^{-}35 - (9) = {}^{-}44$

Player 2 chooses a 6 of spades, a 10 of spades, and 3 of spades, which generates $x = {}^{-}4$, $y = {}^{-}4$ and $x + y + 4$. The value of the expression is ${}^{-}4 + {}^{-}4 + 4 = {}^{-}4$.

The next card chosen is a queen of diamonds. Since it is red, the player with the least value wins the round. Since ${}^{-}44$ is less than ${}^{-}4$, Player 1 wins the round.

Black and Red Card Double Variable Game

Begin with three decks of cards: one containing all of the spades and clubs from ace to 10, another with all of the hearts and diamonds from ace to 10, and another with all of the face cards mixed. Players choose two cards from the black deck. The first card generates the x-value, the second card the y-value. Then a card is chosen from the red deck, which generates the expression. Each player evaluates the expression based on the value of the variables. Once the values of the expressions are determined and validated (a calculator may be used to settle disagreements), a card is chosen from the shuffled deck of face cards. If the card is black, the player with the greatest (or bigger, remember B for black) value wins the round. If the card is red, the player with the least value wins the round. The first player to win five rounds wins the game.

Example:

Player 1 chooses a 9 of clubs, a 10 of spades, and a 4 of hearts, which generates $x = 5$, $y = {}^{-}4$ and $2 + xy$. The value of the expression is $2 + 5({}^{-}4) = 2 + {}^{-}20 = {}^{-}18$.

Player 2 chooses a 5 of clubs, a 5 of spades, and a 5 of diamonds, which generates $x = 7$, $y = {}^{-}6$ and $3x + y^2$. The value of the expression is $3(7) + ({}^{-}6)^2 = 21 + 36 = 57$.

The card chosen from the face card deck is a jack of spades. Since it is a black card, the player with the greater value wins the round. Since $57 > {}^{-}18$, Player 2 wins the round.

Play continues until one player earns 5 points.

"The Evaluation Game" Variable and Expression Generator– Day 65

	Column 1	Column 2	Column 3
Ace♣	$x = 4$	$y = 3$	$x - 4y$
2♣	$x = 3$	$y = 0$	$3x + 5y$
3♣	$x = 0$	$y = 1$	$x - 4y$
4♣	$x = 1$	$y = 7$	$6y + 2x$
5♣	$x = 7$	$y = 6$	$3x - 4y$
6♣	$x = 8$	$y = 5$	$3y + 6y$
7♣	$x = 2$	$y = 4$	$y + 8x$
8♣	$x = 9$	$y = 9$	$y - 4x$
9♣	$x = 5$	$y = 2$	$5y - 9x$
10♣	$x = 6$	$y = 8$	$3x + 2y$
Ace♠	$x = {}^{-}2$	$y = {}^{-}1$	$2x - y$
2♠	$x = {}^{-}3$	$y = {}^{-}3$	$3 + x - y$
3♠	$x = {}^{-}6$	$y = {}^{-}9$	$x + y + 4$
4♠	$x = {}^{-}7$	$y = {}^{-}7$	$x - 7y$
5♠	$x = {}^{-}9$	$y = {}^{-}6$	$7x + 2y$
6♠	$x = {}^{-}4$	$y = {}^{-}5$	$4x - 2y$
7♠	$x = {}^{-}8$	$y = {}^{-}8$	$x - 3y$
8♠	$x = 0$	$y = 0$	$5x - y$
9♠	$x = {}^{-}1$	$y = {}^{-}2$	$4x - 2y + 2$
10♠	$x = {}^{-}5$	$y = {}^{-}4$	$1 - 5x + y$
Ace♥	$x + 3$	$y + 3$	$2(x + y)$
2♥	$2x + 3$	$3y + 2$	$xy + y$
3♥	$x - 3$	$y - 4$	$(2 + x)y$
4♥	$5 + 2x$	$6 + 3y$	$2 + xy$
5♥	$3x - 1$	$3y + 1$	$(x - 3)2y$
6♥	$2x + 6$	$2y + 6$	$(3x + 2y)(x + y)$
7♥	$x + 3$	$y + 5$	$2x + 3xy$
8♥	$x - 7$	$2y - 4$	$5(3x - y)$
9♥	$5x - 9$	$3y + 7$	$4x - (2y + 3)$
10♥	$3 + 2x$	$3 + 5y$	$5x + 2y$
Ace♦	$x^2 + 3$	$4 + y^2$	$x^2 + y$
2♦	x^2	y^2	$x + y^2$
3♦	$3x^2$	${}^{-}3y^2$	$2x + y^2$
4♦	${}^{-}2x^2$	$2y^2$	$x + y^2$
5♦	$4x^2 - 3$	$4y^2 - 3$	$3x + y^2$
6♦	$x^2 - 10$	$2y^2 - 10$	$x^2 + y^2$
7♦	$x^2 + 5$	$y^2 + 7$	$x^2 - 3y$
8♦	$6x^2 + 1$	$y^2 - 1$	$x^2 - y$
9♦	$x^3 + 1$	y^3	$x^2 + 2y^2$
10♦	x^3	$y^3 - 4$	$x^3 - y$

Evaluating Expressions – Day 65

Name: ______________________________ Date: ______________

1. Evaluate $3x + 2$ for $x = 4$. ____________

2. Evaluate $^{-}5x + 3$ for $x = 3$. ____________

3. Evaluate $9x - 42$ for $x = {}^{-}2$. ____________

4. Evaluate $3 + 2y$ for $y = 10$. ____________

5. Evaluate $6 - 4y$ for $y = {}^{-}2$. ____________

6. Evaluate $9 - 2y$ for $x = 4$. ____________

7. Evaluate $3x + 2$ for $x = 4$. ____________

8. Evaluate $3x + 2y$ for $x = {}^{-}3$ and $y = 4$. ____________

9. Evaluate $2x - y$ $x = {}^{-}3$ and $y = 5$. ____________

10. Evaluate $(x + 2)(3x + 1)$ for $x = {}^{-}2$. ____________

11. Evaluate $(x - 4)(2y + 3)$ for $x = 1$ and $y = 4$. ____________

Pre-Algebra Concepts – Assessment – Day 66

Name: ______________________________ Date: ______________

1. What is the value of $4 + 2 \cdot 6$?

   (A) 1 (B) 12 (C) 16 (D) 36

2. What is the value of $18 \div 2 \times 9 \div 3$?

   (A) $\frac{1}{3}$ (B) 3 (C) 27 (D) 108

3. What is the value of $3 \cdot 2^2$?

   (A) 10 (B) 12 (C) 25 (D) 36

4. Which of the following has a value of 10?

   (A) $24 \div (2^2 \cdot 3) \cdot 5$ (B) $(2 + 3)^2$ (C) 2×5^2 (D) $2 \times 5^2 \div 10$

5. What is the value of $8 \div (4 \times 2) \cdot 3^2$?

   (A) 2 (B) 9 (C) 36 (D) 324

6. $10 \cdot 2^2 \div 10 \cdot 2 =$

   (A) 8 (B) 20 (C) 72 (D) 160

7. What is the value of $16 \div (4 \cdot 2) \cdot (12 \div 4)^2$?

   (A) $1\frac{1}{3}$ (B) 4 (C) 18 (D) 48

8. $(6 + 18) \div (2 \cdot 3) =$

   (A) 4 (B) 5 (C) 24 (D) 36

9. What is the value of $3x - 6$ if $x = 5$?

(A) $^{-}48$ (B) 2 (C) 9 (D) 21

10. If the pattern below were to continue, how many toothpicks would be needed for the 10th term?

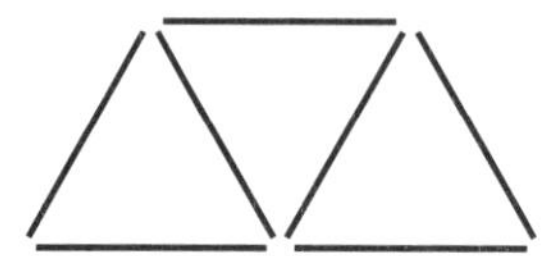

(A) 20 (B) 21 (C) 29 (D) 30

11. Which phrase best describes the algebraic expression below?

$$2(x + 3)$$

(A) The sum of 2 times a number and 3.

(B) The sum of 2 times a number and 6.

(C) Six times the sum of a number and 6.

(D) The product of any number and 3.

12. Which of the expressions represents the general term if the pattern below continued?

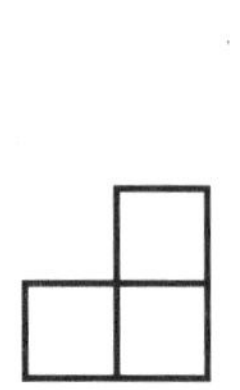
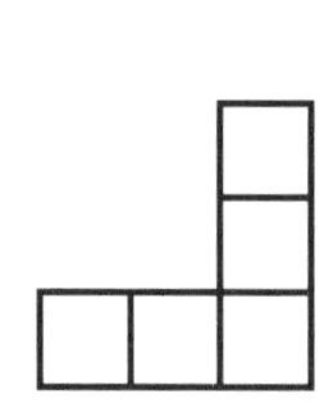
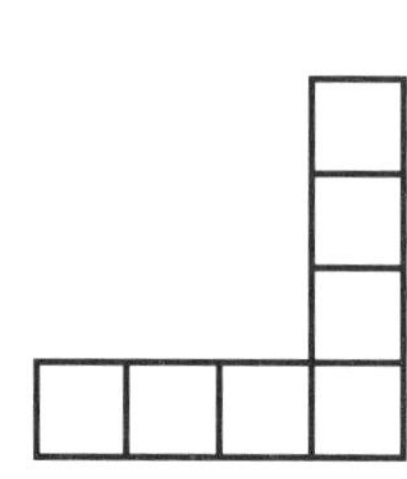
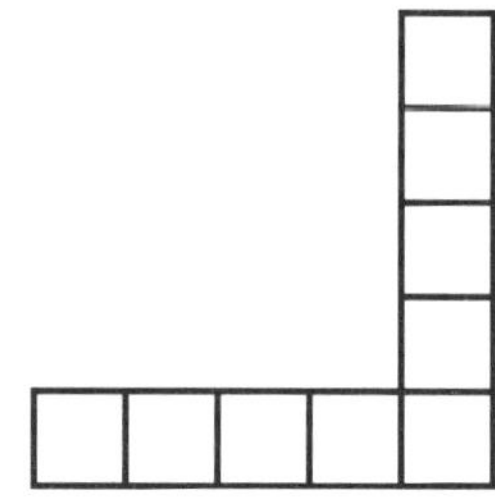

(A) $n + 3$ (B) $2n - 1$ (C) $2n + 1$ (D) $2n + 3$

Integer Practice – Day 67

Name: ______________________________ Date: ______________

Use mental math to complete the following.

1. $(^-7)(^-3) =$ ____________
2. $(^-7) + (^-3) =$ ____________
3. $(^-7) - (^-3) =$ ____________
4. $(^-9) \div (^-3) =$ ____________
5. $(^-7)(9) =$ ____________
6. $(15) - (^-3) =$ ____________
7. $(5)(^-5) =$ ____________
8. $(^-18) \div (^-9) =$ ____________
9. $(4) + (^-3) =$ ____________
10. $(^-27) + 27$ ____________
11. $19 + 7 =$ ____________
12. $(4) - (^-3) =$ ____________
13. $(^-5) - (17) =$ ____________
14. $(6)(7) =$ ____________
15. $(^-9) - (8) =$ ____________
16. $(36) \div (4) =$ ____________
17. $(19) \div (^-19) =$ ____________
18. $(^-9)(^-6) =$ ____________
19. $(12) \div (^-4) =$ ____________
20. $(^-29) + 5 =$ ____________

Properties of Equality – Day 68

Name: ______________________________ Date: ______________

As directed by your teacher, use the first blank to tell whether the actions below will keep the equality balanced. Use the second blank to record the result after the action is performed on the equality.

Equality: 15 = 15

1. Add $^{-}6$ to the right side and 6 to the left side. ____________ ____________

2. Add $^{-}3$ and $^{+}3$ to the right side. ____________ ____________

3. Subtract $^{-}3$ from the right side and subtract $^{-}3$ from the left side. ____________ ____________

4. Multiply each side by 4. ____________ ____________

5. Divide each side by $^{-}5$. ____________ ____________

6. Add $^{-}5$ and $^{+}5$ to the left side. ____________ ____________

7. Multiply the right side by $^{-}3$ and the left side by 3. ____________ ____________

8. Divide the left side by $\frac{3}{4}$ and multiply the right side by $\frac{3}{4}$. ____________ ____________

Keep It Balanced – Day 68

Name: ______________________________ Date: ____________

Tell whether each of the statements below would keep the equation 4 = 4 balanced or make it unbalanced.

1. Add a 3 to the left side and a $^{-}3$ to the right side. ____________
2. Multiply $^{-}5$ by the left side and right side. ____________
3. Add $^{-}3$ and $^{+}3$ to the left side. ____________
4. Add 16 to the right side and subtract 16 from the left side. ____________
5. Multiply the left side and right side by $\frac{1}{4}$. ____________
6. Multiply the left side by $\frac{1}{4}$ and divide the right side by $^{-}\frac{1}{4}$. ____________
7. Multiply the right side by 3 and add $\frac{1}{3}$ to the left side. ____________
8. Subtract $^{-}6$ from the left side and $^{-}6$ from the right side. ____________

---

9. The additive inverse of $^{-}3$ is: ____________
10. The multiplicative inverse of $^{-}3$ is: ____________
11. The multiplicative inverse of $\frac{3}{7}$ is: ____________
12. The additive inverse of $^{-}\frac{3}{7}$ is: ____________

Active Algorithms – Day 69

Name: ______________________________ Date: ______________

Complete the input and output values for each of the function machines described below. The bold solid outline is the input value. The dotted outline is the output value.

1. [ ] + 5 = [ ]

Input	Output
$^-4$	
6	
	3
	9

2. [ ] ÷ $^-3$ = [ ]

Input	Output
6	
12	
	$^-2$
	8

3. 4 × [ ] – 2 = [ ]

Input	Output
$^-1$	
2	
	10
	$^-10$

4. $^-3$ × [ ] + 2 = [ ]

Input	Output
$^-2$	
5	
	$^-7$
	17

Solving Equations – Day 70

Name: ______________________________ Date: ______________

Solve the equations below. Show all the necessary steps.

1. $3x + 4 = 12$

2. $5 = 4x - 3$

3. $15 = -3x$

4. $7 = x + 10$

5. $-2x - 11 = 1$

6. $-11 = 3x + 6$

7. $x + 7 = -13$

8. $4x = 15$

9. $2x - 4 = -11$

10. $5 + x = -3$

Solving Equations – Day 71

Name: ______________________________ Date: ______________

Show all necessary steps when solving the equations below.

1. $2x + 3 = x - 4$

2. $-3x - 4 = x - 8$

3. $5x + 1 = 3x + 4$

4. $2x - 5 = 6x - 4$

5. $3x + 5 = -x + 1$

6. $-3x + 4 = x - 10$

7. $-x + 2 = x$

8. $4x + 9 = 7x + 3$

Integers and Equations - Assessment – Day 72

Name: ______________________________________ Date: ______________

1. Solve for x: $2x + 3 = 17$

   Ⓐ $^{-}5$ Ⓑ 7 Ⓒ 10 Ⓓ 20

2. Solve for x: $3x - 5 = 7x - 3$

   Ⓐ $^{-}2$ Ⓑ $^{-}\frac{1}{2}$ Ⓒ $\frac{1}{2}$ Ⓓ 2

3. Which of the following equations could be solved without applying the addition property of equality?

   Ⓐ $2x + 3 = 9$ Ⓑ $2x + 4 = 5 - 6x$ Ⓒ $3x = {^{-}7}$ Ⓓ $9 = {^{-}4} + x$

4. Which of the pairs of equations below shows the correct result after an application of either the addition or multiplication property of equality?

   Ⓐ $3x + 4 = 10$, $3x = 14$ Ⓑ $2 = 4x$, $^{-}2 = x$ Ⓒ $x - 4 = 12$, $x = 16$ Ⓓ $x + 4 = 8$, $x = 2$

5. Solve for x: $17 = 5x + 2$

   Ⓐ $^{-}3$ Ⓑ 3 Ⓒ 10 Ⓓ $\frac{19}{5}$

Guess My Rule 1 – Day 73

Name: ______________________________ Date: ______________

Provide both a verbal and algebraic description of the relationship between x and y for each of the tables below.

Table 1	
x	y
– 10	– 13
– 4	– 7
0	– 3
4	1
10	7

Table 1

____

____

____

____

Table 2	
x	y
– 9	18
– 6	12
– 1	– 2
4	– 8
8	– 16

Table 2

____

____

____

____

Table 3	
x	y
8	12
6	10
1	5
–7	–3
–11	–7

Table 3

____

____

____

____

Table 4	
x	y
– 9	$-2\frac{1}{4}$
– 8	-2
2	$\frac{1}{2}$
3	$\frac{3}{4}$
12	3

Table 4

____

____

____

____

Guess My Rule 2 – Day 74

Name: ______________________________ Date: ______________

Provide both a verbal and algebraic description of the relationship between x and y for each of the tables below.

Table 1	
x	y
– 6	– 15
– 2	– 7
0	– 3
5	7
8	13

Table 1

____

____

____

____

Table 2	
x	y
– 8	– 1
– 3	$1\frac{1}{2}$
0	3
2	4
7	$6\frac{1}{2}$

Table 2

____

____

____

____

Table 3	
x	y
– 5	16
– 3	10
0	1
3	– 8
6	– 17

Table 3

____

____

____

____

Table 4	
x	y
7	$-7\frac{1}{2}$
2	– 5
0	– 4
– 5	$-1\frac{1}{2}$
– 8	0

Table 4

____

____

____

____

Generating Tables of Values – Day 75

Name: ______________________________ Date: ______________

Use each of the equations to determine the corresponding y-values.

Table 1: $y = 2x - 1$	
x	y
– 4	
– 1	
3	
7	
10	

Table 2: $y = \frac{1}{2}x - 3$	
x	y
– 8	
– 4	
0	
4	
8	

For Tables 3 and 4, choose x-values between $^{-}5$ and 5. Then find the corresponding y-values.

Table 3: $y = -3x + 1$	
x	y

Table 4: $y = -\frac{1}{2}x + 3$	
x	y

Connecting Equations to Graphs – Day 76

Name: ______________________________ Date: ______________

Match the graphs below to the correct equation. (Using the equations to determine some *x*- and *y*-values can help with the matching process.)

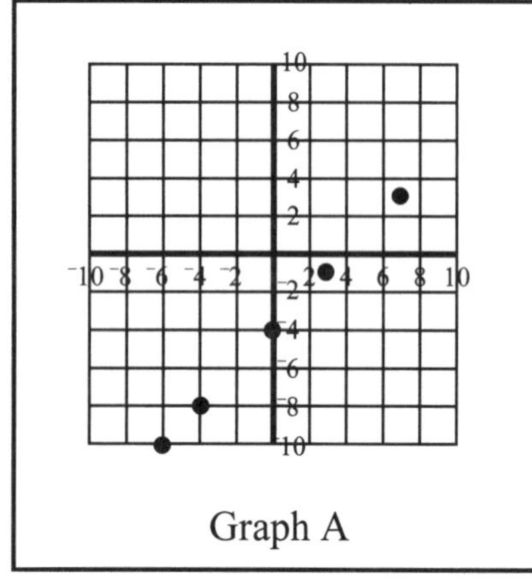

Graph A

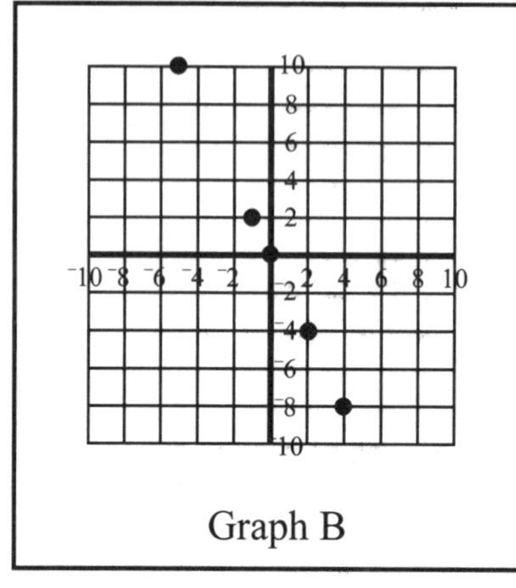

Graph B

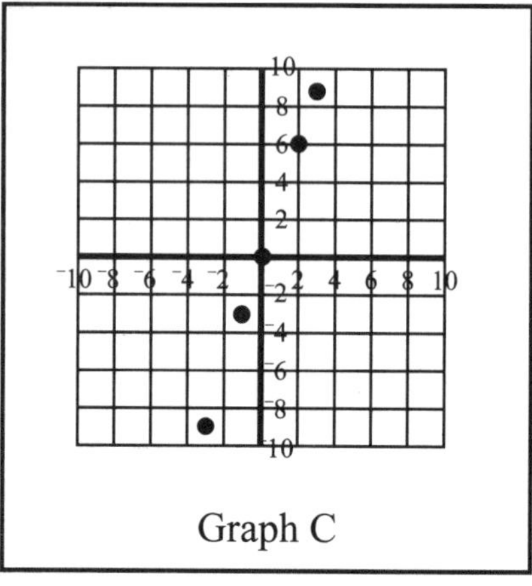

Graph C

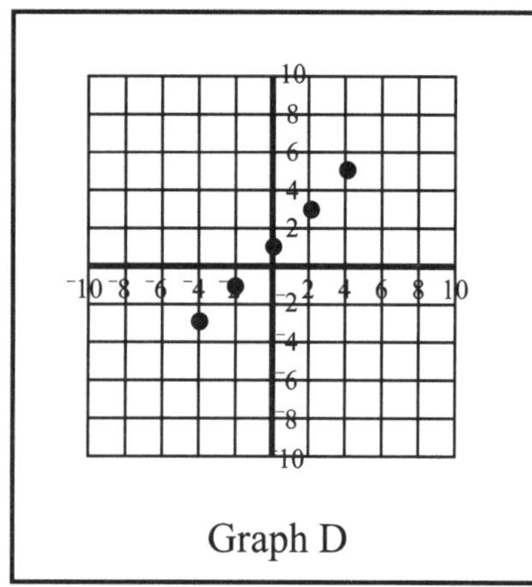

Graph D

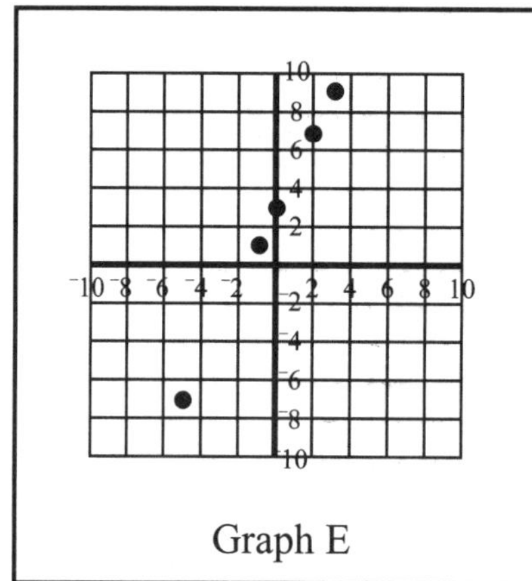

Graph E

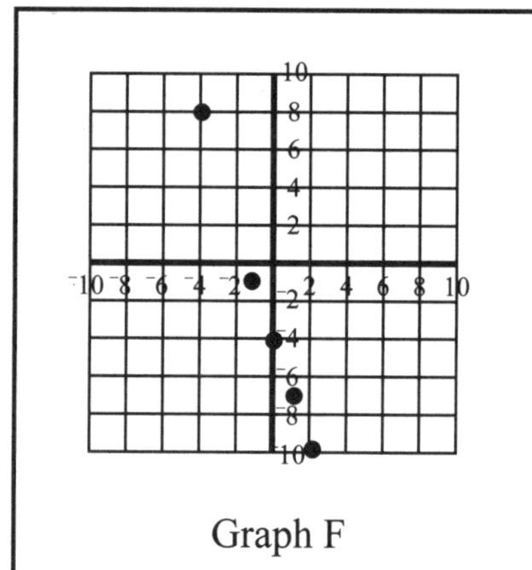

Graph F

1. ______________ $y = 3x$

2. ______________ $y = {}^{-}2x$

3. ______________ $y = {}^{-}3x - 4$

4. ______________ $y = 2x + 3$

5. ______________ $y = x + 1$

6. ______________ $y = x - 4$

Linear Functions – Assessment – Day 77

Name: ______________________________ Date: ______________

1. Which of the tables below can be represented by the equation $y = 2x - 4$?

(A)

x	y
$^-3$	14
$^-2$	10
0	4
1	$^-2$
4	$^-14$

(B)

x	y
$^-3$	10
$^-2$	8
0	4
1	2
4	$^-4$

(C)

x	y
$^-3$	$^-10$
$^-2$	$^-8$
0	$^-4$
1	$^-2$
4	4

(D)

x	y
$^-3$	$^-2$
$^-2$	0
0	4
1	6
4	12

2. Which of the equations below describes the table of values shown?

x	y
$^-3$	$^-7$
$^-2$	$^-5$
0	$^-1$
2	3
3	5

(A) $y = 2x - 1$ (B) $y = x - 2$ (C) $y = 2x + 1$ (D) $y = x + 1$

3. Which of the tables shown is represented by the graph below?

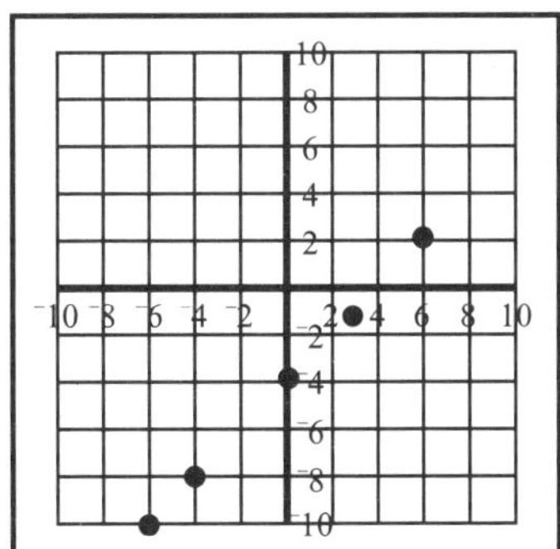

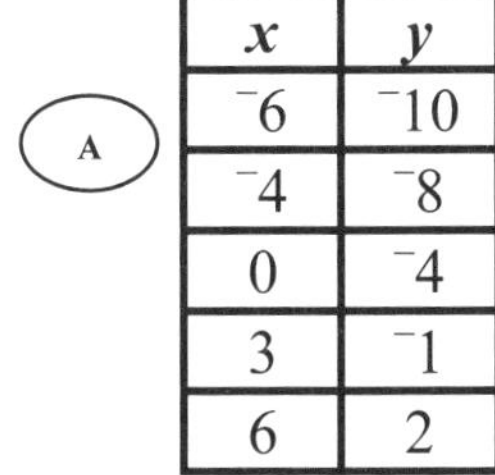

(A)

x	y
$^-6$	$^-10$
$^-4$	$^-8$
0	$^-4$
3	$^-1$
6	2

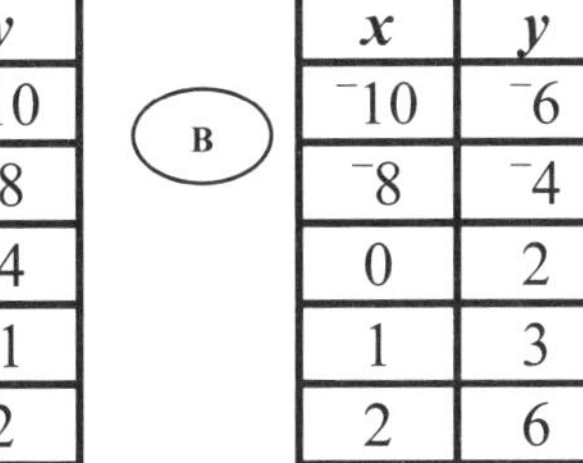

(B)

x	y
$^-10$	$^-6$
$^-8$	$^-4$
0	2
1	3
2	6

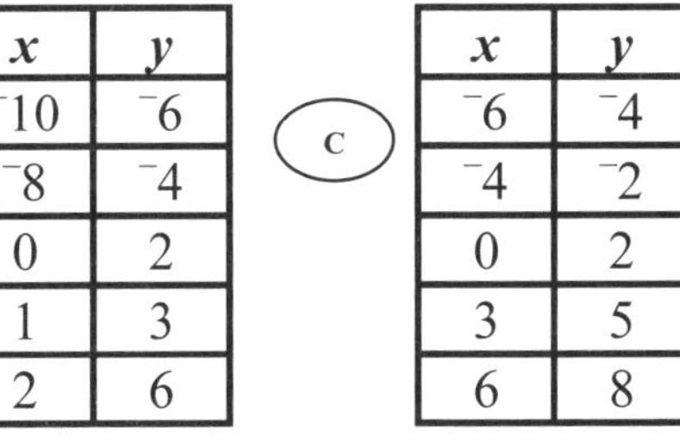

(C)

x	y
$^-6$	$^-4$
$^-4$	$^-2$
0	2
3	5
6	8

(D)

x	y
10	6
8	4
4	0
1	$^-3$
$^-2$	$^-6$

4. The relationship between x and y is described by the following: To find the value of y, multiply the value of x by 3 and then subtract 2 from that product.

   - What would be the value of y if $x = 2$?

   (A) $^{-}4$ (B) 4  (C) 7 (D) 12

5. Study the table of values below and give a written description of the relationship between x and y.

x	y
$^{-}6$	$^{-}8$
$^{-}3$	$^{-}5$
0	$^{-}2$
3	1
5	3

6. Determine the y-values in the table below for the equation $y = {}^{-}3x - 1$.

x	y
$^{-}4$	
$^{-}2$	
0	
1	
3	

Computation in Context – Day 78

Name: ______________________ Date: ____________

Study the eight problems below, and decide whether to use mental math, paper and pencil, or estimation and a calculator to complete each by circling the method. Write answers or estimates in the blanks at the right.

		Estimate / Exact Answer
1. $1\frac{2}{3} \div \frac{7}{16}$ MM PP EC	2. $3\frac{3}{10} + 1\frac{3}{5}$ MM PP EC	1. ____ ____ 2. ____ ____
3. $2\frac{1}{3} \times \frac{3}{14}$ MM PP EC	4. $5\frac{3}{5} - 2\frac{4}{7}$ MM PP EC	3. ____ ____ 4. ____ ____
5. $4\frac{3}{8} + 3\frac{7}{10}$ MM PP EC	6. $\frac{3}{4} \div 1\frac{3}{8}$ MM PP EC	5. ____ ____ 6. ____ ____
7. $2\frac{7}{8} \times 4\frac{4}{5}$ MM PP EC	8. $5\frac{13}{16} - 2\frac{5}{8}$ MM PP EC	7. ____ ____ 8. ____ ____

Investigating Slopes and Intercepts – Day 79

Name: ____ Date: __________________

Parameters for all graphs: x-min: $^{-}47$, x-max: 47, x-scale: 4, y-min: $^{-}31$, y-max: 31, y-scale: 4.

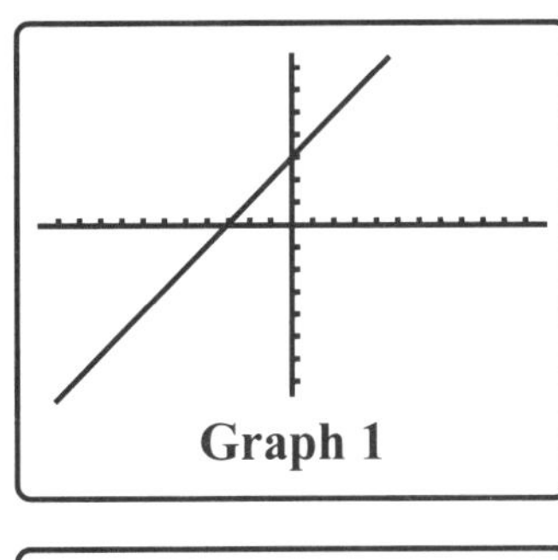
Graph 1

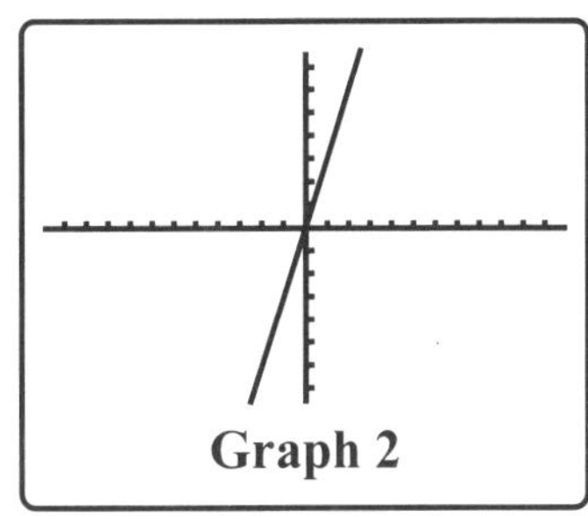
Graph 2

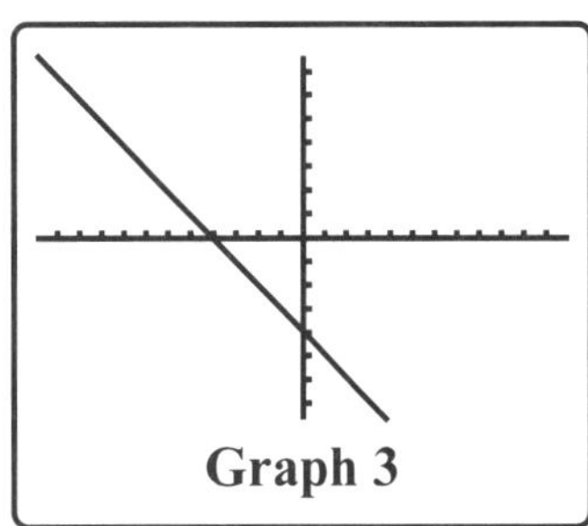
Graph 3

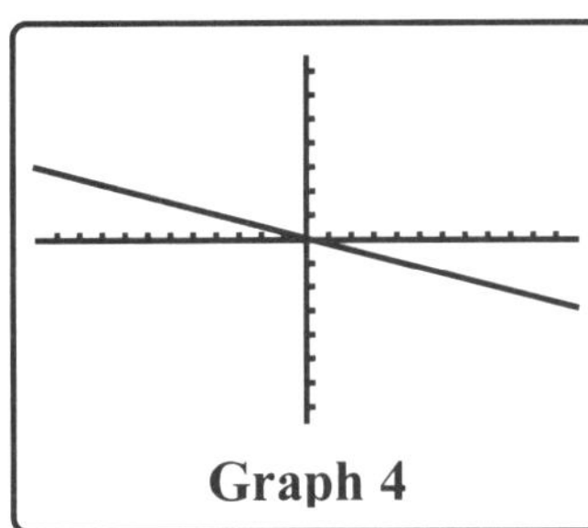
Graph 4

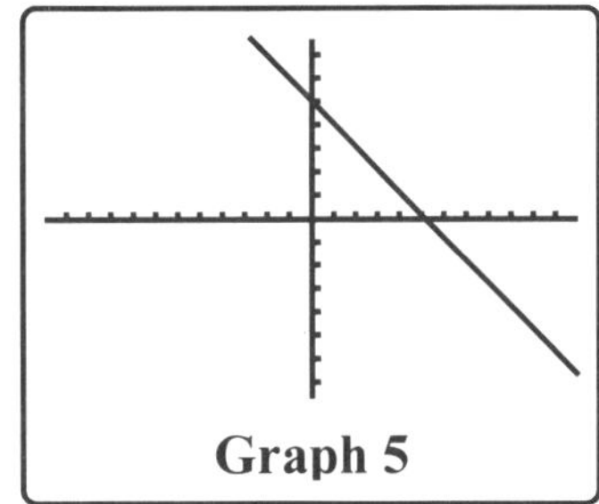
Graph 5

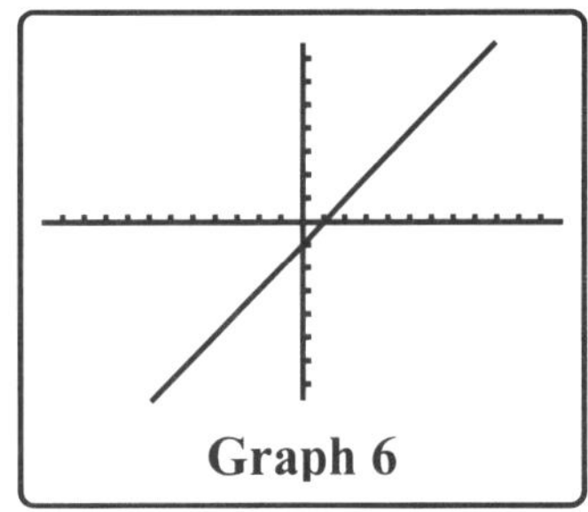
Graph 6

1. Which graphs pass through the origin? ________________________

2. Which graphs have a positive y-intercept? ________________________

3. Which graphs have a negative y-intercept? ________________________

4. How do Graphs 1, 2 and 6 differ from Graphs 3, 4, and 5?

5. Which graph shows the steepest line? ________________________

6. Which graph shows the least steep line? ________________________

7. Which graphs would show parallel lines if they were plotted on the same axes?

Connecting Equations and Graphs – Day 80

Name: ______________________________ Date: ______________

Parameters for all graphs: x-min: $^-47$, x-max: 47, x-scale: 4, y-min: $^-31$, y-max: 31, y-scale: 4.

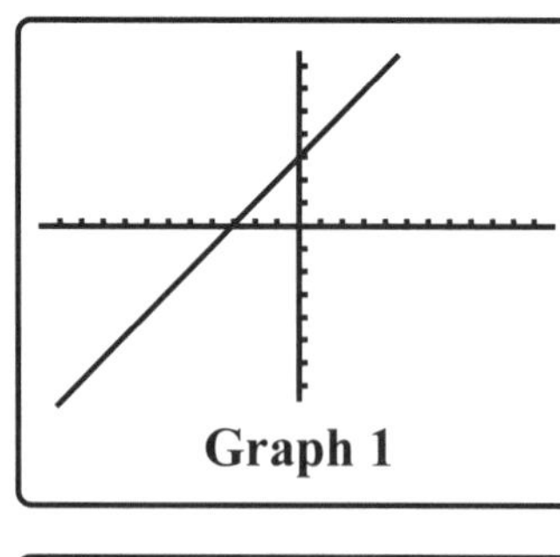
Graph 1

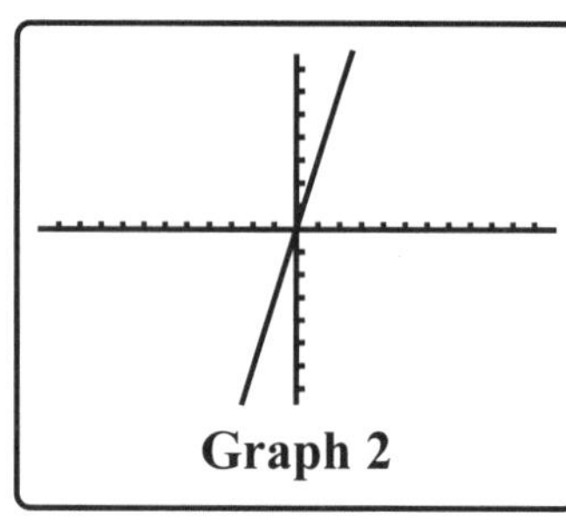
Graph 2

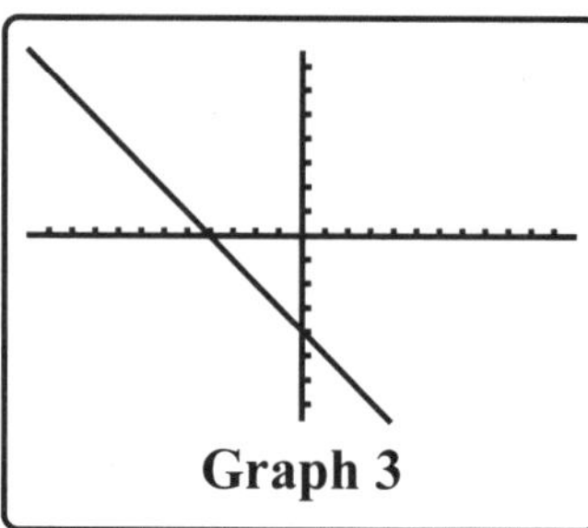
Graph 3

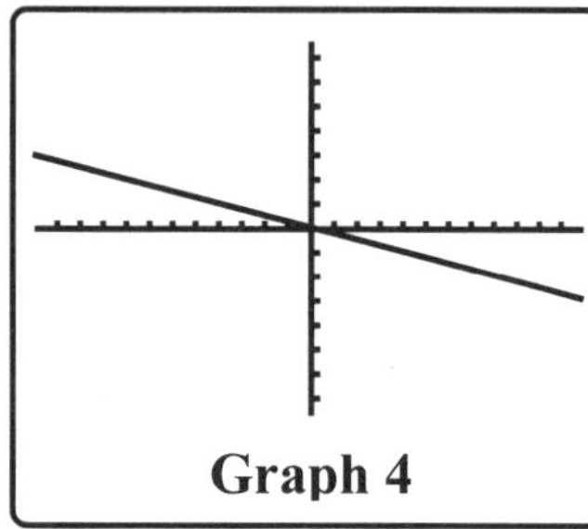
Graph 4

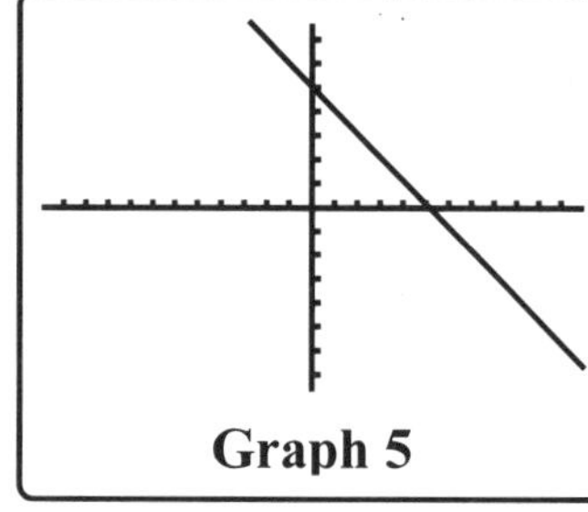
Graph 5

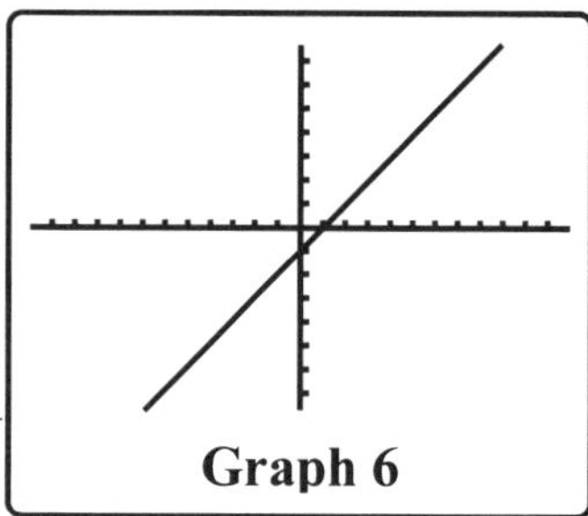
Graph 6

Match the graphs above to the equations below by writing the correct graph number next to the equation.

1. $y = 2x$ ____________

2. $y = {}^-\frac{1}{4}x$ ____________

3. $y = {}^-x + 20$ ____________

4. $y = x - 4$ ____________

5. $y = x + 12$ ____________

6. $y = {}^-x - 16$ ____________

7. Explain the effect the m has on the graph of an equation written as $y = mx + b$.

8. Explain the effect b has on the graph of an equation written as $y = mx + b$.

Graphing by the Slope-Intercept Method – Day 81

Name: ______________________________ Date: ______________

Graph each of the equations below using the slope-intercept method.

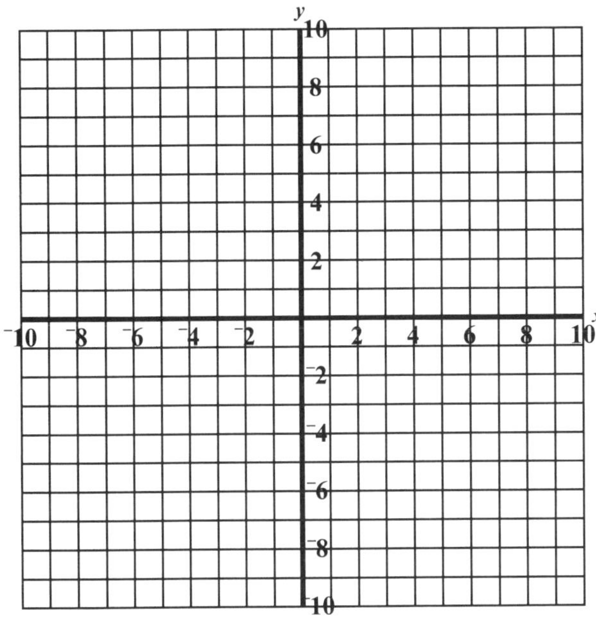

1. $y = \frac{3}{5}x$

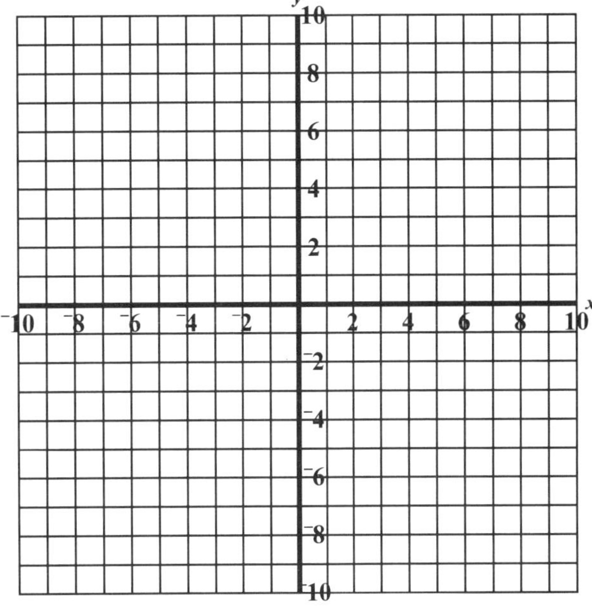

2. 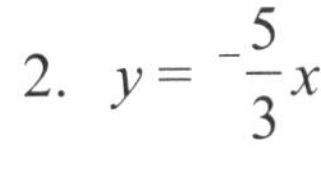 $y = -\frac{5}{3}x$

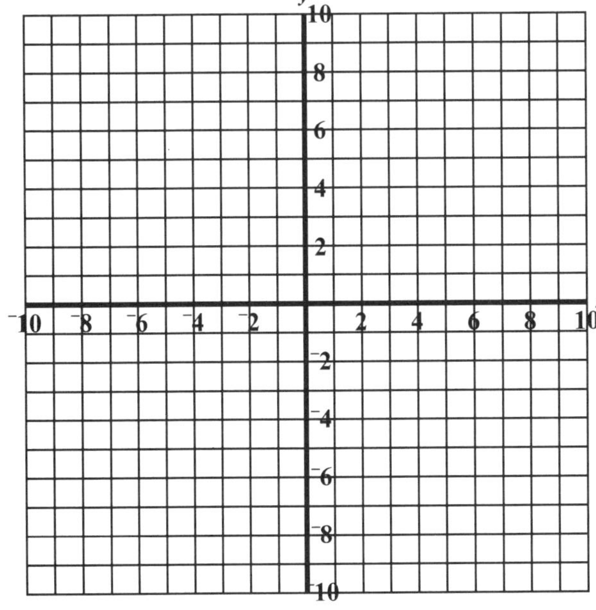

3. $y = -3x$

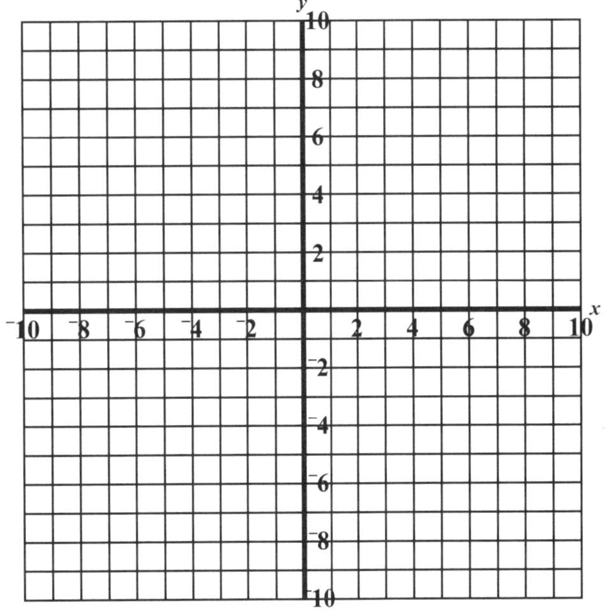

4. $y = \frac{1}{3}x$

Graphing by the Slope-Intercept Method – Day 82

Name: ______________________________ Date: ______________

Graph each of the equations below using the slope-intercept method.

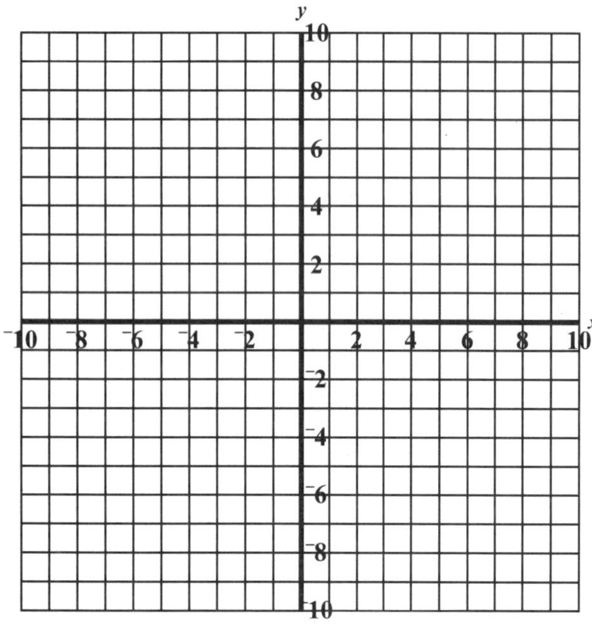

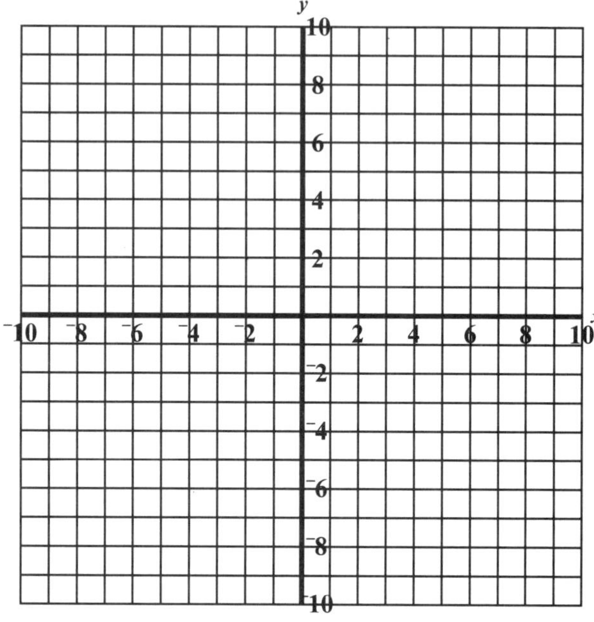

1. $y = \frac{1}{5}x + 3$

2. $y = {}^{-}\frac{1}{3}x - 5$

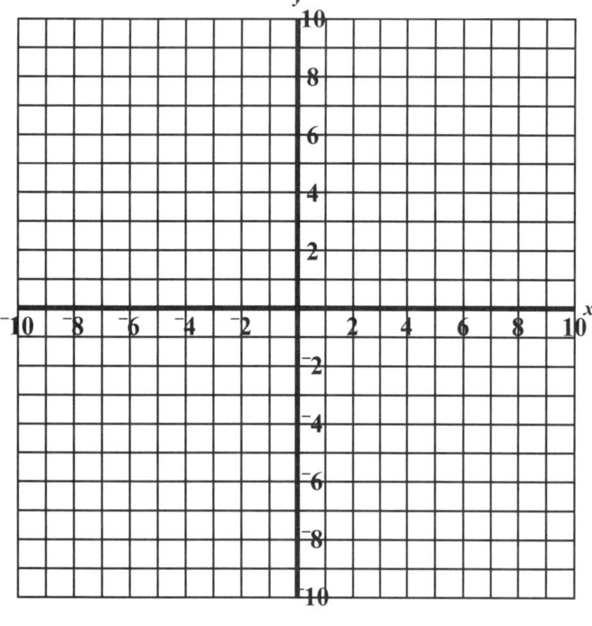

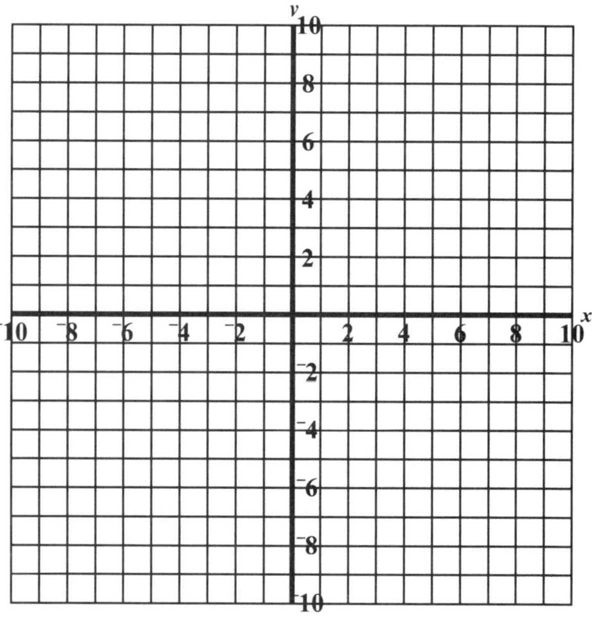

3. $y = 2x - 4$

4. $y = {}^{-}\frac{4}{3}x + 1$

Slope and Intercept – Assessment – Day 83

Name: ______________________________ Date: ______________

1. Which of the following shows the graph for $y = \frac{1}{2}x - 2$?

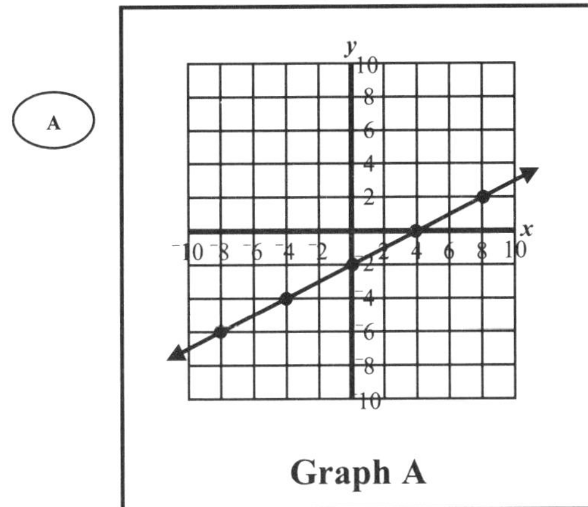

Graph A

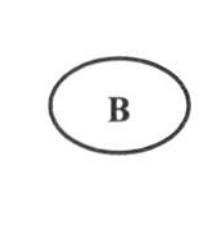

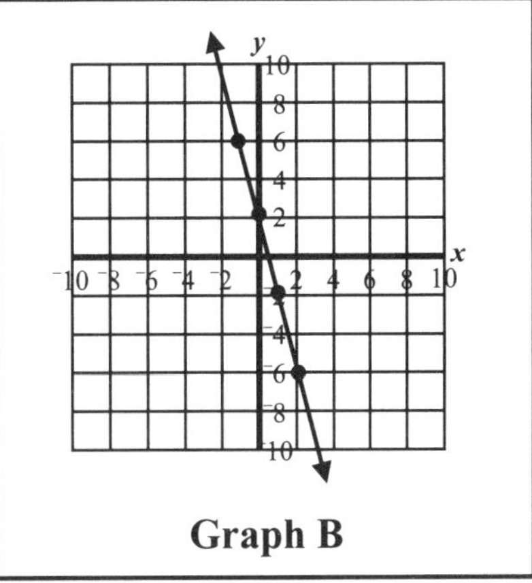

Graph B

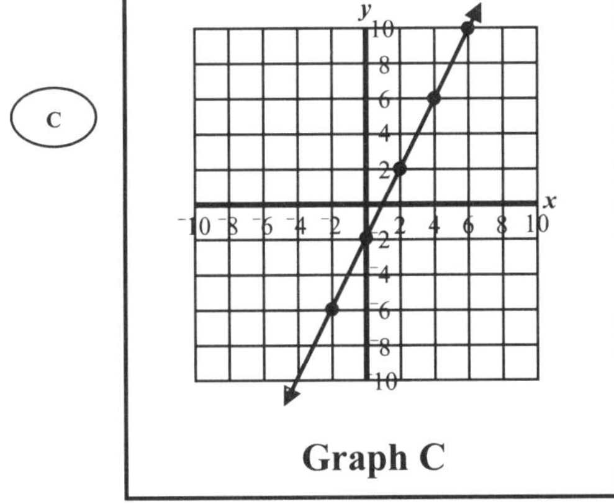

Graph C

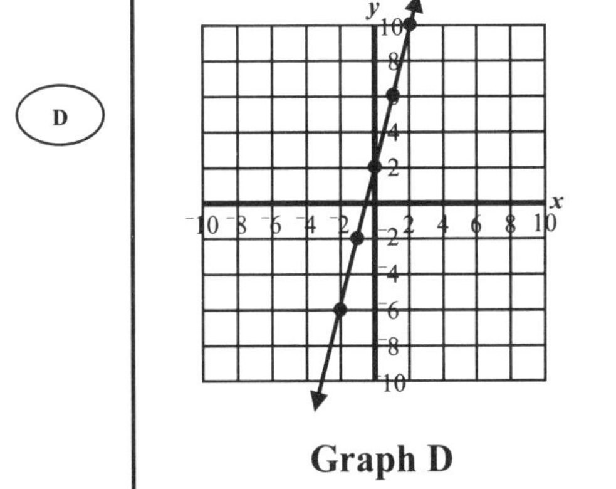

Graph D

2. Which of the equations below represents a line that passes through the point (0,4) and falls from left to right?

(A) $y = \frac{1}{2}x + 4$ (B) $y = \frac{-1}{2}x + 4$ (C) $y = 2x - 4$ (D) $y = \frac{-2}{3}x - 4$

3. Which equation describes the table of values below?

x	y
¯3	¯7
¯2	¯5
0	¯1
2	3
3	5

(A) $y = x - 2$ (B) $y = 2x - 1$ (C) $y = 2x + 1$ (D) $y = x + 1$

4. Which of the tables below is represented by the graph shown?

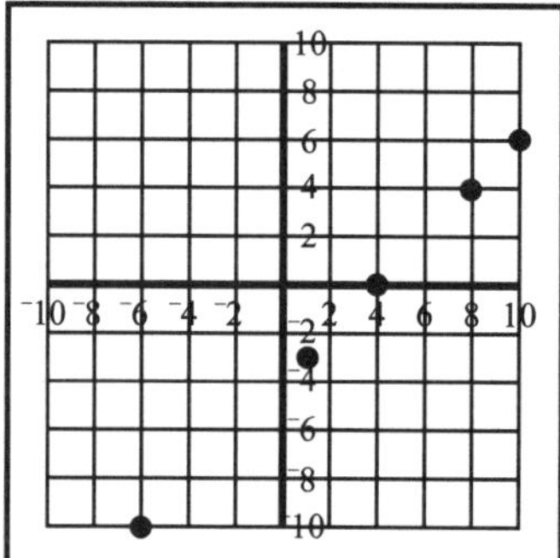

(A)

x	y
10	6
8	4
4	0
1	¯3
¯6	¯10

(B)

x	y
¯10	¯6
¯3	1
0	4
4	8
6	10

(C)

x	y
¯6	10
¯4	8
0	4
3	1
6	¯2

(D)

x	y
¯6	¯10
¯4	¯8
0	¯4
3	¯1
6	2

5. If $\Delta y = 3$ and $\Delta x = 4$, then what must the slope be?

(A) $-\frac{4}{3}$ (B) $\frac{3}{4}$ (C) 1 (D) $\frac{4}{3}$

Computation in Context – Day 84

Name: ______________________________ Date: ______________

Study the eight problems below, and decide whether to use mental math, paper and pencil, or estimation and a calculator to complete each by circling the method. Write answers or estimates in the blanks at the right.

		Estimate / Exact Answer
1. $100 - 29.75$ MM PP EC	2. $53.6 + 1001.2 + 0.421 + 15.64 + 243.089$ MM PP EC	1. ______ ______ 2. ______ ______
3. $0.14\overline{)713.87}$ MM PP EC	4. $0.625 \times 32{,}000$ MM PP EC	3. ______ ______ 4. ______ ______
5. 405.21×29.2 MM PP EC	6. $233{,}427.132 - 8{,}544.786$ MM PP EC	5. ______ ______ 6. ______ ______
7. $0.6 + 0.3 + 8.2 + 1.4$ MM PP EC	8. $2.5\overline{)525.75}$ MM PP EC	7. ______ ______ 8. ______ ______

Real Data - Day 85

Name: ______________________________ Date: ______________

Think about each of the descriptions below and tell whether they would be represented by a continuous or non-continuous graph.

1. Movies Online charges $12.00 per month and $1.00 per movie that is rented. Which chart shows the total cost based on the number of movies rented? ______________

2. Ashmed needs to convert feet to inches. Which table will help him make these conversions? ______________

3. Which graph shows the amount of gasoline left in a tank relative to the number of miles traveled? ______________

4. Mr. Aguero bases his test scores on 100 points and always rounds grades so they are whole numbers. Which graph shows the grade based on the number of questions that a student gets correct? ______________

5. At the beginning of each marking period, Ms. Geissler gives every student 99 points as a homework grade. However, she subtracts 3 points for each homework assignment that is not completed. Which graph should a student use to calculate a homework grade based on missed assignments? ______________

6. Talk More phone company charges 19.95 per month and a rate of $0.04 per minute for the exact number of minutes (including partial minutes) used during the month. Which graph shows the total monthly charges? ______________

7. Anitha averages 3 miles per hour while hiking. Which graph shows her total miles with respect to the number of hours hiked? ______________

8. Hector averages 3 miles per hour while hiking. Which graph shows the total miles left to hike on a 48-mile hike? ______________

Interpreting Real Data – Day 86

Name: ______________________________ Date: ______________

Think about each of the descriptions below. Match each to one of the graphs on Discovery Templates 37 and 38 that most accurately represents them. (Make sure you are able to tell how you know the description matches the graph you selected.)

1. Movies Online charges $12.00 per month and $1.00 per movie that is rented. Which chart shows the total cost based on the number of movies rented?

2. Ashmed needs to convert feet to inches. Which table will help him make these conversions?

3. Which graph shows the amount of gasoline left in a tank relative to the number of miles traveled?

4. Mr. Aguero bases his test scores on 100 points and always rounds grades so they are whole numbers. Which graph shows the grade based on the number of questions that a student gets correct?

5. At the beginning of each marking period, Ms. Geissler gives every student 99 points as a homework grade. However, she subtracts 3 points for each homework assignment that is not completed. Which graph should a student use to calculate a homework grade based on missed assignments?

6. Talk More phone company charges 19.95 per month and a rate of $0.04 per minute for the exact number of minutes used during the month. Which graph shows the total monthly charges?

7. Anitha averages 3 miles per hour while hiking. Which graph shows her total miles with respect to the number of hours hiked?

8. Hector averages 3 miles per hour while hiking. Which graph shows the total miles left to hike on a 48-mile hike?

Connecting Slope to Real Data – Day 87

Name: ______________________________ Date: ______________

1. Based on the graphs below, tell which fast food chain has the most calories from fat per ounce and which has the least calories from fat per ounce. Tell how you know.

2. Tell how many calories from fat per ounce there are for each of the fast food chains. Describe how you determined the answer.

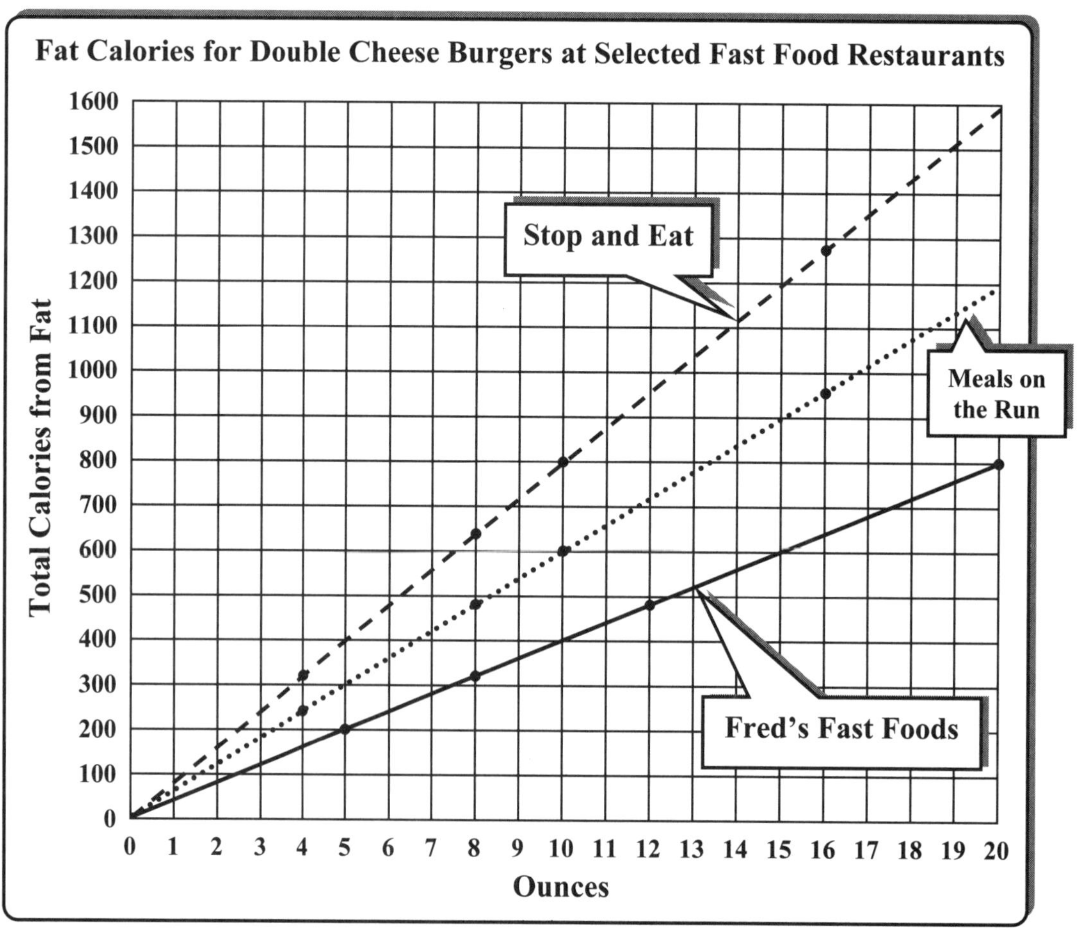

Scatter Plots – Day 88

Name: ______________________________ Date: ______________

Use the graphs below to answer the questions on the following page.

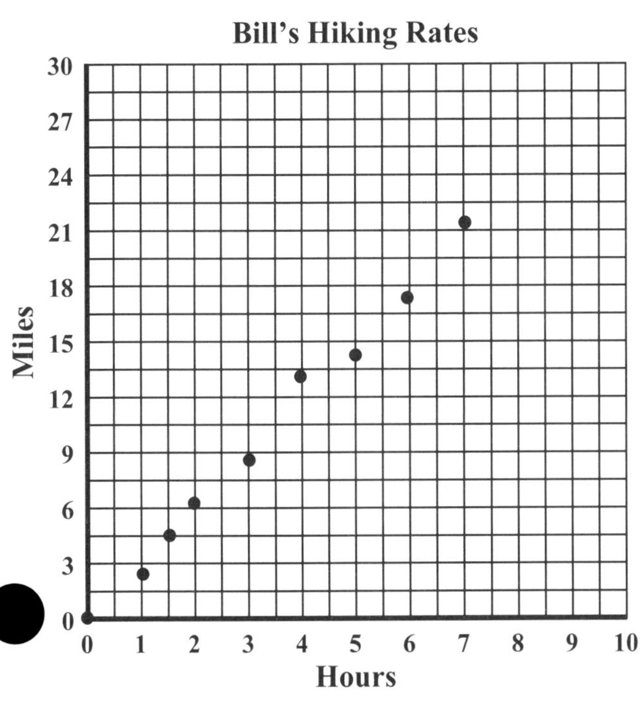

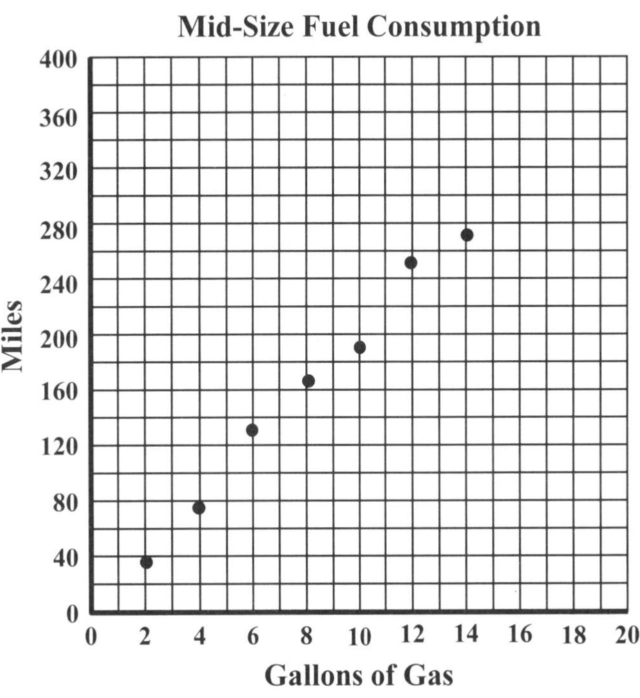

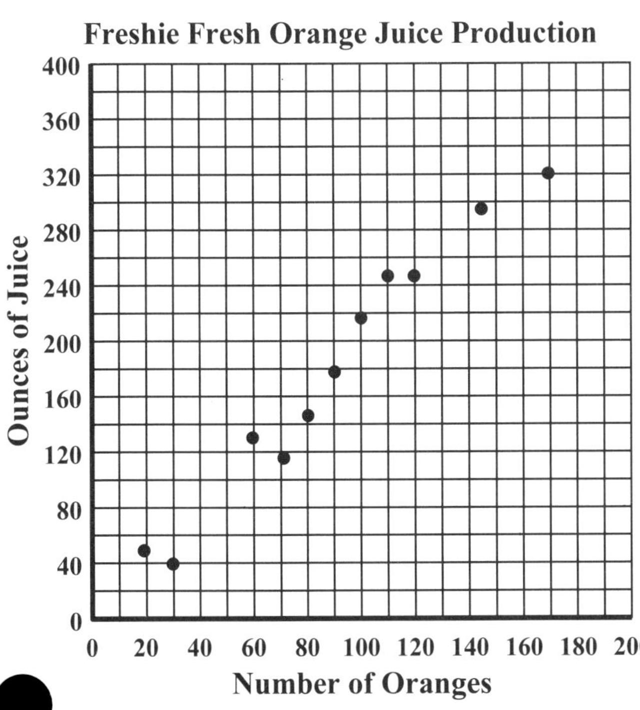

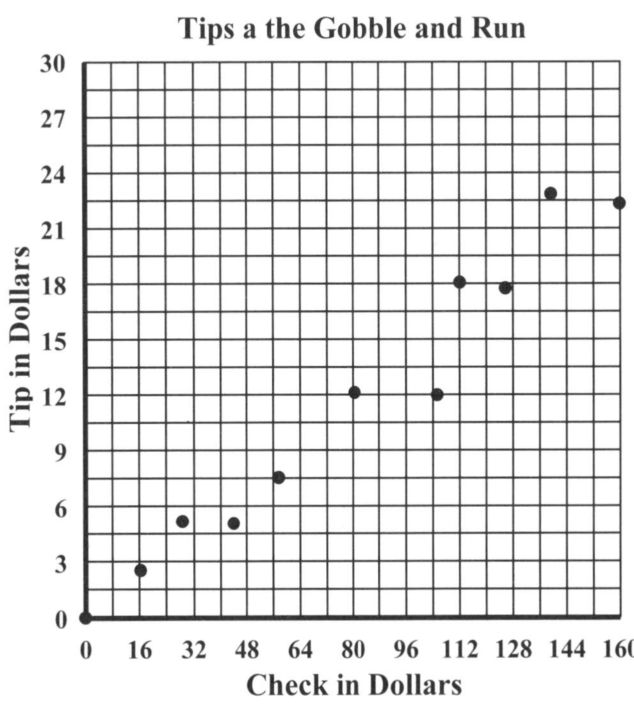

1. Based on the graph, about how much juice was obtained from 30 oranges?

2. Based on the graph, about how much was the tip for the $112 check?

3. Based on the graph how many miles were traveled on 4 gallons of gas?

4. Based on the graph how many miles were hiked in 3 hours?

Draw the trend lines for each of the graphs on the previous page.

5. Based on the trend line, what would be tip for an $88 check?

6. Based on the trend line, what how many miles would be traveled on 16 gallons of gas?

7. Based on the trend line, how far would Bill hike in 3.5 hours?

8. Based on the trend line, how many ounces of orange juice would 130 oranges produce?

9. Based on the trend line, what is the average miles per gallon?

10. Based on the trend line, how much juice does the average orange yield?

11. Based on the trend line, about what percent tip was received?

Real Data – Assessment – Day 89

Name: ______________________________ Date: ______________

1. The DVD Internet Movie Line charges a fixed price of \$4.95 per month and a rental fee of \$2.98 for each DVD. Which graph below shows the total cost for renting up to 25 movies for the month?

(A)
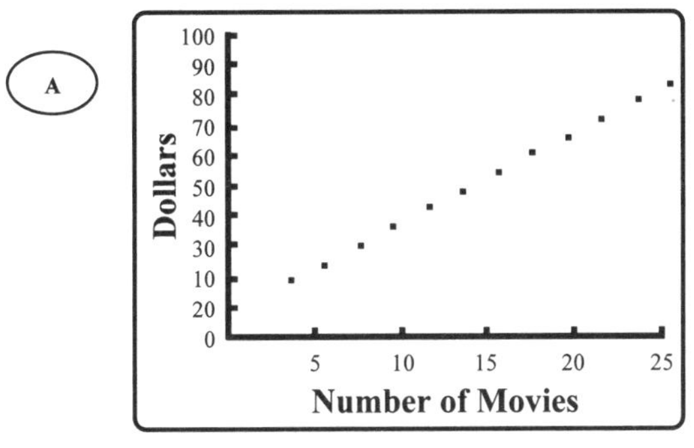

(B)
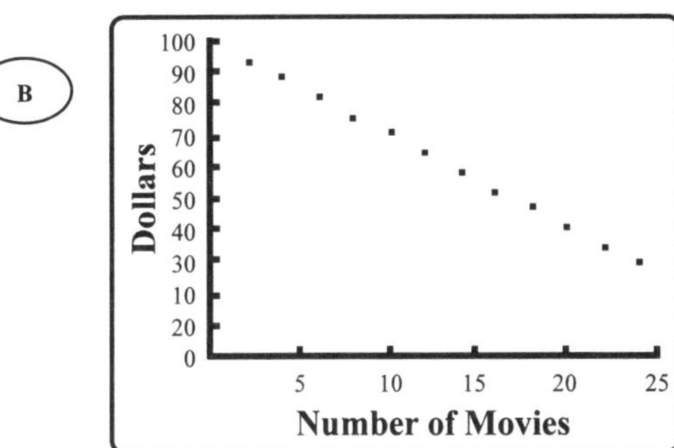

(C)
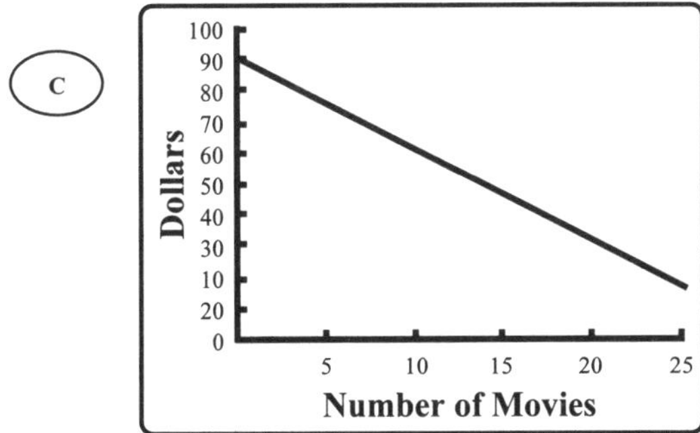

(D)
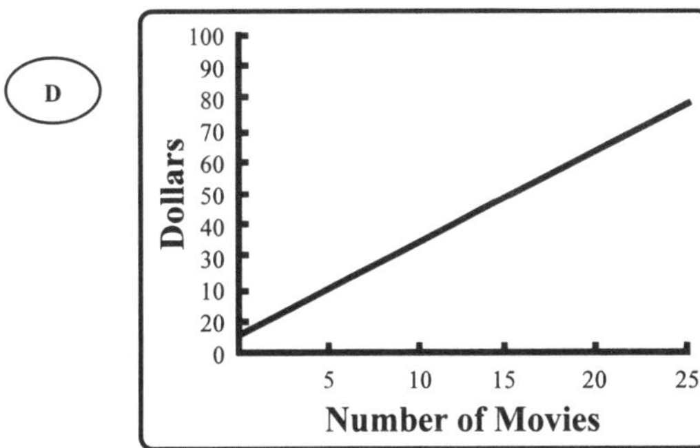

2. During his ten-hour journey, Myron recorded the total number of miles he had traveled after each hour. He then drew a line of best fit to help him determine his average rate. Based on this line, what is Myron's average rate of speed in miles per hour?

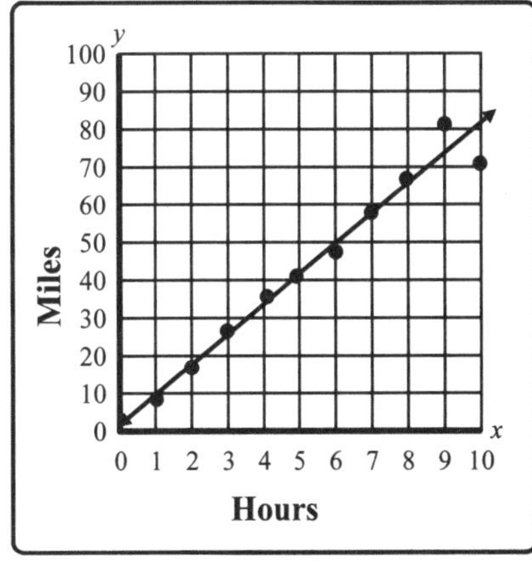

(A) 6 mph (B) 7 mph (C) 8 mph (D) 10 mph

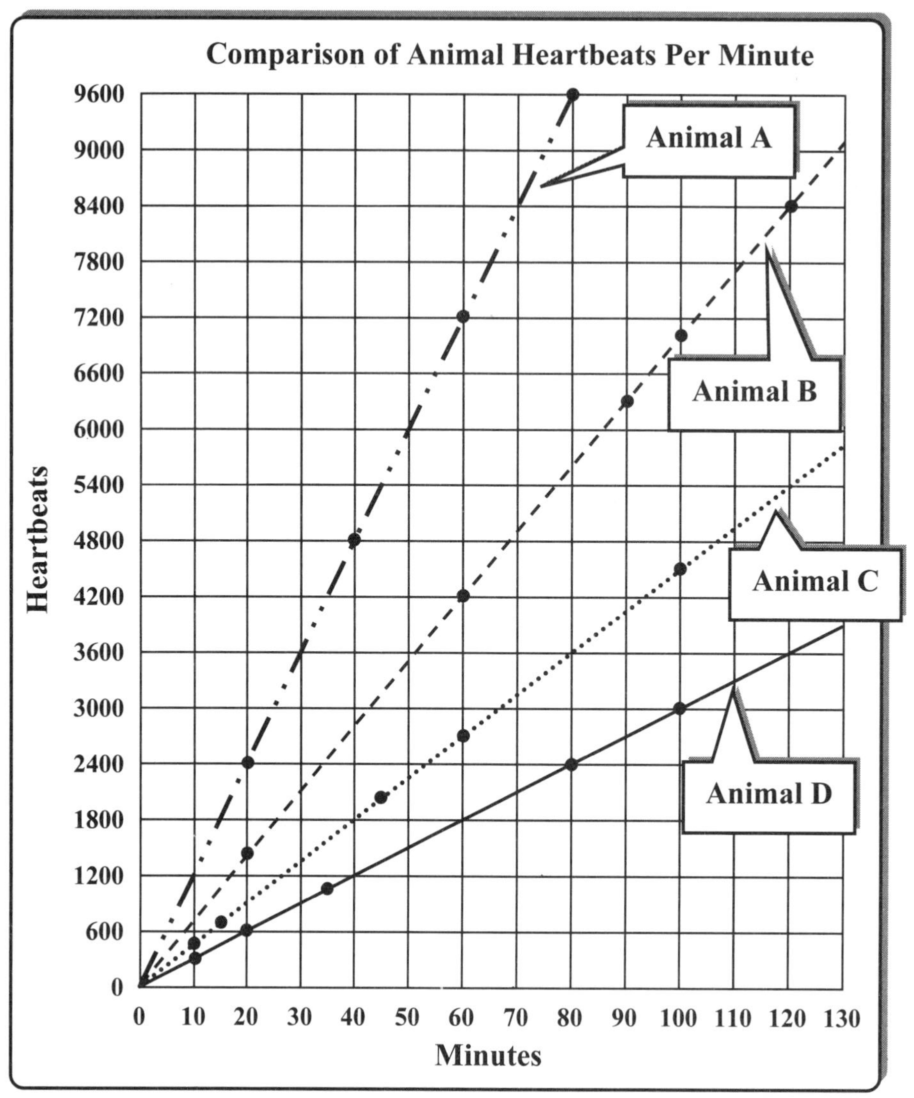

3. The graph above shows the total number of heartbeats of various animals for various periods of time. Based on this chart, which animal has a heart rate of 45 beats per minute?

(A) Animal A (B) Animal B (C) Animal C (D) Animal D

4. Based on the graph, which animal has the slowest heart rate?

(A) Animal A (B) Animal B (C) Animal C (D) Animal D

5. Mr. Gore developed the graph below when he purchased his new solar-powered sports car Echowheels. Based on the data about how many miles should he be able to travel on 8 gallons of gas?

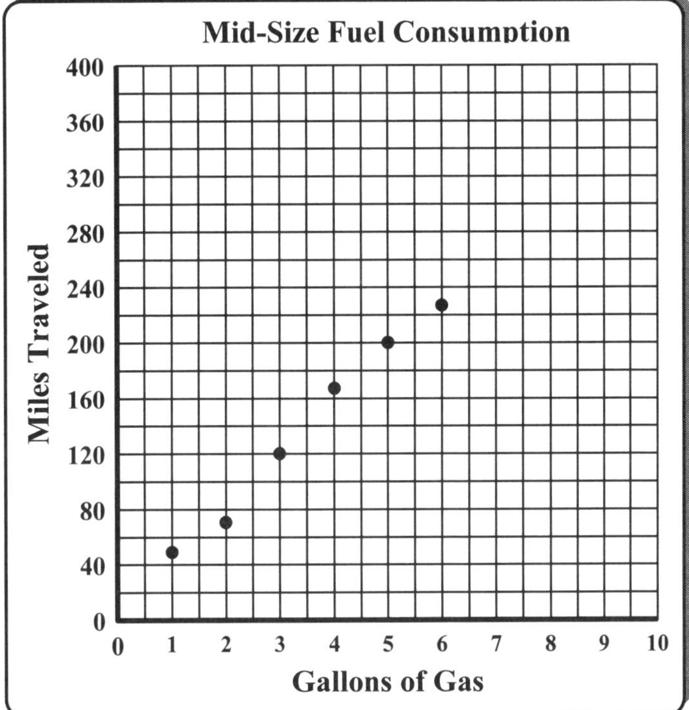

(A) 280 (B) 320 (C) 360 (D) 400

Computation in Context – Day 90

Name: ______________________________ Date: ______________

Study the eight problems below, and decide whether to use mental math, paper and pencil, or estimation and a calculator to complete each by circling the method. Write answers or estimates in the blanks at the right.

Problem	Problem	Estimate / Exact Answer
1. $0.25 \times 28{,}000$ MM PP EC	2. $0.33\overline{)814.87}$ MM PP EC	1. ____ ____ 2. ____ ____
3. $\begin{array}{r} 4.123 \\ 5.2 \\ 0.653 \\ 15.54 \\ +\ 453.0892 \\ \hline \end{array}$ MM PP EC	4. $9 - 7.24$ MM PP EC	3. ____ ____ 4. ____ ____
5. $\begin{array}{r} 32.78 \\ \times\ 19.8 \\ \hline \end{array}$ MM PP EC	6. $0.3 + 0.4 + 1.2 + 4.8$ MM PP EC	5. ____ ____ 6. ____ ____
7. $1.2\overline{)72.12}$ MM PP EC	8. $\begin{array}{r} 123.876 \\ -\ 44.987 \\ \hline \end{array}$ MM PP EC	7. ____ ____ 8. ____ ____

Primes, Composites, and Perfect Squares - Day 91

Name: ______________________________ Date: ______________

1. List all the perfect squares less than 250 that are missing from Data Source 1.

____

____

____

2. List all the prime numbers less than 50 that are missing from Data Source 1.

____

____

____

Data Source 1

	1	2	3	4
5	6	7	8	9
	10	11	12	13
14	15	16	17	18
	19	20	21	22
25	42	50	60	72
	80	90	96	100
101	120	150	200	250

3. List all the factors of 21. ______________________

4. List all the factors of 50. ______________________

5. List all the multiples of 6 that are shown on Data Source 1. ______________________

6. List all the multiples of 7 that are shown on the Data Source 1. ______________________

7. How many factors does a prime number have? ______________________

8. Why does a perfect square have an odd number of factors?

9. List all the factors of 150. ______________________

10. Give an example of a number from Data Source 1 that has eight factors.

Factors – Day 92

Name: ______________________________ Date: ______________

Evaluate each of the expressions below.

1. $3 \cdot 5^2 =$ ______________ 2. $2 \cdot 10^2 =$ ______________

3. $2 \cdot 5^2 =$ ______________ 4. $3 \cdot 2^3 =$ ______________

5. $3 \cdot 10^3 =$ ______________ 6. $5 \cdot 3^2 =$ ______________

7. $2^3 \cdot 5 =$ ______________ 8. $3^3 \cdot 2^2 =$ ______________

9. $3^2 \cdot 10^3 =$ ______________ 10. $2^3 \cdot 10^4 =$ ______________

11. $2 \cdot 7^2 \cdot 5 =$ ______________ 12. $5^2 \cdot 3^2 =$ ______________

Give the prime factors in exponential form for each of the numbers below .

13. 45 ______________________

14. 32 ______________________

15. 24 ______________________

16. 100 ______________________

17. 18 ______________________

18. 56 ______________________

GCFs and LCMs – Day 93

Name: ______________________________ Date: ______________

Determine the greatest common factor for each set of numbers.

1. 35 and 45 ______________________

2. 6 and 25 ______________________

3. 27 and 36 ______________________

4. 8 and 12 ______________________

5. 24 and 54 ______________________

6. 42 and 49 ______________________

Determine the LCM for each of the problems below.

7. 4 and 5 __________

8. 6 and 7 __________

9. 2 and 9 __________

10. 4 and 20 __________

11. 7 and 21 __________

12. 2 and 10 __________

13. 4 and 6 __________

14. 6 and 21 __________

15. What relationship does the greatest common factor have to the least common multiple?

16. If the least common multiple between two denominators is 210, and the greatest common factor is 6, what must be the original denominators?

Patterns with GCFs and LCMs – Day 94

Name: ______________________________ Date: ____________

Use efficient strategies to determine the LCM of each set of fractions.

1. $\frac{1}{12} + \frac{1}{4}$ ____________

2. $\frac{5}{9} + \frac{1}{4}$ ____________

3. $\frac{5}{12} + \frac{1}{8}$ ____________

4. $\frac{7}{18} + \frac{5}{6}$ ____________

5. $\frac{3}{8} + \frac{4}{5}$ ____________

6. $\frac{5}{9} + \frac{4}{21}$ ____________

7. $\frac{17}{40} + \frac{9}{16}$ ____________

8. $\frac{4}{7} + \frac{5}{8}$ ____________

9. $\frac{7}{20} + \frac{11}{36}$ ____________

10. $\frac{3}{10} + \frac{11}{21}$ ____________

11. $\frac{5}{21} + \frac{2}{3}$ ____________

12. $\frac{5}{12} + \frac{11}{14}$ ____________

Patterns with Primes and Composites – Assessment – Day 95

Name: ______________________________ Date: ______________

1. What is the value of $2^3 \times 3^2$?

   (A) 17 (B) 36 (C) 54 (D) 72

2. Which of the following has a value of 36?

   (A) $2^3 \cdot 2^3$ (B) $2 \cdot 3^2$ (C) $2^2 \cdot 3^2$ (D) 3^{12}

3. Which of the following has the same value as $2 \cdot 2 \cdot 2 \cdot 3 \cdot 5 \cdot 5$?

   (A) $2^3 \cdot 3 \cdot 5^2$ (B) $3^2 \cdot 1^3 \cdot 2^5$ (C) $2^3 \cdot 5^2$ (D) $2^3 \cdot 3^{10}$

4. What is the greatest common factor of 12 and 18?

   (A) 2 (B) 3 (C) 6 (D) 36

5. What is the least common multiple between 8 and 6?

   (A) 2 (B) 10 (C) 12 (D) 24

6. Which of the following is the only true statement?

   (A) Each prime number can be represented by exactly two arrays.

   (B) An even number cannot be a prime number.

   (C) One is a prime number.

   (D) Every perfect square is also a prime number.

Computation in Context – Day 96

Name: ______________________ Date: ____________

Study the twelve problems below, and decide whether to use mental math, paper and pencil, or estimation and a calculator to complete each by circling the method. Write answers or estimates in the blanks at the right.

			Estimate / Exact Answer
1. $\begin{array}{r} 420.01 \\ 1038.9 \\ 522.83 \\ +\ 319. \\ \hline \end{array}$ PP MM EC	2. $\frac{14}{15} \div \frac{2}{15}$ PP MM EC	3. $41\overline{)23{,}083}$ PP MM EC	1. ____ 2. ____ 3. ____
4. $21\frac{1}{8} - 9\frac{2}{3}$ PP MM EC	5. $\begin{array}{r} 32{,}908{,}419 \\ +\ 5{,}109{,}381 \\ \hline \end{array}$ PP MM EC	6. $\begin{array}{r} 272.59 \\ -\ 50.13 \\ \hline \end{array}$ PP MM EC	4. ____ 5. ____ 6. ____
7. $13\frac{2}{9} \times \frac{3}{5}$ PP MM EC	8. $0.7\overline{)844.921}$ PP MM EC	9. $\begin{array}{r} 2{,}591 \\ \times\ 3 \\ \hline \end{array}$ PP MM EC	7. ____ 8. ____ 9. ____
10. $\begin{array}{r} 163{,}081 \\ -\ 17{,}172 \\ \hline \end{array}$ PP MM EC	11. $\begin{array}{r} 1.843 \\ \times\ 2.7 \\ \hline \end{array}$ PP MM EC	12. $11\frac{1}{6} + 3\frac{11}{12}$ PP MM EC	10. ____ 11. ____ 12. ____

Working with Negative Exponents – Day 97

Name: ______________________________ Date: ______________

1. Based on the patterns established with negative exponents, what fraction would be formed by the expression $2^3 \cdot 3^{-2}$? Explain how you determined the answer.

2. How could the fraction $\frac{25}{49}$ be written in exponential form? Explain how you determined the answer.

Evaluate each of the following without a calculator.

1. $11^{-1} =$ __________ 2. $7^{-2} =$ __________ 3. $4^{-3} =$ __________

4. $7 \cdot 10^{-1} =$ __________ 5. $13 \cdot 10^{-2} =$ __________ 6. $71 \cdot 10^{-3} =$ __________

7. $2^4 \cdot 5^{-2} =$ __________ 8. $3^3 \cdot 10^{-2} =$ __________ 9. $5^1 \cdot 2^{-3} =$ __________

Write each of the following in exponential form.

10. $\frac{1}{10} =$ __________ 11. $\frac{1}{25} =$ __________ 12. $\frac{1}{121} =$ __________

13. $\frac{219}{1000} =$ __________ 14. $\frac{3}{10} =$ __________ 15. $\frac{51}{100} =$ __________

16. $\frac{8}{25} =$ __________ 17. $\frac{49}{1000} =$ __________ 18. $\frac{25}{27} =$ __________

A Different Look at Numbers – Day 98

Name: ______________________________ Date: ______________

1. How many complete 1000s are in 3.4 thousands? ______________
2. What is 0.4 of 1000? ______________
3. How many complete 10,000s are in 9.3 ten-thousands? ______________
4. What is 0.3 of ten-thousand? ______________
5. How many complete 100,000s are in 7.8 hundred-thousands? ______________
6. What is 0.8 of a hundred-thousand? ______________
7. How many complete 0.01s are in 5.1 hundredths? ______________
8. What is 0.1 of a hundredth? ______________
9. How many complete 0.0001s are in 6.2 ten-thousandths? ______________
10. What is 0.2 of one ten-thousandth? ______________

Write the following in standard form:

11. 4.8 thousands ______________
12. 8.5 tenths ______________
13. 9.6 million ______________
14. 5.3 thousandths ______________
15. 7.8 billion ______________
16. 9.1 ten-thousands ______________
17. 1.6 millionths ______________
18. 4.2 tens ______________
19. 3.6 hundreds ______________
20. 8.4 hundredths ______________

Number Equivalencies – Day 99

Name: ____ Date: __________________

Match the numbers below to the correct description by writing the letter next to the description.

A. 3.4×10^3	B. 4.3×10^5	C. 5.3×10^{-3}	D. 2.4×10^2
E. 1.7×10^{-1}	F. 8.6×10^{-2}	G. 3.2×10^5	H. 1.7×10^9
I. 2.4×10^4	J. 3.4×10^{-3}	K. 4.3×10^{-6}	L. 3.2×10^6

1. _______________ This number has 3 complete hundred-thousands.
2. _______________ This number has 200,000 as part of its standard form.
3. _______________ This number can be written as 0.0000043.
4. _______________ This number has 3 complete thousands.
5. _______________ This number can be written as 240.
6. _______________ This number has 3 complete thousandths.
7. _______________ This number has 0.0003 as part of its standard form.
8. _______________ This number has 4000 as part of its standard form.
9. _______________ This number has one complete tenth.
10. _______________ This number can be written as 430,000.
11. _______________ This number has 8 complete hundredths.
12. _______________ This number has 700,000,000 as part of its standard form.

Scientific Notation and Standard Form– Day 100

Name: ______________________________ Date: ______________

Write each of Problems 1 – 10 in standard form. Write each of the Problems 11 – 20 in scientific notation.

1. $8.5 \times 10^{4} =$ ______________
2. $6.9 \times 10^{-3} =$ ______________
3. $3.4 \times 10^{2} =$ ______________
4. $2.5 \times 10^{-1} =$ ______________
5. $9.7 \times 10^{5} =$ ______________
6. $7.6 \times 10^{-2} =$ ______________
7. $5.4 \times 10^{4} =$ ______________
8. $1.67 \times 10^{2} =$ ______________
9. $4.23 \times 10^{-1} =$ ______________
10. $4.58 \times 10^{9} =$ ______________
11. 45,000 ______________
12. 0.0012 ______________
13. 67,000 ______________
14. 3800 ______________
15. 0.937 ______________
16. 29,000 ______________
17. 760 ______________
18. 0.055 ______________
19. 1,400,000 ______________
20. 0.00024 ______________

More Conversions – Day 101

Name: ______________________________ Date: ______________

Fill in the missing values.

Scientific Notation	Standard Form
1. 3.6×10^{-2}	
2.	0.32
3.	0.054
4. 3.7×10^{-1}	
5. 1.8×10^{-3}	
6.	0.004
7.	5,300
8. 8.0×10^{4}	
9.	240
10. 2.6×10^{1}	
11.	4,300,000
12. 9.4×10^{5}	

Scientific Notation – Assessment - Day 102

Name: ______________________________ Date: ______________

1. What is the value of 2.34×10^3

Ⓐ 0.00234 Ⓑ 32.34 Ⓒ 2340 Ⓓ 234,000

2. Siobon set his calculator to display numbers in scientific notation. What did his calculator display when he put in 0.042 and pressed enter?

Ⓐ 4.2 E^{-}3 Ⓑ 4.2 E^{-}2 Ⓒ 4.2 E2 Ⓓ 4.2 E3

3. What digit is in the hundreds place when 7.51×10^3 is written in standard form?

Ⓐ 0 Ⓑ 1 Ⓒ 5 Ⓓ 7

4. What is three tenths of one thousand?

Ⓐ 0.3 Ⓑ 3 Ⓒ 30 Ⓓ 300

5. Which of the following is equivalent to 1.27×10^4?

Ⓐ 0.000127

Ⓑ 1,270

Ⓒ 12,700

Ⓓ 1270000

Basic Patterns – Day 103

Name: ______________________________ Date: ______________

1. If the pattern below were to continue, what digit would be in the 19th position?

   706706706706... ____________

2. If the pattern below were to continue, what digit would be in the 118th position?

   METRICMETRICMETRICMETRIC... ____________

3. If the pattern below were to continue, what digit would be in the 44th position?

   3487348734873487... ____________

4. If the pattern below were to continue, what digit would be in the 203rd position?

   ANGLEANGLEANGLEANGLEANGLE... ____________

5. If the pattern below were to continue, what digit would be in the 1001st position?

   232323232323...____________

6. If the pattern below were to continue, what letter would be in the 531st position?

   RAYRAYRAYRAYRAYRAY... ____________

7. If the pattern below were to continue, what digit would be in the 38th position?

   358853358853358853358853... ____________

8. If the pattern below were to continue, what letter would be in the 88th position?

   SCALENESCALENESCALENE... ____________

Forming and Describing Patterns – Day 104

Name: ______________________________ Date: ______________

1. What digit is in the units place of 8^{79}?

2. If 5 were the first term of a pattern, and each term after that were doubled, what would be the seventh term of the pattern?

3. What is the 12th digit in the decimal value of $\frac{4}{7}$?

4. If the pattern below were to continue, how many *N*s would be in the pattern?

   DEEFFFGGGG…

5. If the pattern below were to continue, what digit would be in the 25th place?

   69111611116111111…

6. How many 1s would appear after the twentieth 2 in the pattern below?

   211211121111...

Describing Patterns – Day 105

Name: ____ Date: ________________

Study each of the sequences below. Describe how the pattern is generated. Then determine the next three terms and tell whether the sequence is arithmetic or geometric.

1. 5, 9, 13, 17…

2. $^{-}4, 8, ^{-}16, 32\ldots$

3. 6, 12, 18, 24 …

4. $\frac{1}{8}, \frac{3}{16}, \frac{1}{4}, \frac{5}{16}, \frac{3}{8}, \frac{7}{16}\ldots$

5. 5, 10, 20, 40…

6. $^{-}2, 6, ^{-}18, 54\ldots$

7. 35, 31, 27, 23, 19…

8. 800, 400, 200, 100, …

9. 9, 18, 27, 36

Arithmetic, Geometric, and Fibonacci-type Sequences – Day 106

Name: ______________________________ Date: ______________

Study each of the sequences below. Determine the next three terms for each and describe the pattern. Then state whether each is an arithmetic, a geometric, or a Fibonacci-like sequence.

1. 7, 14, 28… _____ _____ _____ _______________ _______________

2. 7, 10, 13, 16… _____ _____ _____ _______________ _______________

3. 2, $^{-}6$, 18, $^{-}54$… _____ _____ _____ _______________ _______________

4. 16, 8, 4… _____ _____ _____ _______________ _______________

5. 4, 4, 8, 12, 20, 32… _____ _____ _____ _______________ _______________

6. 7, 12, 17, 22… _____ _____ _____ _______________ _______________

7. $^{-}3$, 6, $^{-}12$, 24… _____ _____ _____ _______________ _______________

8. 27, 9, 3… _____ _____ _____ _______________ _______________

9. $\frac{1}{16}, \frac{1}{8}, \frac{3}{16}, \frac{1}{4}, \frac{5}{16}\ldots$ _____ _____ _____ _______________ _______________

10. $\frac{1}{5}$, 1, 5… _____ _____ _____ _______________ _______________

11. 40, 35, 30… _____ _____ _____ _______________ _______________

12. 2, 2, 4, 6, 10… _____ _____ _____ _______________ _______________

13. 0, $^{-}0.5$, $^{-}0.1$, $^{-}1.5$, $^{-}2$… _____ _____ _____ _______________ _______________

14. 10, $^{-}100$, 1,000… _____ _____ _____ _______________ _______________

15. 5, 5, 10, 15, 25, 40… _____ _____ _____ _______________ _______________

Patterns – Assessment – Day 107

Name: ______________________________ Date: ______________

1. What is the units digit of 7^{22}?

(A) 1 (B) 3 (C) 7 (D) 9

2. If the pattern below were to continue, what letter would be in the 37th place?

SPACESPACESPACE ...

(A) A (B) P (C) R (D) S

3. If an arithmetic sequence begins with a 5 and the constant term is 4, what is the fifth term of the sequence?

(A) 13 (B) 17 (C) 21 (D) 3125

4. Which of the following is a Fibonacci-like sequence?

(A) $9, 3, 1, \frac{1}{3}\ldots$ (B) $9, 6, 3, 0, ^{-}3\ldots$ (C) $3, 9, 27, 81\ldots$ (D) $1, 1, 2, 3, 5, 8\ldots$

5. If the fifth term of a geometric sequence is 81, and the sixth term is 243, what is the second term of the sequence?

(A) $\frac{1}{3}$ (B) 1 (C) 3 (D) 9

6. Java Junkies sold 30,000,000 cups of coffee in their first year of operation. They expect to sell 10,000,000 cups more each year. In which year of operation will the sales be double those of the first year?

(A) Third (B) Fourth (C) Fifth (D) Sixth

Computation in Context – Day 108

Name: ______________________________ Date: ______________

Study the twelve problems below, and decide whether to use mental math, paper and pencil, or estimation and a calculator to complete each by circling the method. Write answers or estimates in the blanks at the right.

			Estimate / Exact Answer
1. $1.4\overline{)84.042}$ PP MM EC	2. $12\frac{1}{2} \times 3\frac{4}{5}$ PP MM EC	3. 6300×0.04 PP MM EC	1. ___ ___ 2. ___ ___ 3. ___ ___
4. $13{,}475.618 - 9{,}821.74$ PP MM EC	5. $17\frac{4}{9} - 11\frac{1}{3}$ PP MM EC	6. $52\overline{)19{,}708}$ PP MM EC	4. ___ ___ 5. ___ ___ 6. ___ ___
7. $12{,}501.98 + 4{,}204.16 + 54{,}690.56 + 23{,}790.29$ PP MM EC	8. $5{,}372 + 4{,}126$ PP MM EC	9. $10\frac{1}{5} \div \frac{3}{7}$ PP MM EC	7. ___ ___ 8. ___ ___ 9. ___ ___
10. $63{,}247 - 8{,}153$ PP MM EC	11. 5432×39 PP MM EC	12. $14\frac{5}{12} + 7\frac{7}{8}$ PP MM EC	10. ___ ___ 11. ___ ___ 12. ___ ___

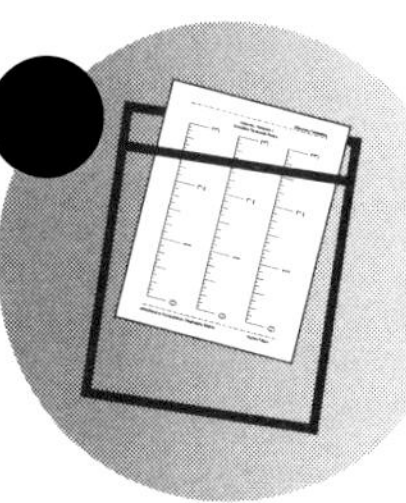

Discovery Templates

Discovery Template 1
Fraction/Decimal Equivalence Bars

1

$\frac{1}{2}$ $\frac{1}{2}$

$\frac{1}{3}$ $\frac{1}{3}$ $\frac{1}{3}$

$\frac{1}{4}$ $\frac{1}{4}$ $\frac{1}{4}$ $\frac{1}{4}$

$\frac{1}{5}$ $\frac{1}{5}$ $\frac{1}{5}$ $\frac{1}{5}$ $\frac{1}{5}$

$\frac{1}{6}$ $\frac{1}{6}$ $\frac{1}{6}$ $\frac{1}{6}$ $\frac{1}{6}$ $\frac{1}{6}$

$\frac{1}{7}$ $\frac{1}{7}$ $\frac{1}{7}$ $\frac{1}{7}$ $\frac{1}{7}$ $\frac{1}{7}$ $\frac{1}{7}$

$\frac{1}{8}$ $\frac{1}{8}$ $\frac{1}{8}$ $\frac{1}{8}$ $\frac{1}{8}$ $\frac{1}{8}$ $\frac{1}{8}$ $\frac{1}{8}$

$\frac{1}{9}$ $\frac{1}{9}$ $\frac{1}{9}$ $\frac{1}{9}$ $\frac{1}{9}$ $\frac{1}{9}$ $\frac{1}{9}$ $\frac{1}{9}$ $\frac{1}{9}$

$\frac{1}{10}$ $\frac{1}{10}$ $\frac{1}{10}$ $\frac{1}{10}$ $\frac{1}{10}$ $\frac{1}{10}$ $\frac{1}{10}$ $\frac{1}{10}$ $\frac{1}{10}$ $\frac{1}{10}$

$\frac{1}{12}$ $\frac{1}{12}$ $\frac{1}{12}$ $\frac{1}{12}$ $\frac{1}{12}$ $\frac{1}{12}$ $\frac{1}{12}$ $\frac{1}{12}$ $\frac{1}{12}$ $\frac{1}{12}$ $\frac{1}{12}$ $\frac{1}{12}$

$\frac{1}{15}$ $\frac{1}{15}$ $\frac{1}{15}$ $\frac{1}{15}$ $\frac{1}{15}$ $\frac{1}{15}$ $\frac{1}{15}$ $\frac{1}{15}$ $\frac{1}{15}$ $\frac{1}{15}$ $\frac{1}{15}$ $\frac{1}{15}$ $\frac{1}{15}$ $\frac{1}{15}$ $\frac{1}{15}$

$\frac{1}{16}$ $\frac{1}{16}$ $\frac{1}{16}$ $\frac{1}{16}$ $\frac{1}{16}$ $\frac{1}{16}$ $\frac{1}{16}$ $\frac{1}{16}$ $\frac{1}{16}$ $\frac{1}{16}$ $\frac{1}{16}$ $\frac{1}{16}$ $\frac{1}{16}$ $\frac{1}{16}$ $\frac{1}{16}$ $\frac{1}{16}$

$\frac{1}{20}$ $\frac{1}{20}$ $\frac{1}{20}$ $\frac{1}{20}$ $\frac{1}{20}$ $\frac{1}{20}$ $\frac{1}{20}$ $\frac{1}{20}$ $\frac{1}{20}$ $\frac{1}{20}$ $\frac{1}{20}$ $\frac{1}{20}$ $\frac{1}{20}$ $\frac{1}{20}$ $\frac{1}{20}$ $\frac{1}{20}$ $\frac{1}{20}$ $\frac{1}{20}$ $\frac{1}{20}$ $\frac{1}{20}$

$\frac{1}{25}$ $\frac{1}{25}$

Discovery Template 2
Fractions, Fractions, Fractions

Set A: $\frac{1}{2}$ $\frac{1}{4}$ $\frac{1}{5}$ $\frac{1}{10}$ $\frac{1}{20}$ $\frac{1}{25}$

Set B: $\frac{1}{16}$ $\frac{1}{15}$ $\frac{1}{12}$ $\frac{1}{11}$ $\frac{1}{9}$ $\frac{1}{6}$

Set C: $\frac{7}{20}$ $\frac{9}{25}$ $\frac{7}{10}$ $\frac{3}{4}$ $\frac{19}{25}$ $\frac{4}{5}$

Set D: $\frac{11}{12}$ $\frac{5}{6}$ $\frac{5}{9}$ $\frac{7}{16}$ $\frac{3}{11}$ $\frac{4}{15}$

Set E: $\frac{5}{12}$ $\frac{9}{20}$ $\frac{3}{8}$ $\frac{5}{9}$ $\frac{7}{25}$ $\frac{5}{6}$

Discovery Template 3
Fraction/Decimal/Percent Randomizer

	A	B	C
Ace♣	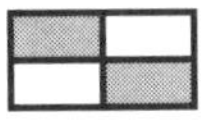	$\frac{6}{10}$	0.40
2♣	$\frac{3}{5}$	$\frac{3}{4}$	$\frac{10}{25}$
3♣	0.6	$\frac{8}{20}$	$\frac{75}{100}$
4♣	$\frac{2}{5}$	$\frac{5}{25}$	0.05
5♣	0.20	$\frac{1}{50}$	
6♣	$\frac{3}{9}$	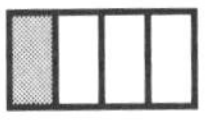	$33\frac{1}{3}\%$
7♣	$\frac{2}{4}$	0.33	$\frac{2}{4}$
8♣	5%	$\frac{1}{20}$	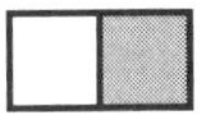
9♣	20%	50%	$\frac{5}{10}$
10♣	2%	60%	0.125
Ace♦	$\frac{1}{4}$	40%	$\frac{5}{8}$
2♦	0.5	0.50	$\frac{4}{20}$
3♦	75%	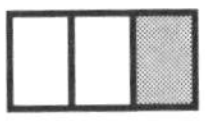	$\frac{2}{3}$
4♦	25%	$\frac{2}{10}$	0.2%
5♦	0.4	0.25	0.25%
6♦	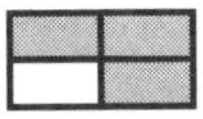	$\frac{1}{2}$	$\frac{5}{20}$
7♦	$\frac{1}{3}$	0.2	$\frac{25}{100}$
8♦	$\frac{1}{5}$	0.75	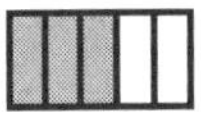
9♦	$\frac{1}{8}$	$66\frac{2}{3}\%$	$\frac{20}{100}$
10♦	62.5%	0.625	12.5%

Discovery Template 4
Fraction Randomizers

Fraction Randomizer #1

$\frac{1}{2}$	$\frac{1}{100}$	$\frac{1}{20}$	$\frac{1}{15}$
$\frac{1}{4}$	$\frac{1}{9}$	$\frac{1}{8}$	$\frac{1}{5}$
$\frac{1}{7}$	$\frac{1}{6}$	$\frac{1}{16}$	$\frac{1}{25}$
$\frac{1}{3}$	$\frac{1}{10}$	$\frac{1}{12}$	$\frac{1}{50}$

Fraction Randomizer #2

$\frac{1}{5}$	$\frac{3}{10}$	$\frac{1}{6}$	$\frac{1}{16}$	$\frac{1}{12}$	$\frac{3}{4}$
$\frac{11}{16}$	$\frac{5}{9}$	$\frac{7}{8}$	$\frac{4}{9}$	$\frac{7}{10}$	$\frac{1}{9}$
$\frac{1}{3}$	$\frac{5}{6}$	$\frac{1}{2}$	$\frac{3}{16}$	$\frac{1}{8}$	$\frac{3}{5}$
$\frac{4}{5}$	$\frac{5}{12}$	$\frac{13}{16}$	$\frac{7}{12}$	$\frac{2}{9}$	$\frac{15}{16}$
$\frac{1}{4}$	$\frac{5}{16}$	$\frac{3}{8}$	$\frac{7}{9}$	$\frac{7}{16}$	$\frac{2}{3}$
$\frac{5}{8}$	$\frac{8}{9}$	$\frac{1}{10}$	$\frac{2}{5}$	$\frac{11}{12}$	$\frac{9}{16}$

Fraction Randomizer #3

$\frac{1}{4}$	$\frac{2}{8}$	$\frac{7}{16}$	$\frac{4}{16}$	$\frac{1}{16}$
$\frac{15}{16}$	$\frac{3}{8}$	$\frac{13}{16}$	$\frac{5}{8}$	$\frac{12}{16}$
$\frac{5}{16}$	$\frac{2}{16}$	$\frac{3}{4}$	$\frac{8}{16}$	$\frac{3}{16}$
$\frac{7}{8}$	$\frac{11}{16}$	$\frac{4}{8}$	$\frac{10}{16}$	$\frac{6}{8}$
$\frac{6}{16}$	$\frac{14}{16}$	$\frac{9}{16}$	$\frac{1}{2}$	$\frac{1}{8}$

Fraction Randomizer #4

$\frac{4}{5}$	$\frac{1}{2}$	$\frac{1}{3}$	$\frac{3}{10}$	$\frac{7}{20}$	$\frac{3}{25}$
$\frac{1}{9}$	$\frac{1}{4}$	$\frac{7}{100}$	$\frac{5}{6}$	$\frac{3}{8}$	$\frac{1}{50}$
$\frac{1}{10}$	$\frac{5}{12}$	$\frac{19}{20}$	$\frac{9}{16}$	$\frac{3}{5}$	$\frac{17}{100}$
$\frac{3}{4}$	$\frac{2}{3}$	$\frac{5}{8}$	$\frac{15}{16}$	$\frac{5}{9}$	$\frac{1}{12}$
$\frac{13}{25}$	$\frac{11}{15}$	$\frac{7}{10}$	$\frac{1}{6}$	$\frac{7}{8}$	$\frac{1}{5}$
$\frac{39}{100}$	$\frac{11}{16}$	$\frac{33}{50}$	$\frac{1}{16}$	$\frac{1}{20}$	$\frac{7}{12}$

Discovery Template 5
Hundredths Grids
("Decimal Get to 5" Record Sheet)

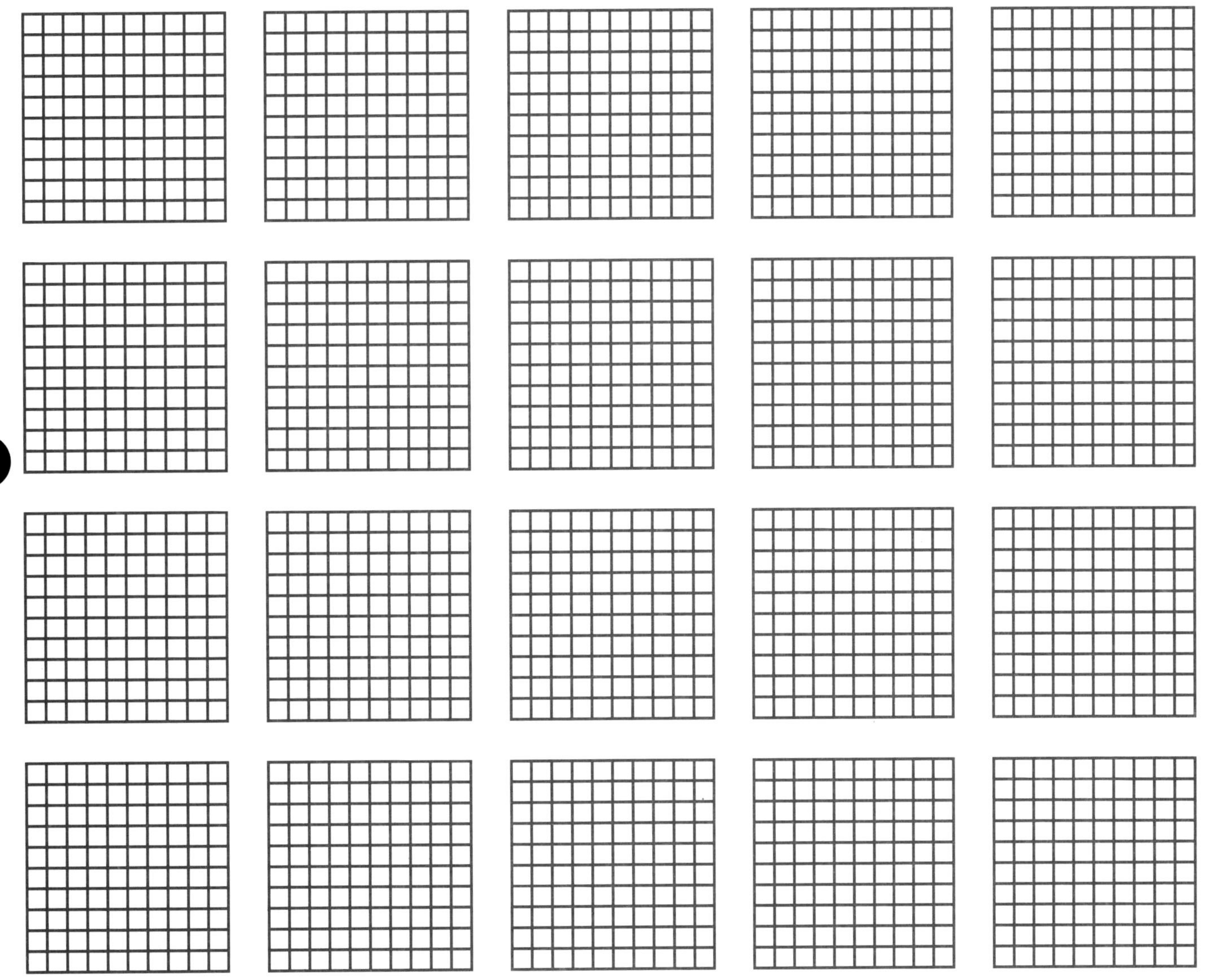

Discovery Template 6
Unit Squares and Fractions, Decimals and Percents

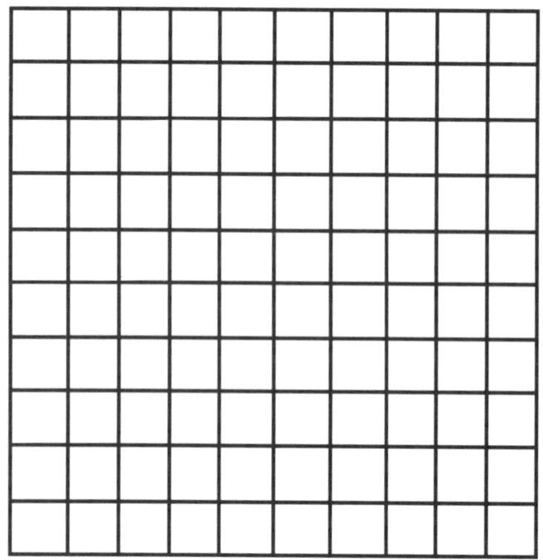

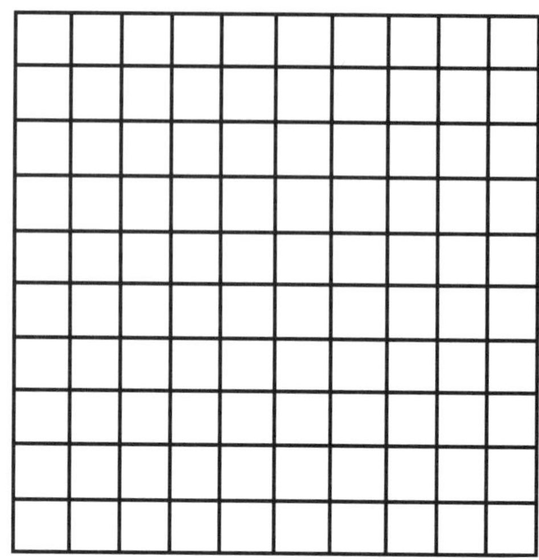

_______________ _______ _______________

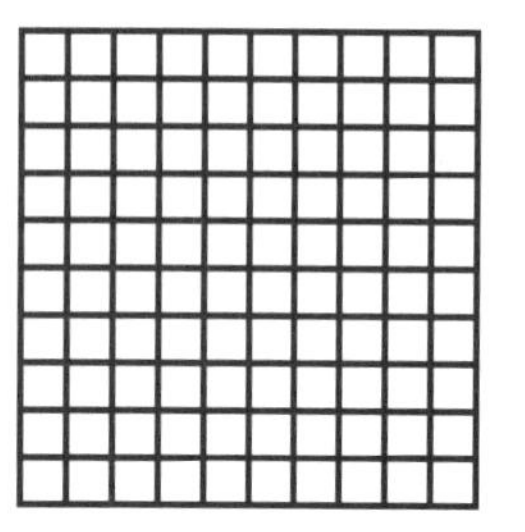

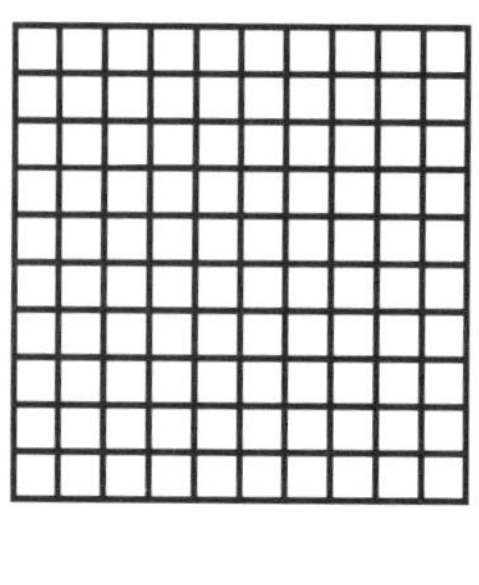

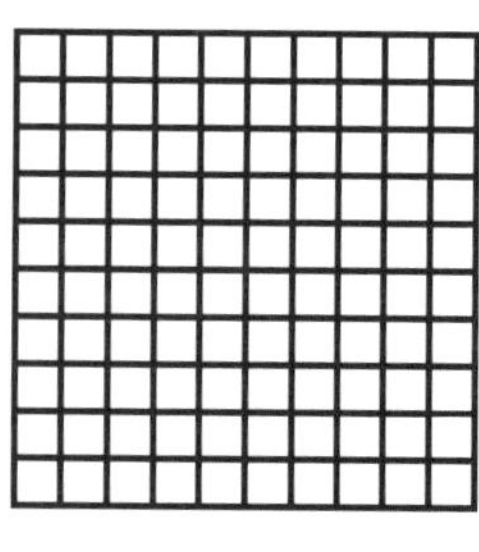

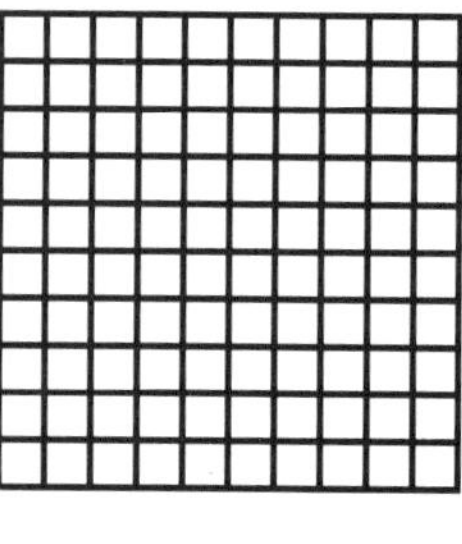

__________ __________ __________ __________

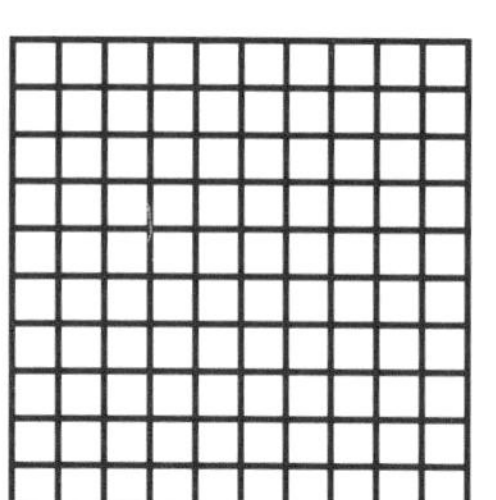

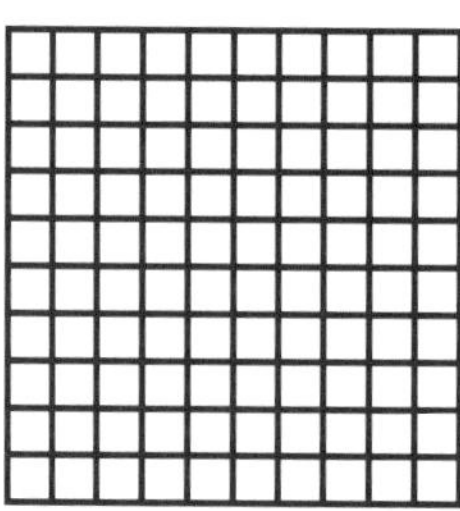

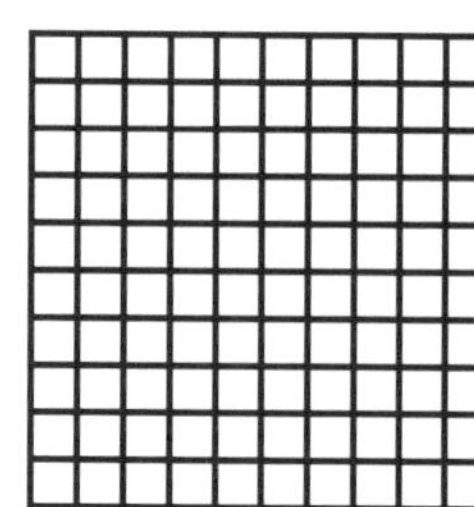

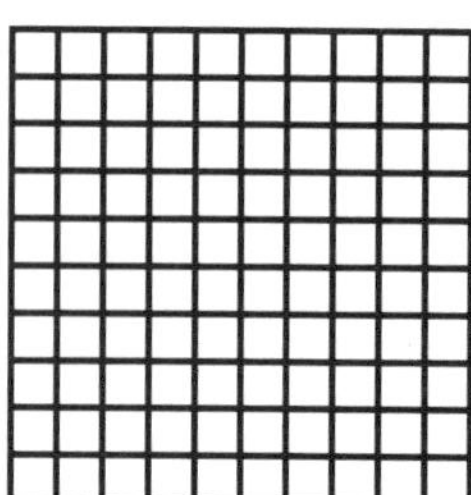

__________ __________ __________ __________

Discovery Template 7
Percent Circle

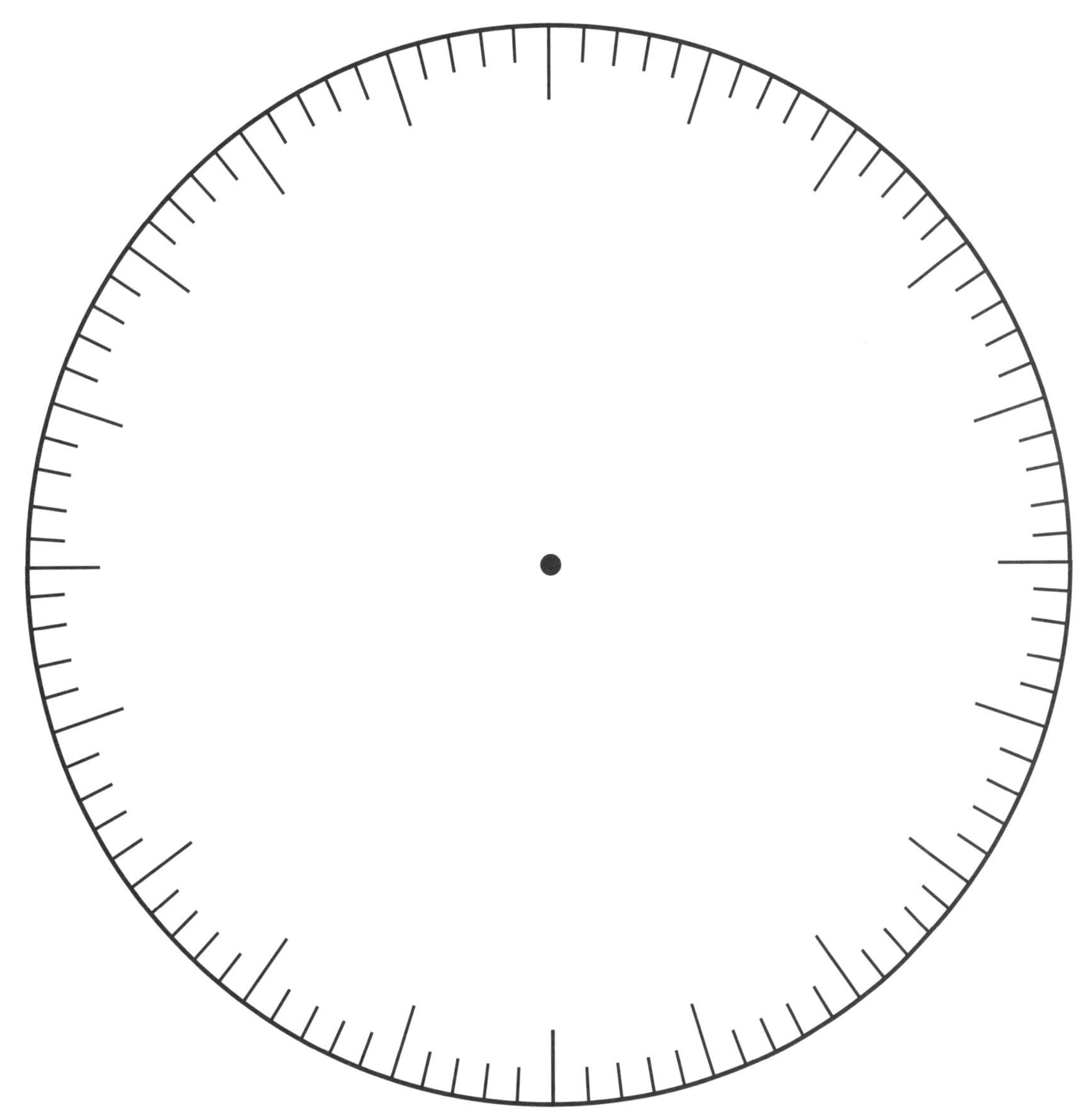

Discovery Template 8
Fraction and Percent Circles I

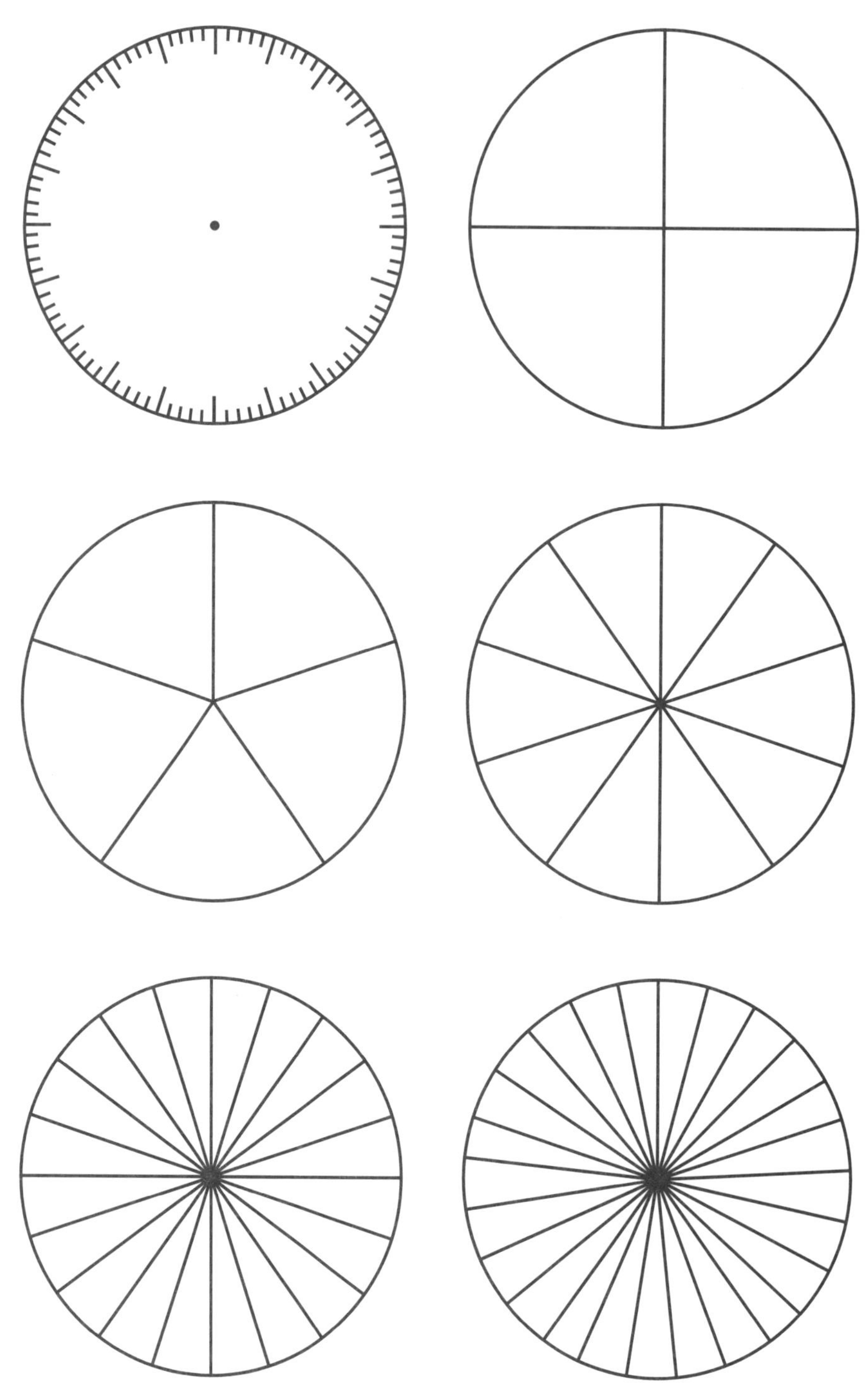

Discovery Template 9
Geoboard Template

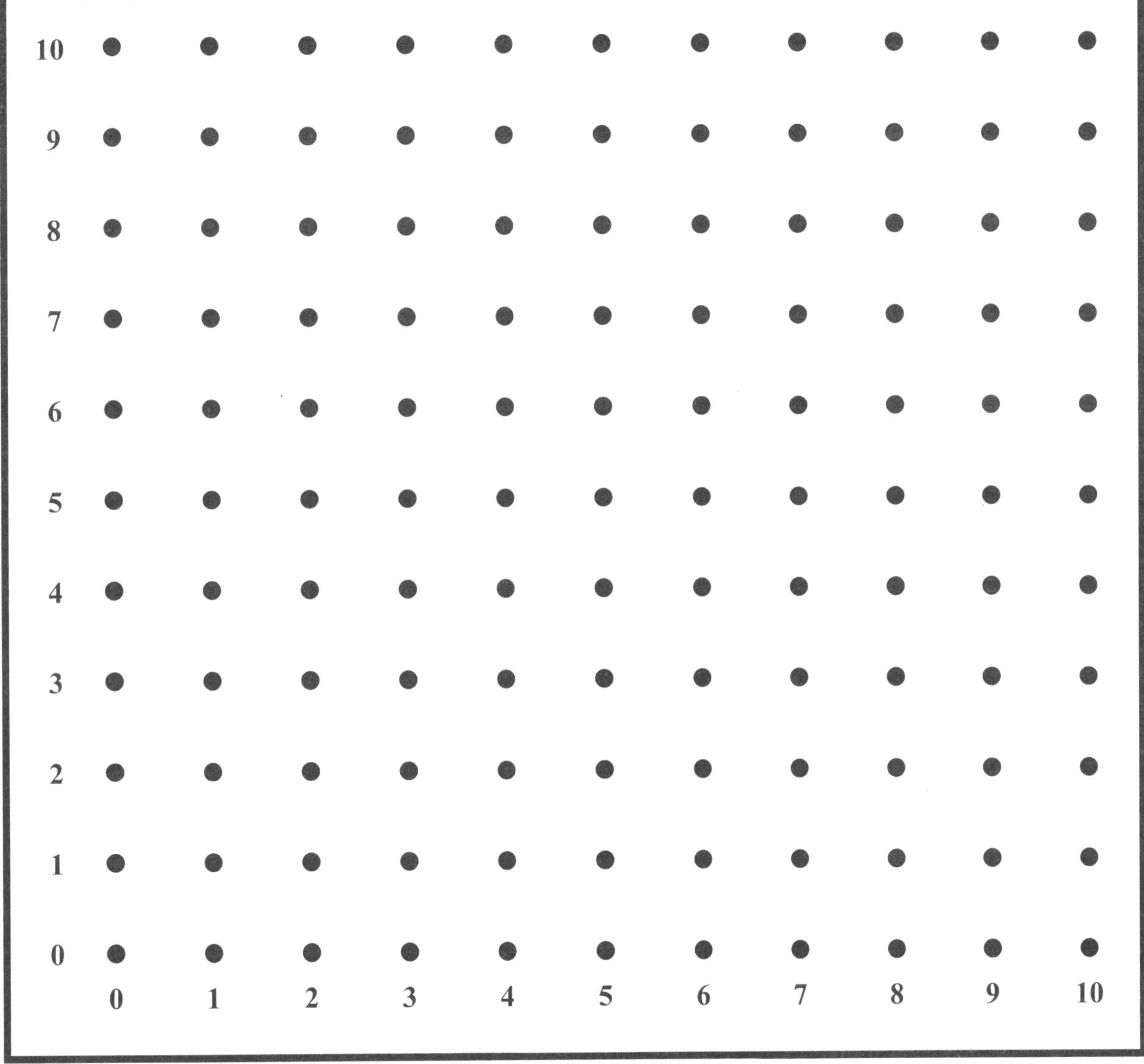

Discovery Template 10
Decimals, Decimals, Decimals 1

1. 5.2915026221291811810032315072785
2. 0.28571428571428571428571428571429
3. 4.1231056256176605498214098559741
4. 0.3125
5. 0.30158730158730158730158730158730158730158730
6. 7.2801098892805182710973024915 27
7. 0.12
8. 14.106735979665884425232163690877
9. 0.95348837209302325581395348837209
10. 6.0827625302982196889996842452021
11. 0.03125
12. 0.10714285714285714285714285714286
13. 10.583005244258362362006463014557
14. 0.11764705882352941176470588235294

Discovery Template 11
Decimals, Decimals, Decimals 2

1. $\sqrt{28}$ 5.2915026221291811810032315072785 5.291502622…

2. $\frac{2}{7}$ 0.28571428571428571428571428571429 $0.\overline{285714}$

3. $\sqrt{17}$ 4.1231056256176605498214098559741 4.123105625…

4. $\frac{9}{16}$ 0.5625 0.5625

5. $\frac{19}{63}$ 0.3015873015873015873015873015873 $0.\overline{301587}$

6. $\sqrt{53}$ 7.280109889280518271097302491527 7.280109889…

7. $\frac{3}{25}$ 0.12 0.12

8. $\sqrt{199}$ 14.106735979665884425232163690877 14.10673597

9. $\frac{41}{43}$ 0.95348837209302325581395348837209 $0.\overline{285714}$

10. $\sqrt{37}$ 6.0827625302982196889996842452021 6.08276253…

11. $\frac{17}{32}$ 0.03125 0.03125

12. $\frac{3}{28}$ 0.10714285714285714285714285714286 $0.107\overline{142857}$

14. $\frac{12}{17}$ 0.11764705882352941176470588235294 $0.\overline{1176470588235294}$

Discovery Template 12
Numbers, Numbers, Numbers

A. ${}^{-}\sqrt{112}$, ${}^{-}5.3458231\ldots$, ${}^{-}0.\overline{285714}$, $\frac{3}{28}$, $\frac{1}{4}$, $3\frac{7}{25}$

B. $2\frac{5}{7}$, $\frac{5}{8}$, $0.\overline{467}$, ${}^{-}\frac{13}{25}$, ${}^{-}1.0043413\ldots$, ${}^{-}\sqrt{53}$

C. ${}^{-}15.87876657\ldots$, ${}^{-}12.4$; ${}^{-}0.\overline{8233}$, $\frac{17}{25}$, $1\frac{14}{57}$, $\sqrt{13}$

D. $\frac{5}{6}$, 0.443, ${}^{-}0.57834\ldots$, ${}^{-}0.\overline{310489}$, ${}^{-}2.0653$, ${}^{-}\sqrt{89}$

E. ${}^{-}\sqrt{39}$, $\frac{9}{16}$, ${}^{-}2.94\overline{21314}$, $5\frac{4}{9}$, ${}^{-}4.57$, $\sqrt{46}$

F. $\frac{3}{10}$, ${}^{-}\frac{7}{12}$, ${}^{-}\sqrt{14}$, ${}^{-}4.23216\ldots$, $0.\overline{21672}$, $\frac{3}{5}$

G. ${}^{-}\frac{7}{20}$, $\frac{3}{17}$, ${}^{-}\frac{1}{5}$, ${}^{-}\sqrt{\frac{1}{7}}$, ${}^{-}0.1543223\ldots$, ${}^{-}0.\overline{34}$

Discovery Template 13
Horizontal Number Line

$^{-}10 \quad ^{-}9 \quad ^{-}8 \quad ^{-}7 \quad ^{-}6 \quad ^{-}5 \quad ^{-}4 \quad ^{-}3 \quad ^{-}2 \quad ^{-}1 \quad 0 \quad ^{+}1 \quad ^{+}2 \quad ^{+}3 \quad ^{+}4 \quad ^{+}5 \quad ^{+}6 \quad ^{+}7 \quad ^{+}8 \quad ^{+}9 \quad ^{+}10$

Discovery Template 14
More Angles

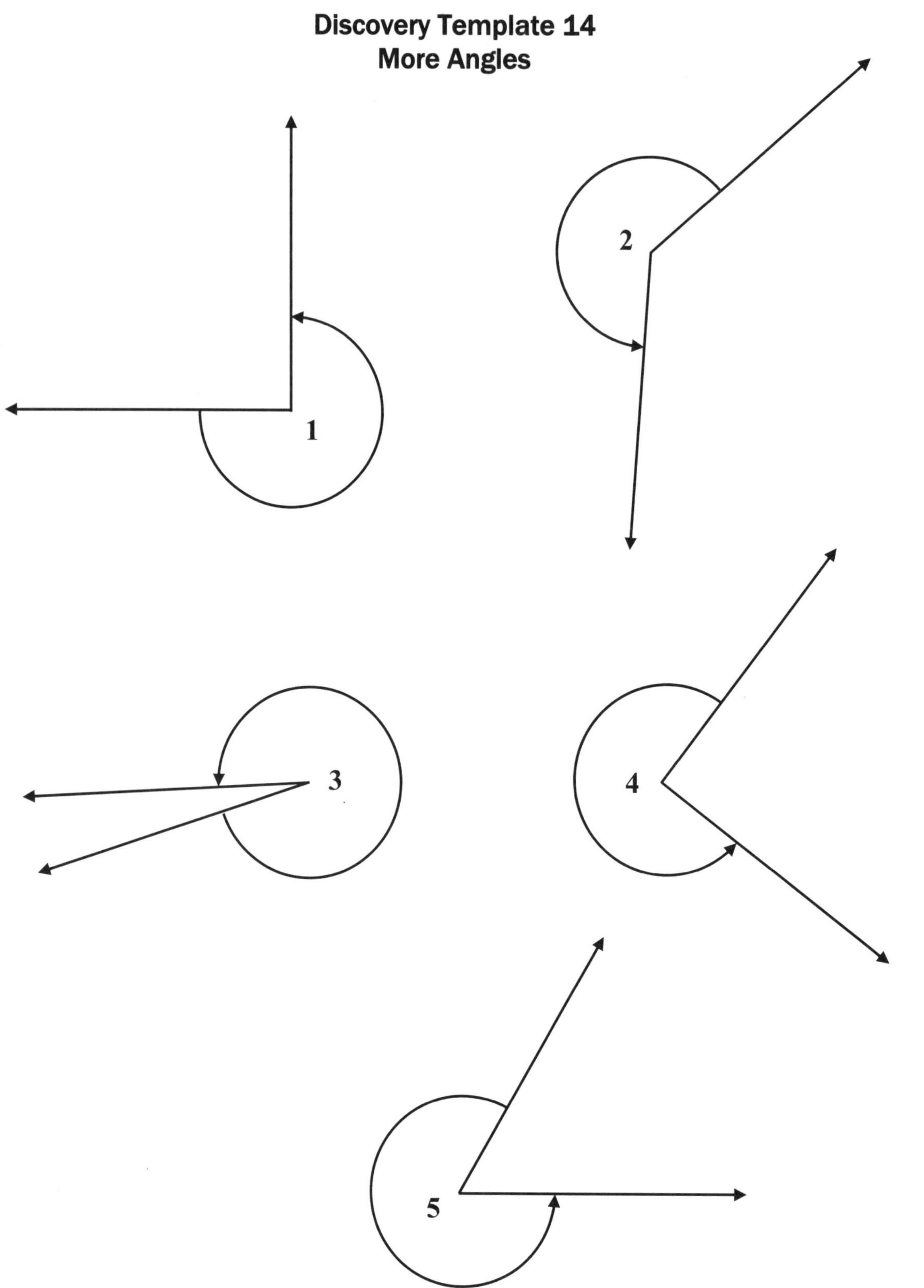

Discovery Template 15
Working with Angles 1

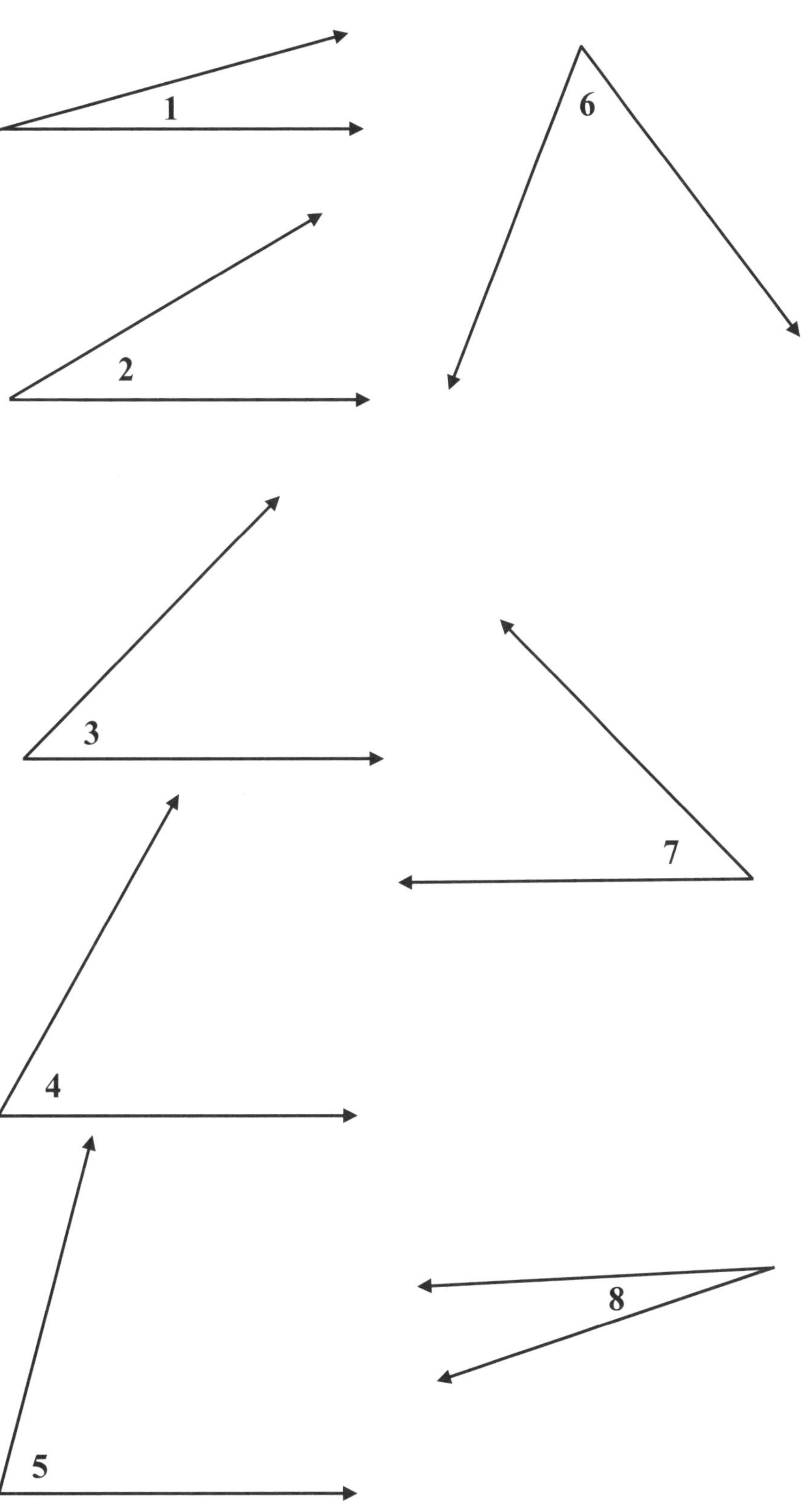

Discovery Template 16
Working with Angles 2

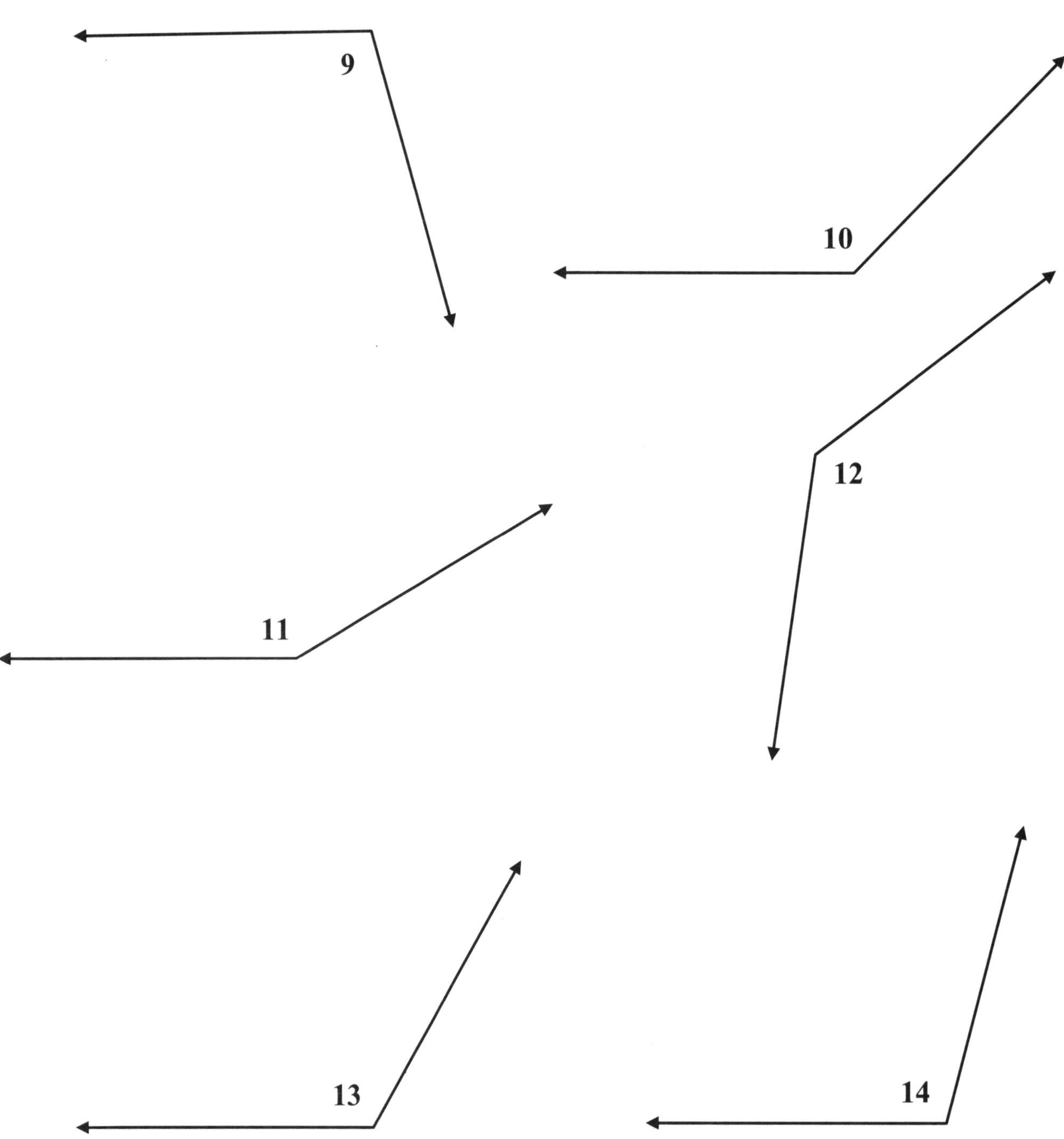

Discovery Template 17
Determining the Sum of Angles in a Polygon I

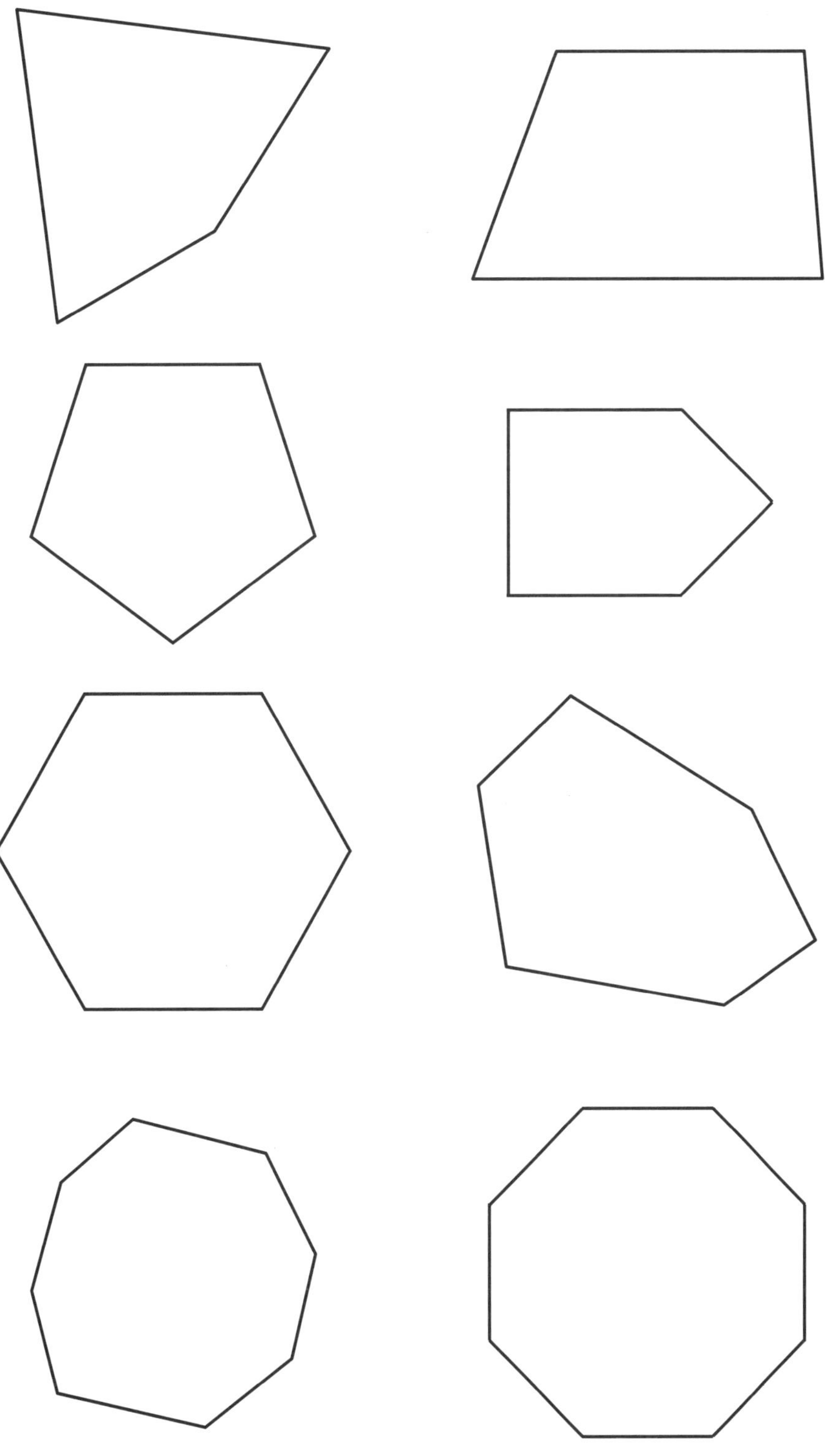

Discovery Template 18
Determining the Sum of Angles in a Polygon 2

Name: ______________________________ Date: ______________

Study the data in the chart. Then answer the questions that follow.

Column 1	Column 2	Column 3	Column 4	Column 5
Polygon	Number of sides	Number of vertex to vertex (non-overlapping) triangles	Number of degrees in each triangle	Number of degrees in the interior of the polygon
Quadrilateral	4	2	180	360
Pentagon	5	3	180	540
Hexagon	6	4	180	720
Octagon	8	6	180	1080

1. Describe any pattern or relationship that you observe between Columns 2 and 3.

2. Describe the relationship among Columns 3, 4 and 5.

3. Describe a process that could be used to determine the sum of the interior angles of any polygon.

4. Using n as the number of sides in a polygon, write an expression that could be used to determine the sum of the interior angles in any polygon.

Discovery Template 19
Irregular Polygons

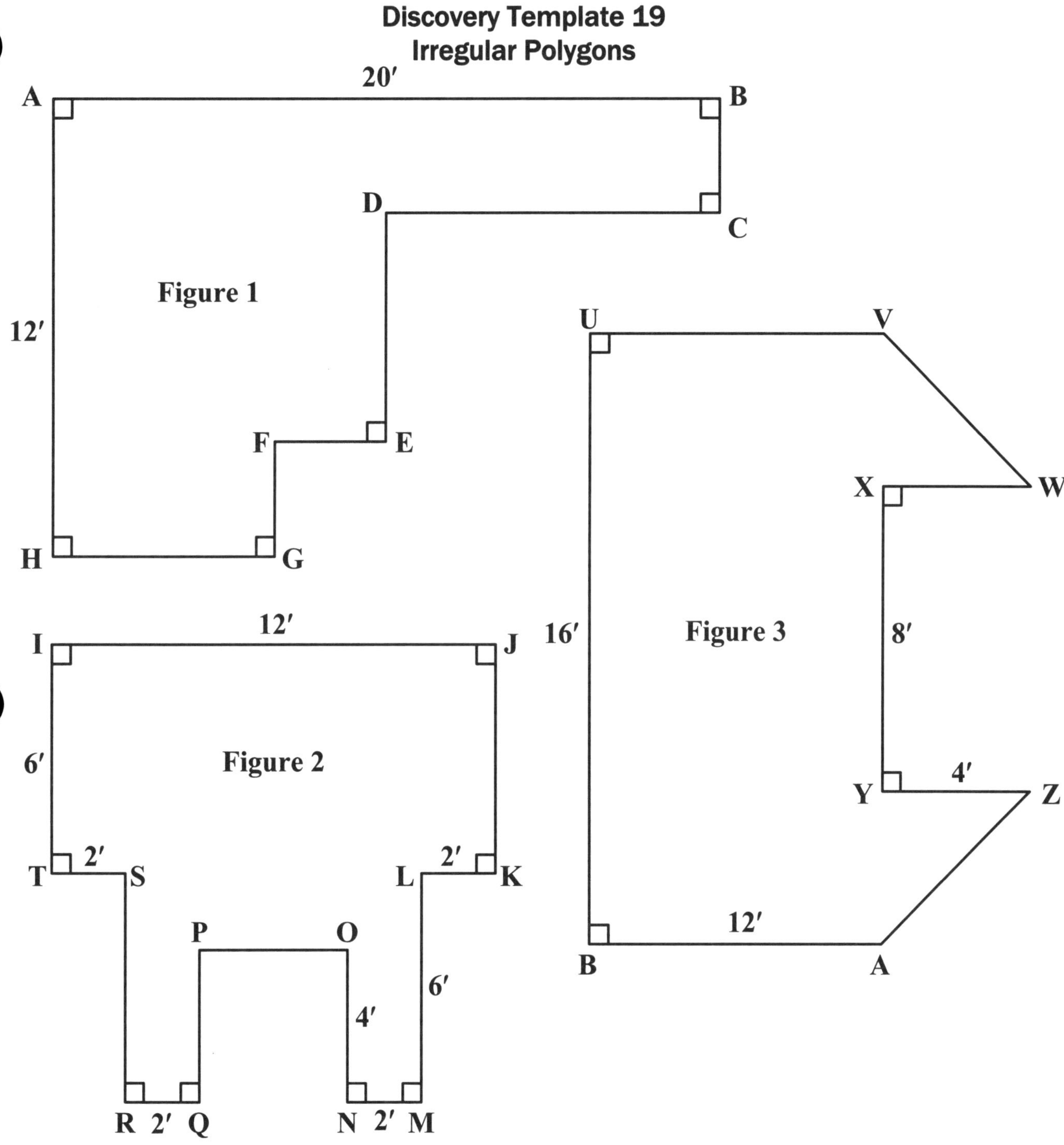

1. How do you know that the perimeter of Figure 1 is 64′?

2. How do you know that the perimeter of Figure 2 is more than 48′?

3. How can you determine the area of Figure 3?

You may want to use a Communicator® clearboard to determine answers.

Discovery Template 20
Volume of Pyramids and Cones

Prism/Cylinder	Volume of Prism/Cylinder	Pyramid/Cone	Volume of Pyramid/Cone
Rectangular Prism	78 cubic units	Rectangular Pyramid	26 cubic units
Triangular Prism	45 cubic units	Triangular Pyramid	15 cubic units
Trapezoidal Prism	126 cubic units	Trapezoidal Pyramid	42 cubic units
Cylinder	226.08 cubic units	Cone	75.36 cubic units
Hexagonal Prism	300 cubic units	Hexagonal Pyramid	200 cubic units

In the chart above, each of the prisms and corresponding pyramids have the same height and base. Study the relationship between the volume of the prism and its corresponding pyramid. Describe the pattern that occurs between the two.

Discovery Template 21
Tessellations 1

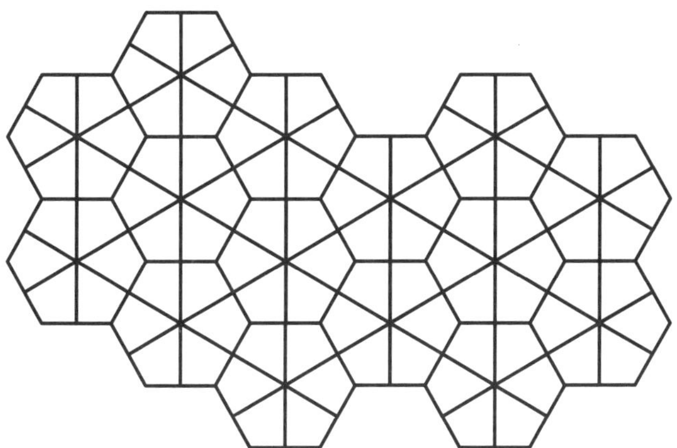

Tessellation 1

Tessellation 2

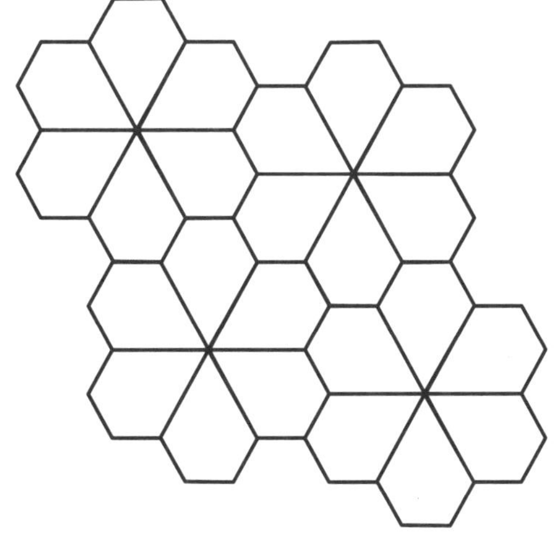

Tessellation 3

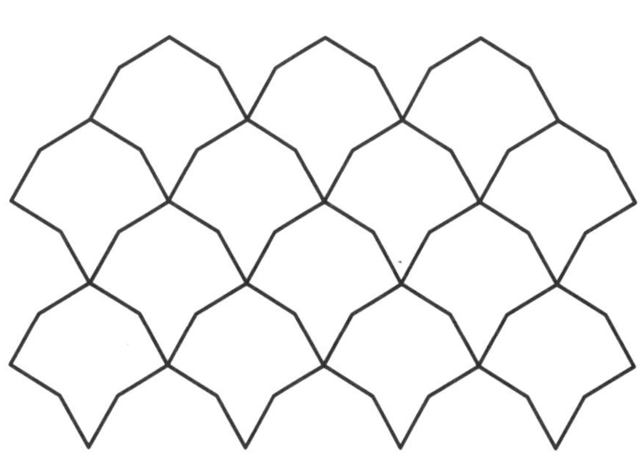

Tessellation 4

Tessellation 5

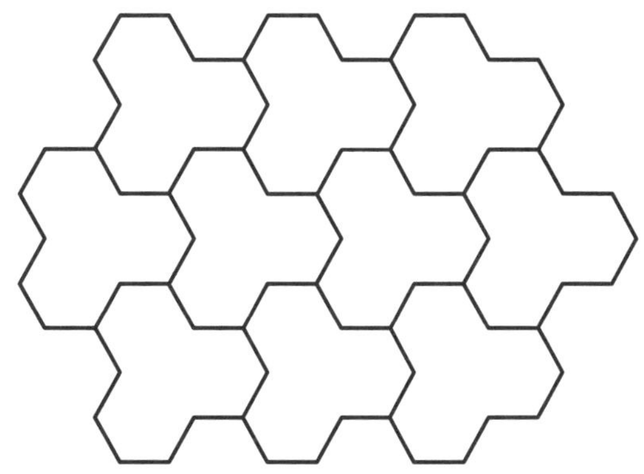

Tessellation 6

Discovery Template 22
Tessellations 2

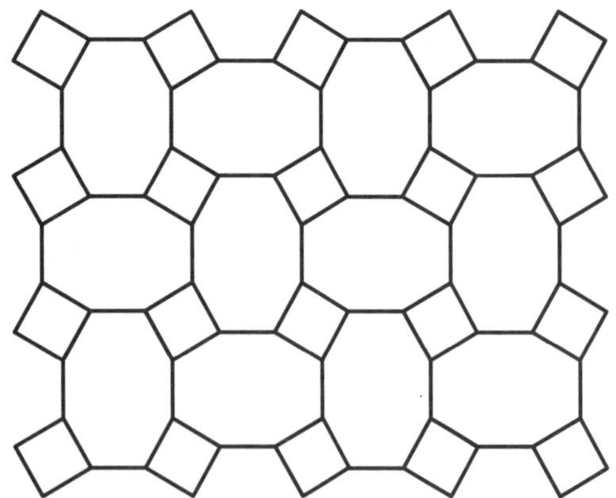

Tessellation 7

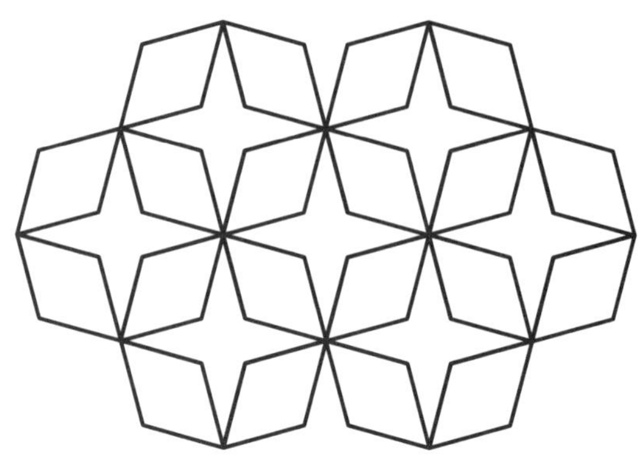

Tessellation 8

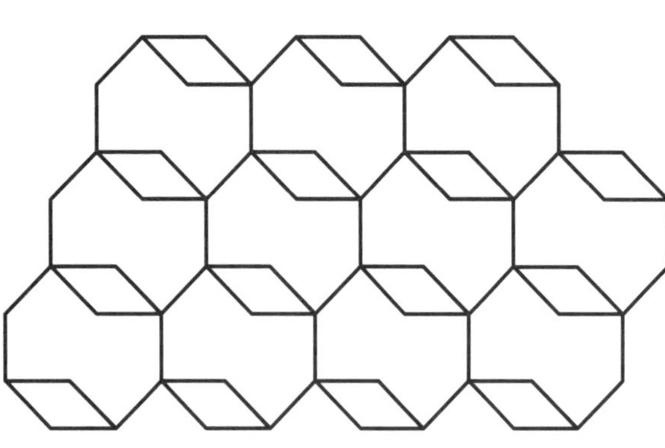

Tessellation 9

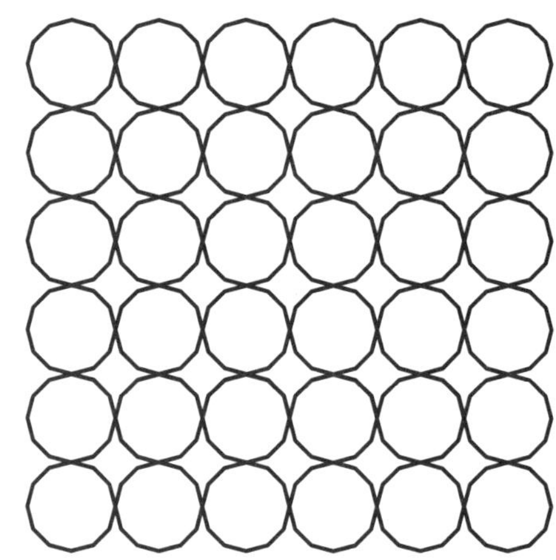

Tessellation 10

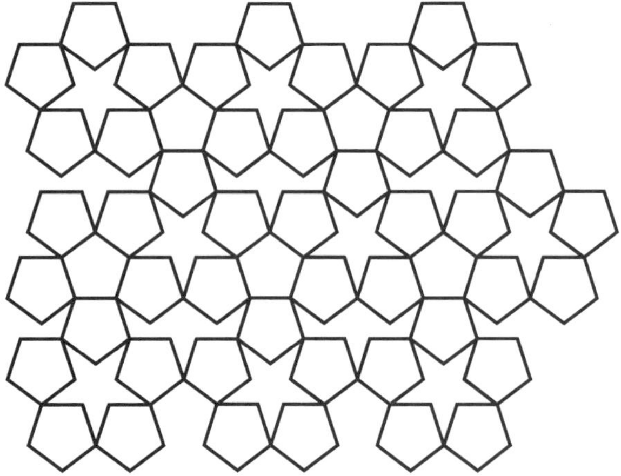

Tessellation 11

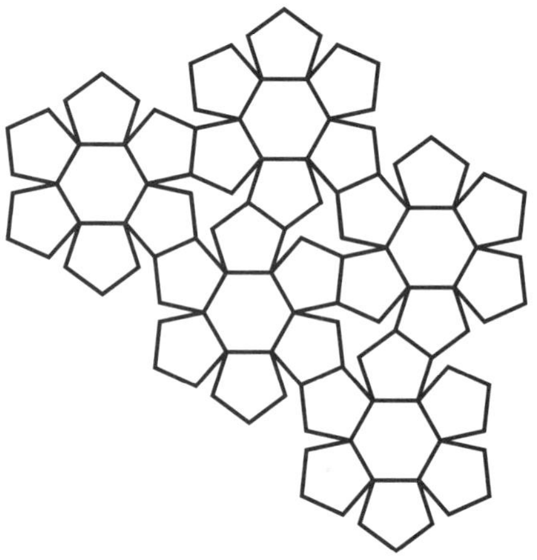

Tessellation 12

Discovery Template 23
Symmetry

A B C D E

F G H I J

K L M N O

P Q R S T

U V W X Y Z

Figure 1

Figure 2

Figure 3

Figure 4

Figure 5

Figure 6

Figure 7

Figure 8

Figure 9

Figure 10

Figure 11

Figure 12

Discovery Template 24
Transformations

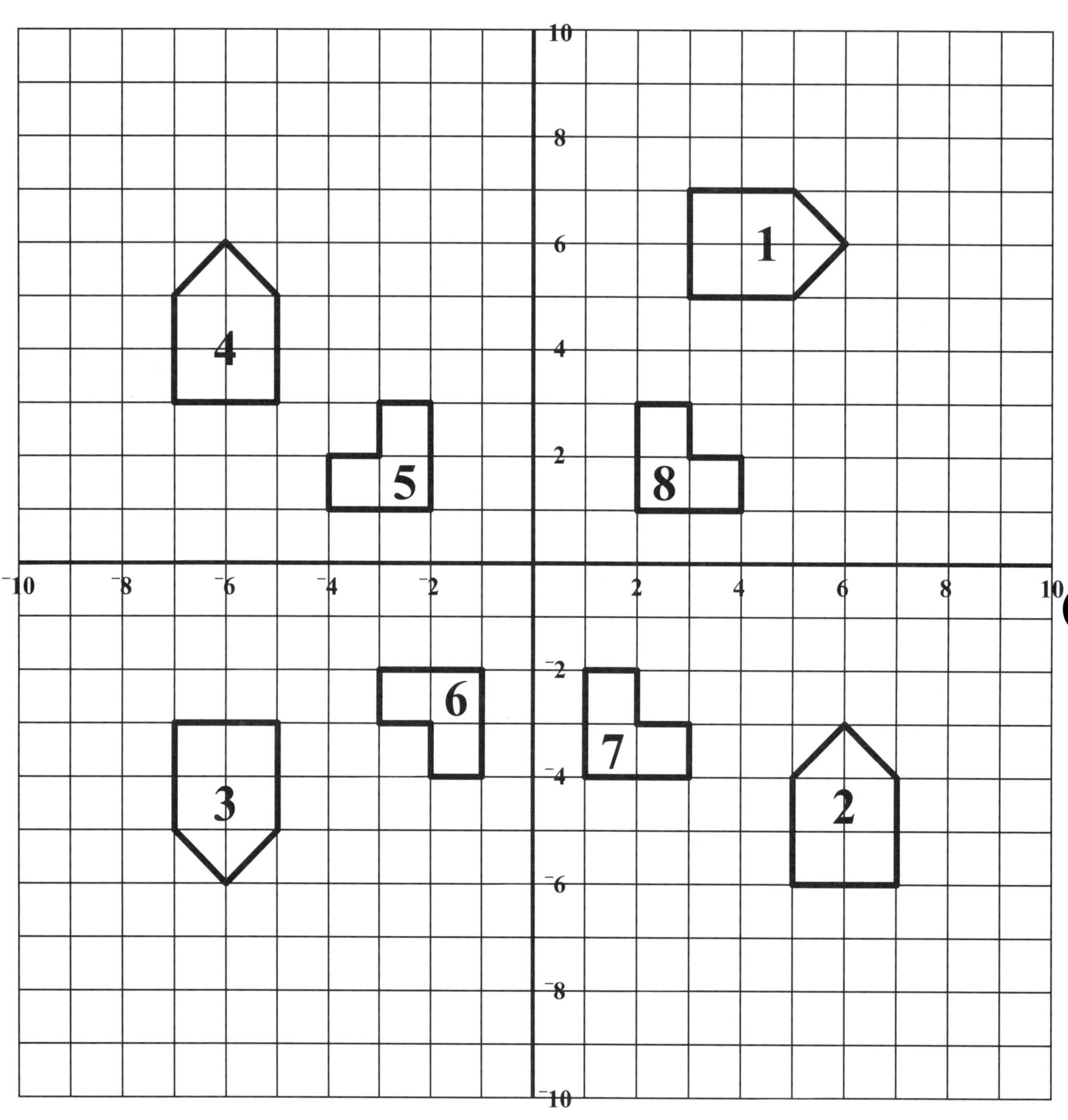

Discovery Template 25
Data Generator

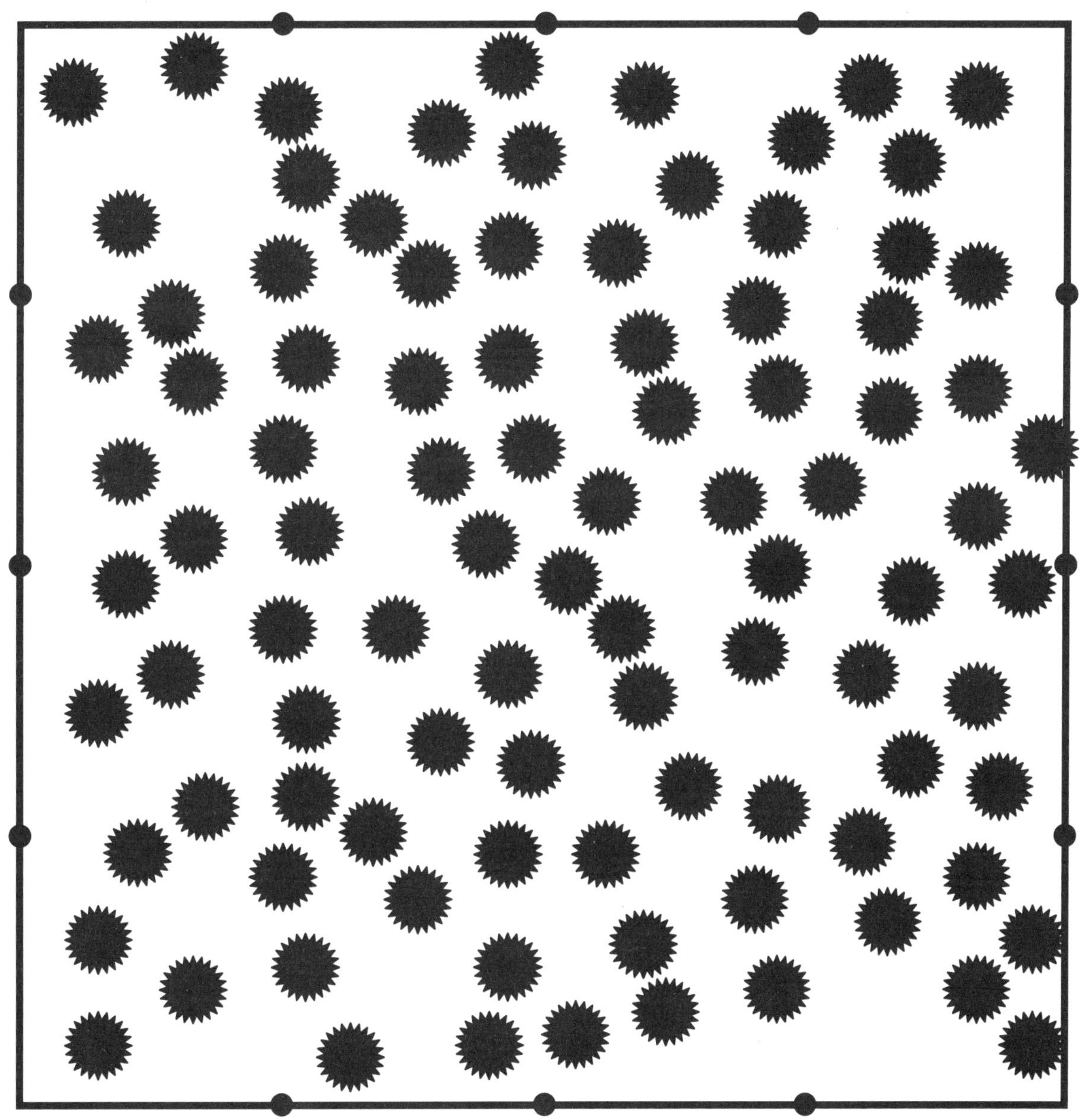

Discovery Template 26
Box-and-Whisker Plots

Grades in Ms. Achieve's class for the last test:

51, 60, 61, 65, 66, 68, 68, 70, 71, 76, 78 79, 80, 81, 83, 83, 85, 87, 88, 90, 93

51, 60, 61, 65, 66, 68, 68, 70, 71, 76, 78 79, 80, 81, 83, 83, 85, 87, 88, 90, 93

51, 60, 61, 65, 66, 68, 68, 70, 71, 76, 78 79, 80, 81, 83, 83, 85, 87, 88, 90, 93

51, 60, 61, 65, 66, 68, 68, 70, 71, 76, 78 79, 80, 81, 83, 83, 85, 87, 88, 90, 93

51, 60, 61, 65, 66, 68, 68, 70, 71, 76, 78 79, 80, 81, 83, 83, 85, 87, 88, 90, 93

51, 60, 61, 65, 66, 68, 68, 70, 71, 76, 78 79, 80, 81, 83, 83, 85, 87, 88, 90, 93

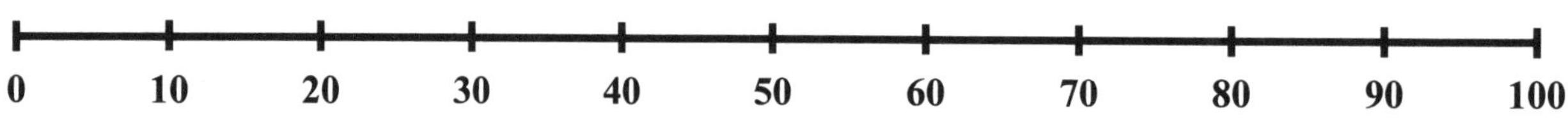

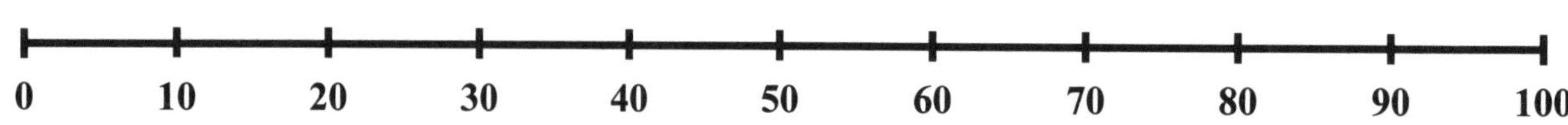

Discovery Template 27
Graphs, Graphs, Graphs

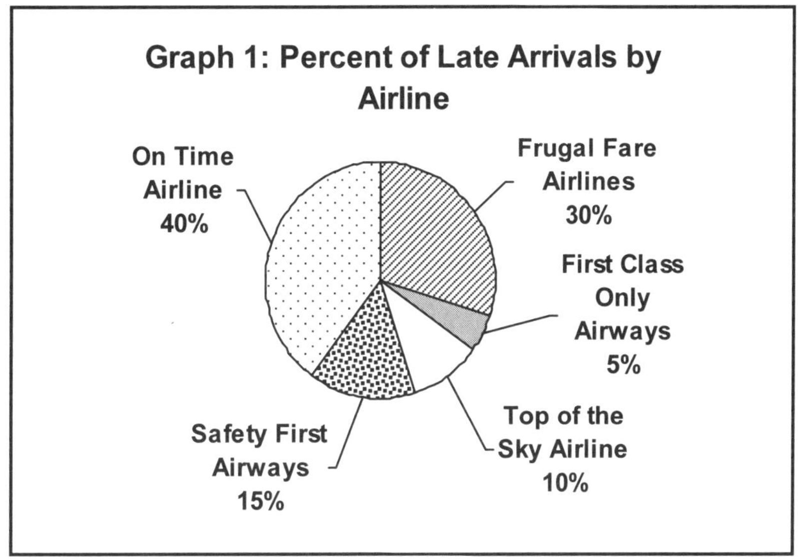

Graph 1: Percent of Late Arrivals by Airline
On Time Airline 40%
Frugal Fare Airlines 30%
First Class Only Airways 5%
Top of the Sky Airline 10%
Safety First Airways 15%

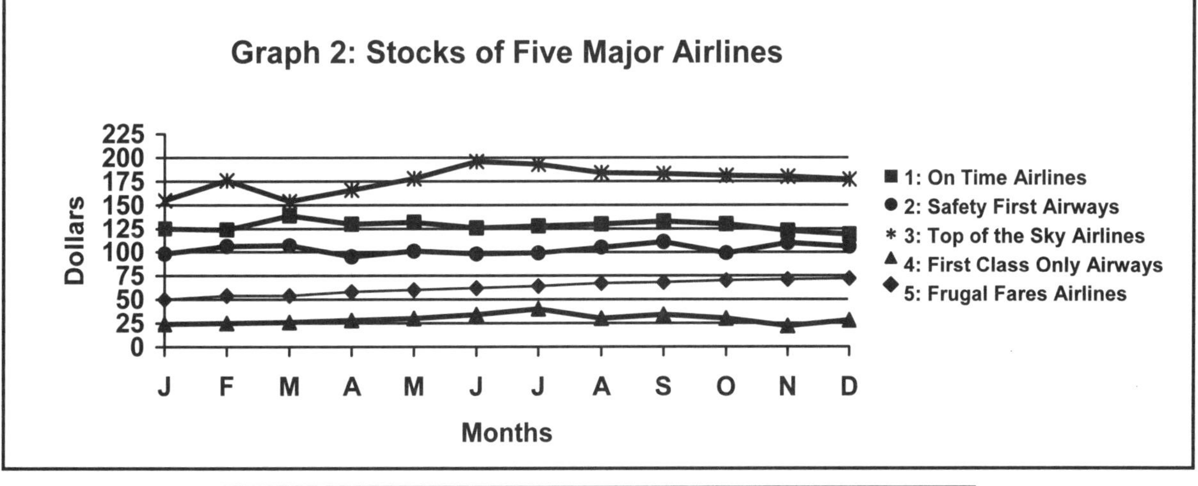

Graph 2: Stocks of Five Major Airlines
Dollars
225
200
175
150
125
100
75
50
25
0
J F M A M J J A S O N D
Months
1: On Time Airlines
2: Safety First Airways
3: Top of the Sky Airlines
4: First Class Only Airways
5: Frugal Fares Airlines

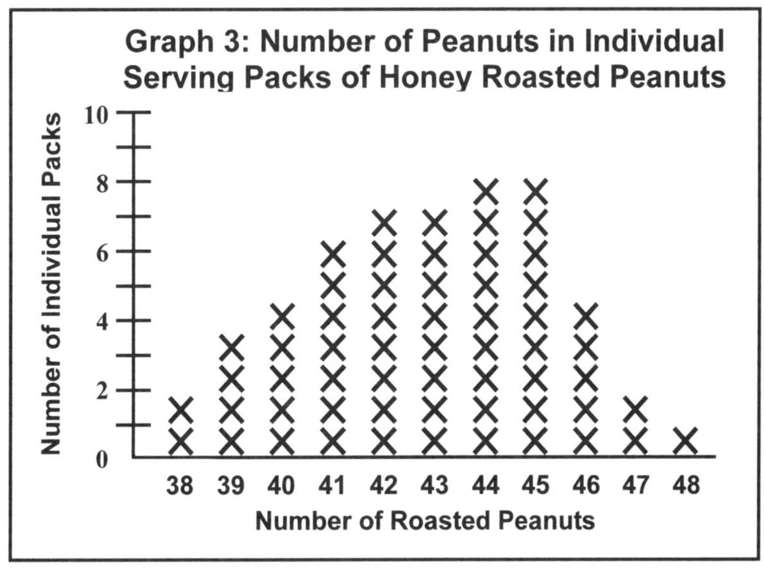

Graph 3: Number of Peanuts in Individual Serving Packs of Honey Roasted Peanuts
Number of Individual Packs
10
8
6
4
2
0
38 39 40 41 42 43 44 45 46 47 48
Number of Roasted Peanuts

Discovery Template 28
Graphs, Graphs, Graphs (continued)

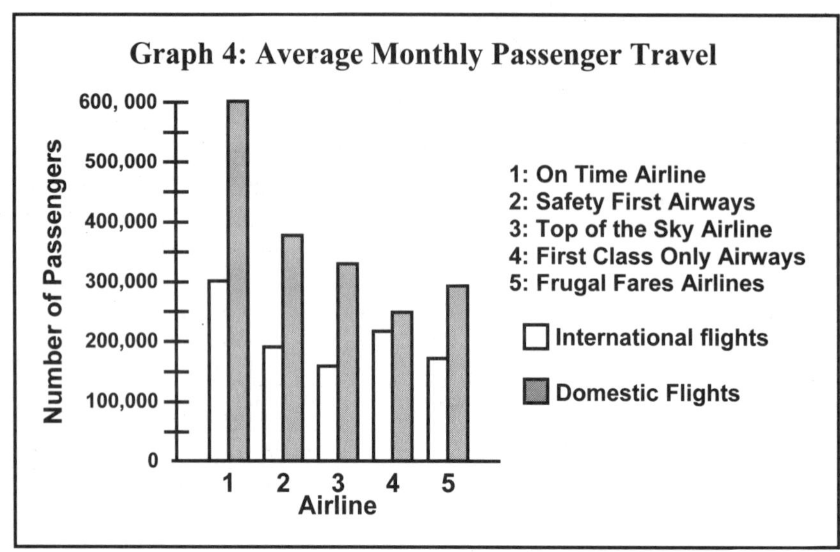

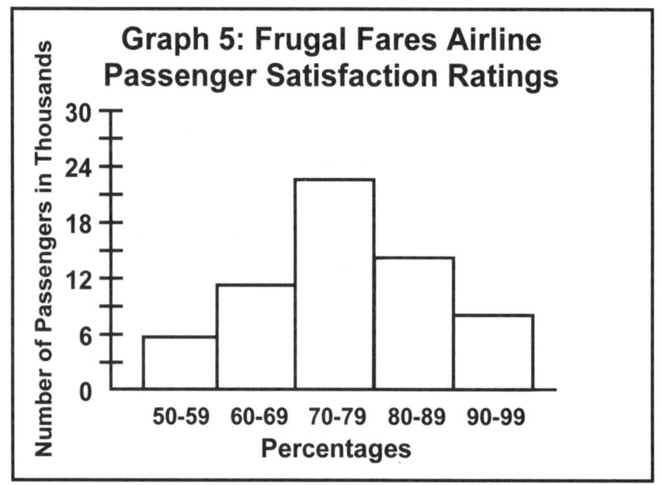

Graph 6: Frugal Fares Airlines Customer Satisfaction Survey in Percents

1	
2	
3	
4	
5	0, 2, 4, 7, 2, 1
6	0, 5, 3, 8, 7, 4, 4, 2, 8, 0, 2, 1,
7	3, 3, 3, 6, 7, 0, 2, 6, 4, 8, 6, 9, 8, 7, 9, 4, 3, 8, 6, 4, 3, 4, 5 9
8	0, 4, 5, 4, 6, 3, 7, 7, 8, 2, 3, 9, 3, 6, 1
9	5,5,7,6,8,3,3,4,0
10	

Discovery Template 29
Graphs, Graphs, Graphs (continued)

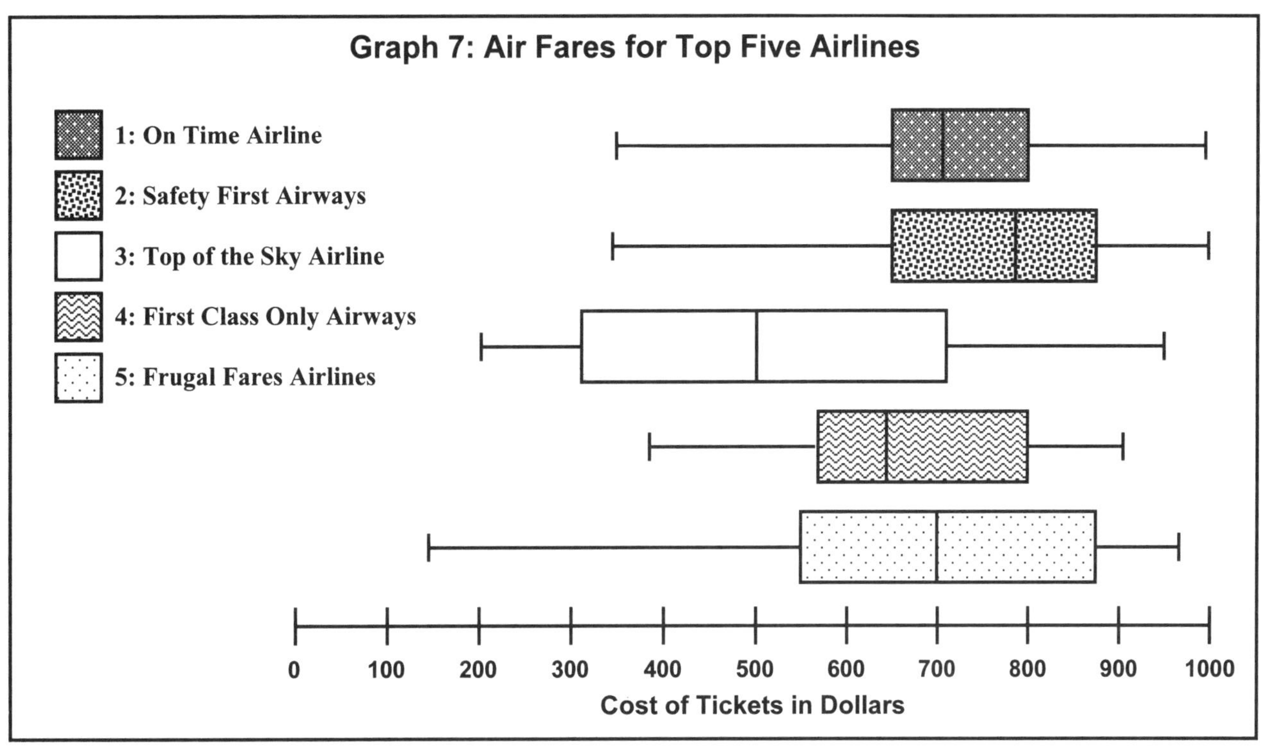

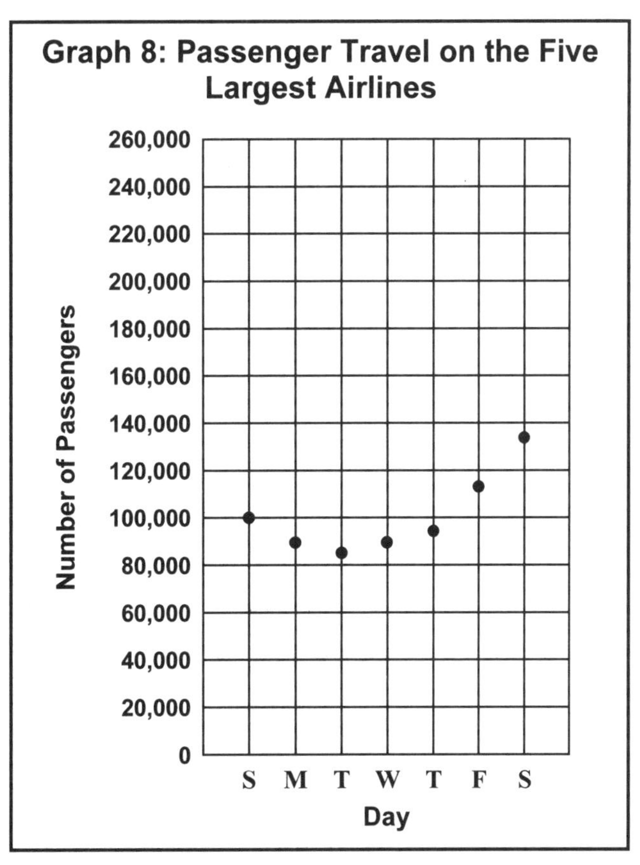

Discovery Template 30
Creating Expressions

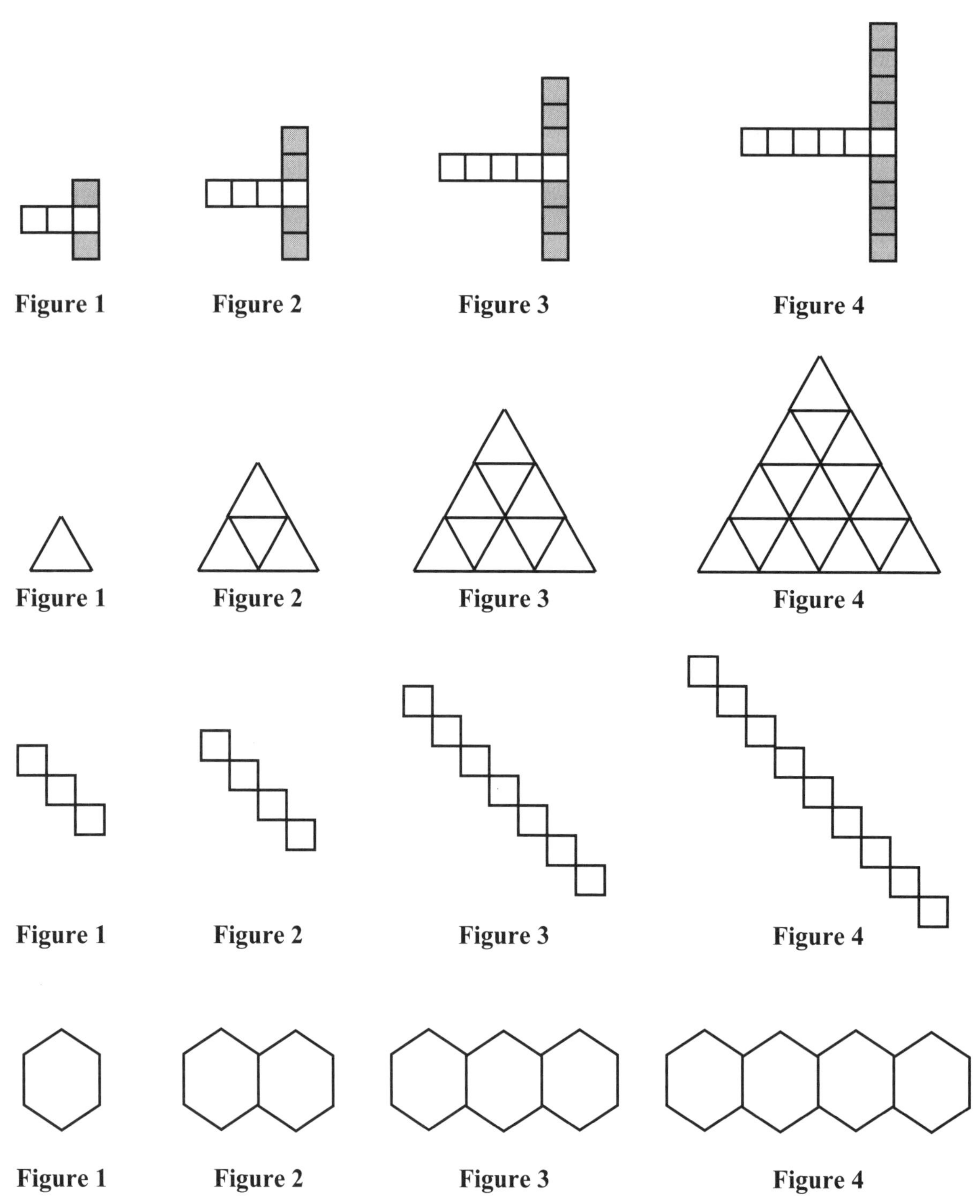

Discovery Template 31
Rules, Rules, Rules

Name: ______________________________ Date: ______________

Use mental math to complete the following:

1. $(^{-}6)(^{-}3) =$ ____________

2. $(^{-}6) + (^{-}3) =$ ____________

3. $(^{-}6) - (^{-}3) =$ ____________

4. $(^{-}6) \div (^{-}3) =$ ____________

5. $(^{-}7)(8) =$ ____________

6. $(15) - (^{-}9) =$ ____________

7. $(7)(^{-}7) =$ ____________

8. $(^{-}18) \div (^{-}6) =$ ____________

9. $(6) + (^{-}3) =$ ____________

10. $(^{-}17) + 17$ ____________

11. $17 + 5 =$ ____________

12. $(8) - (^{-}3) =$ ____________

13. $(^{-}6) - (17) =$ ____________

14. $(9)(4) =$ ____________

15. $(^{-}7) - (8) =$ ____________

16. $(28) \div (4) =$ ____________

17. $(9) \div (^{-}9) =$ ____________

18. $(^{-}8)(^{-}6) =$ ____________

19. $(6) \div (^{-}3) =$ ____________

20. $(^{-}19) + 2 =$ ____________

Discovery Template 32
Active Algorithms

=

=

=

=

Discovery Template 33
Matching Equations to Graphs

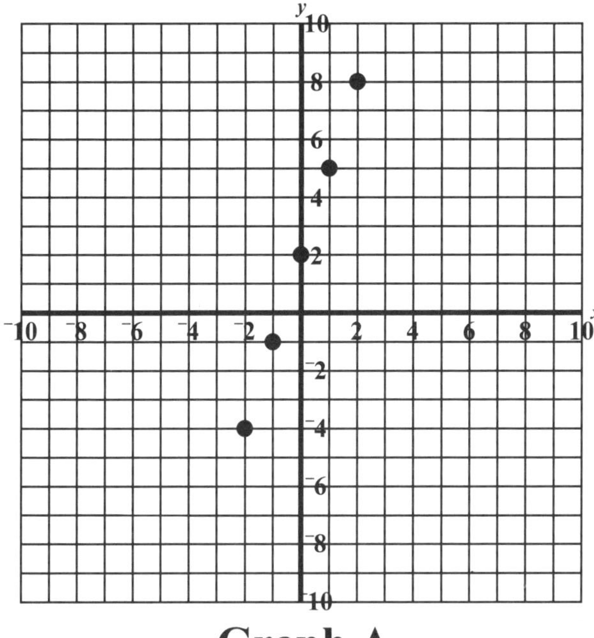

Graph A

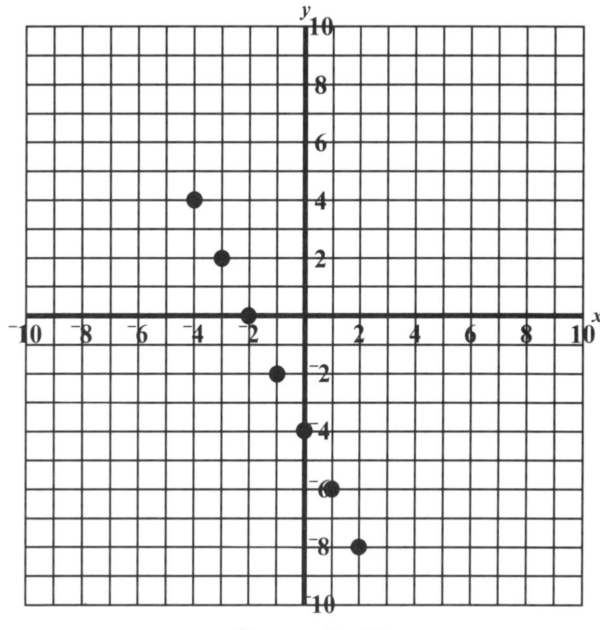

Graph B

1. $y = {}^{-}2x - 4$

Table	
x	y

2. $y = 3x + 2$

Table	
x	y

Discovery Template 34
Amazing Discoveries 1

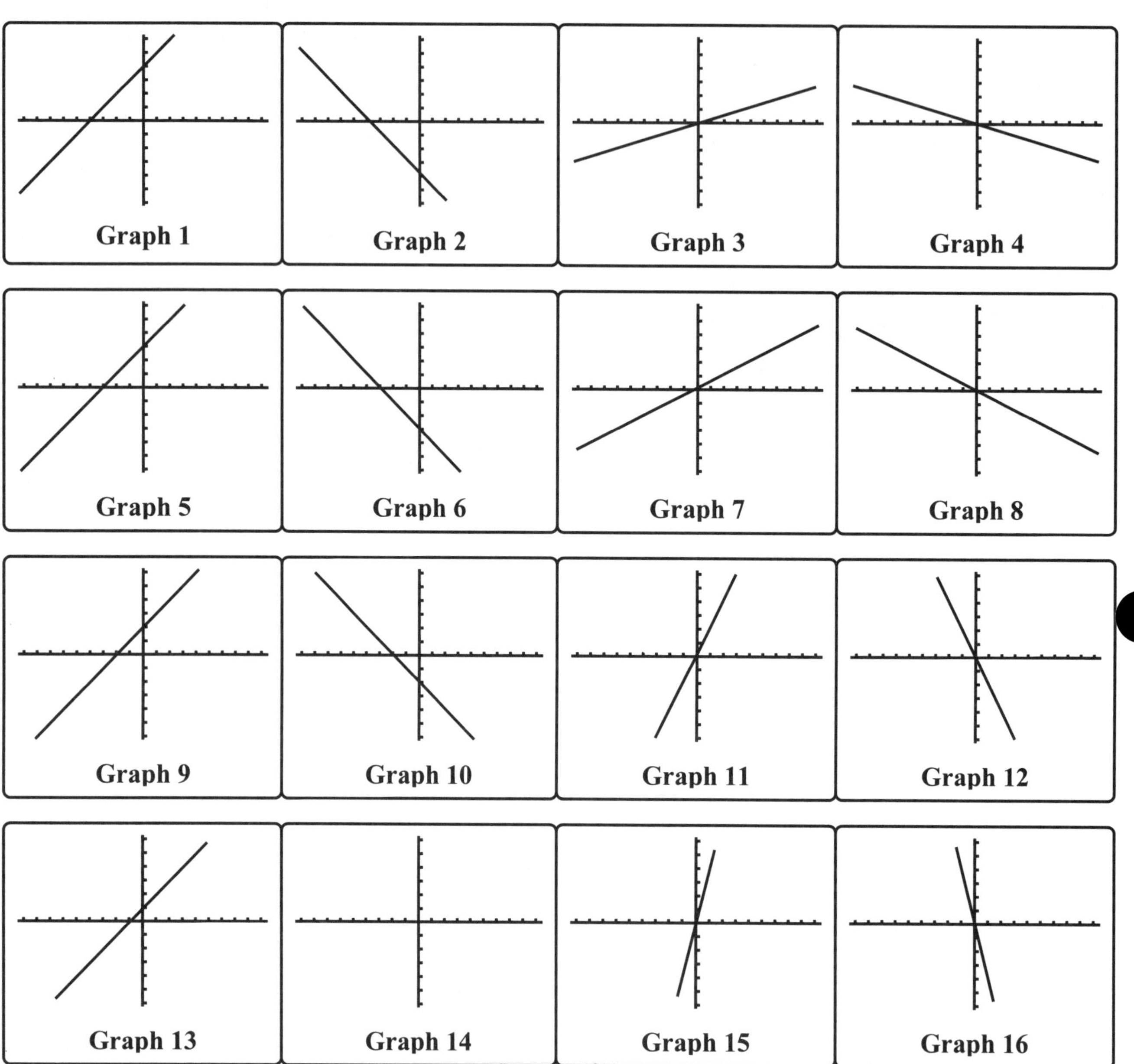

Discovery Template 35
The Coordinate Grid

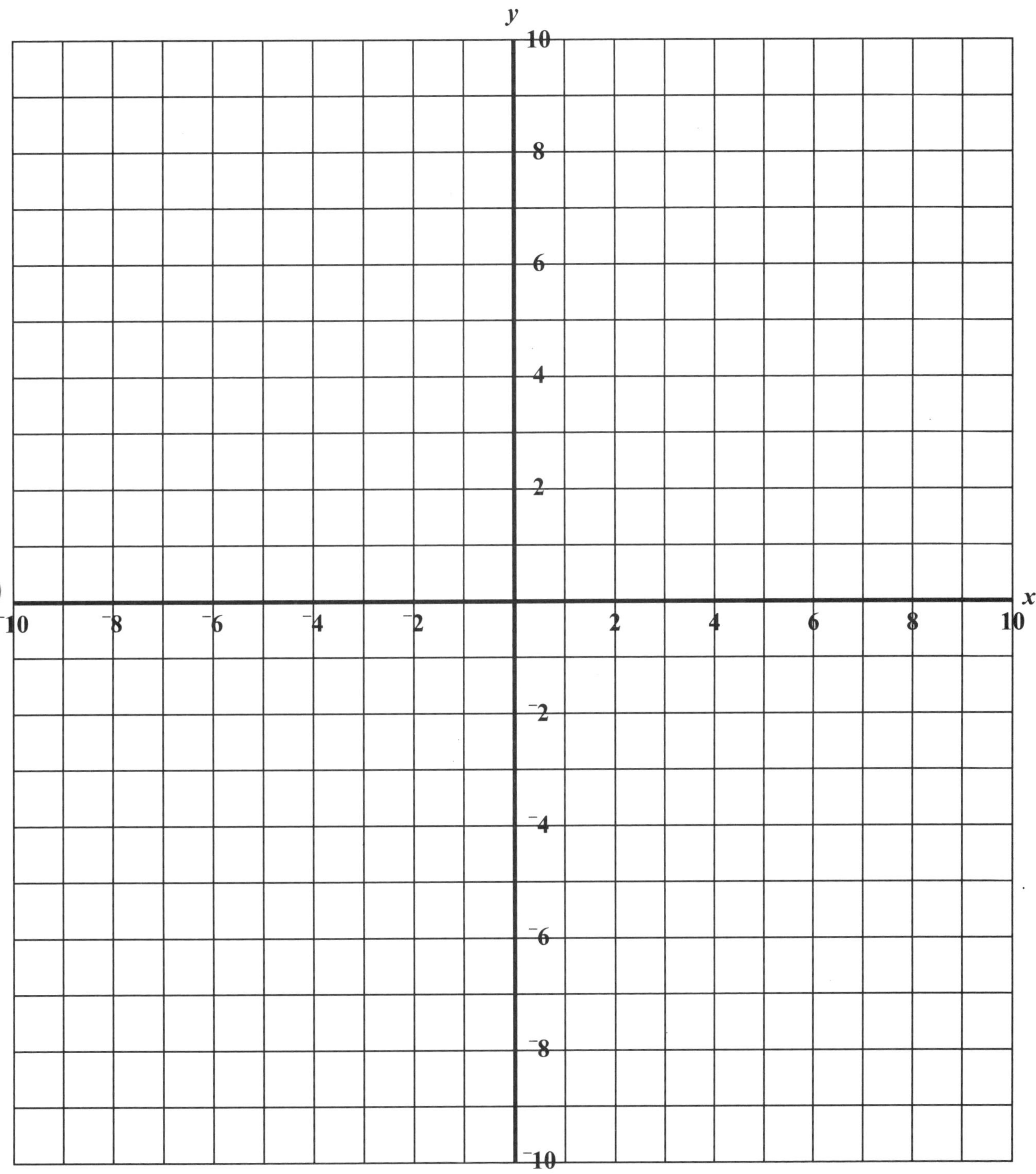

Discovery Template 36
Real Data A

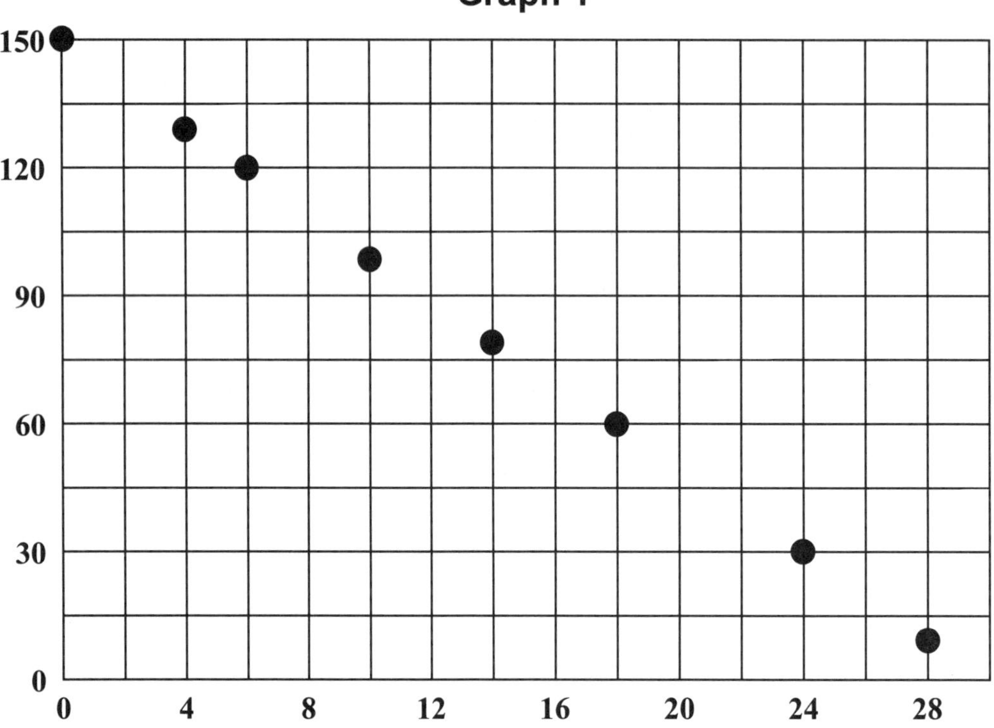

Graph 2

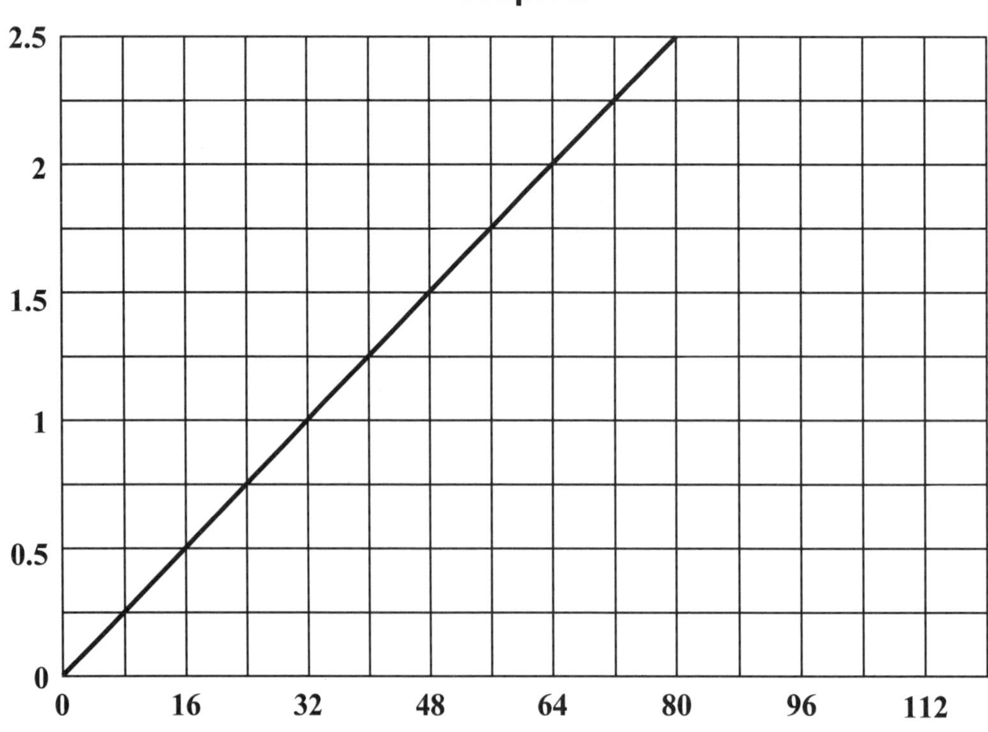

Discovery Template 37
Real Data B

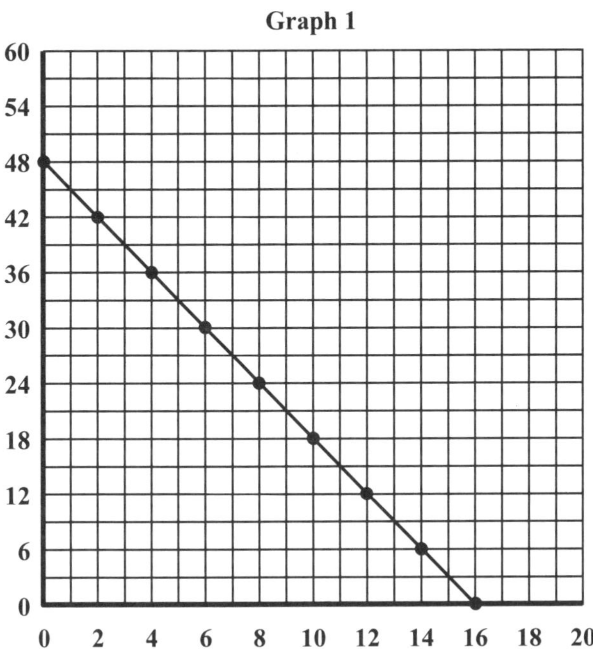

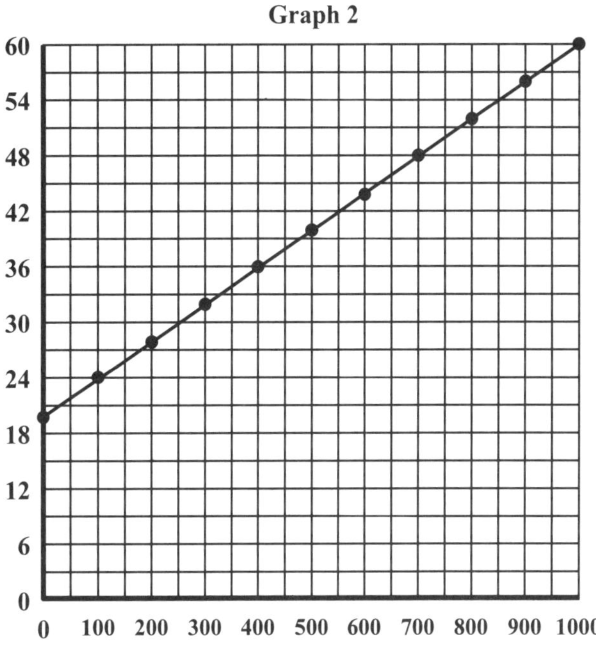

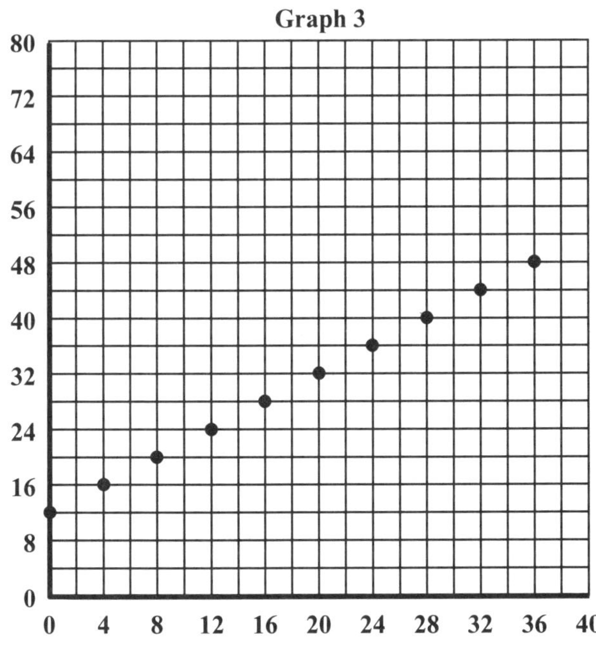

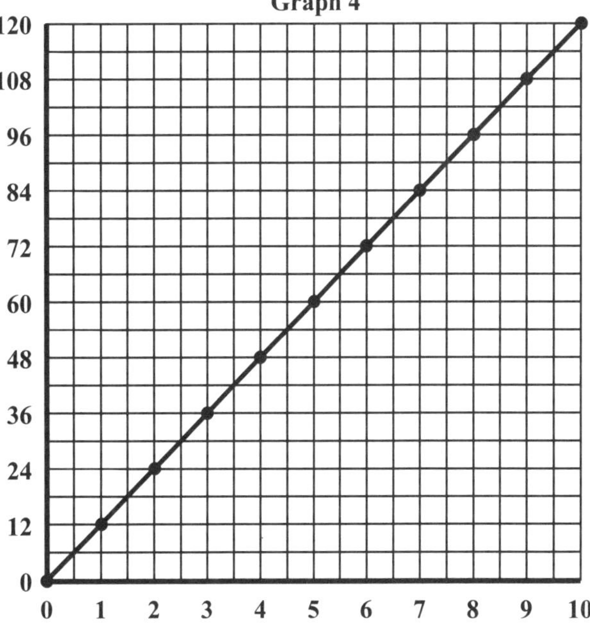

Discovery Template 38
Real Data C

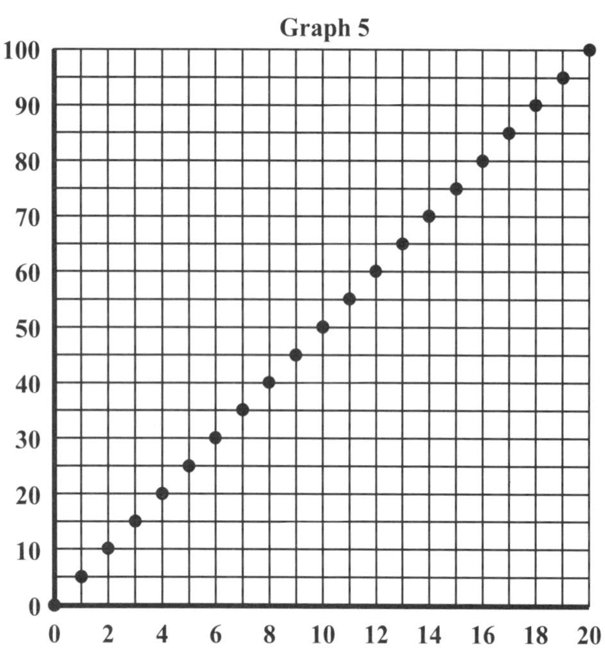

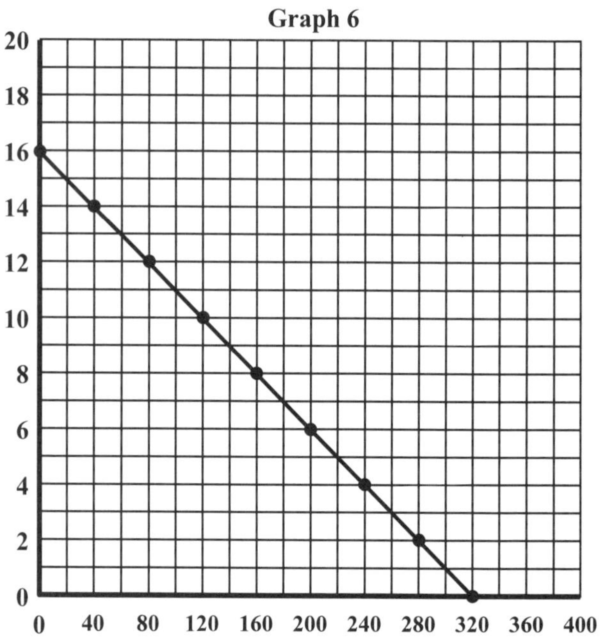

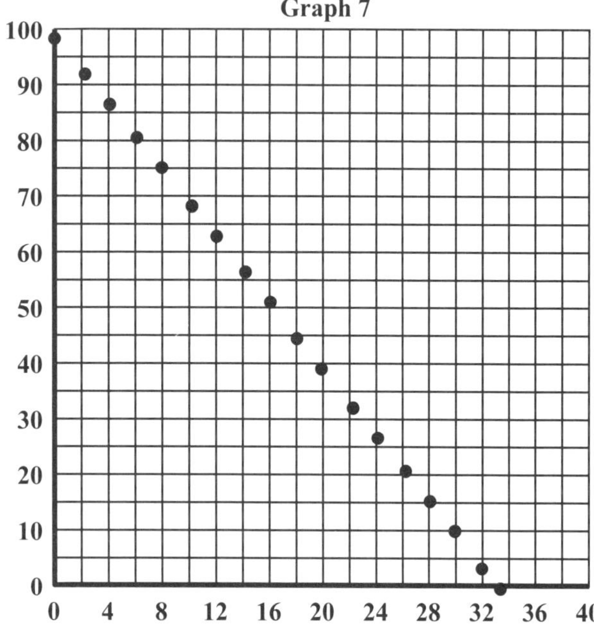

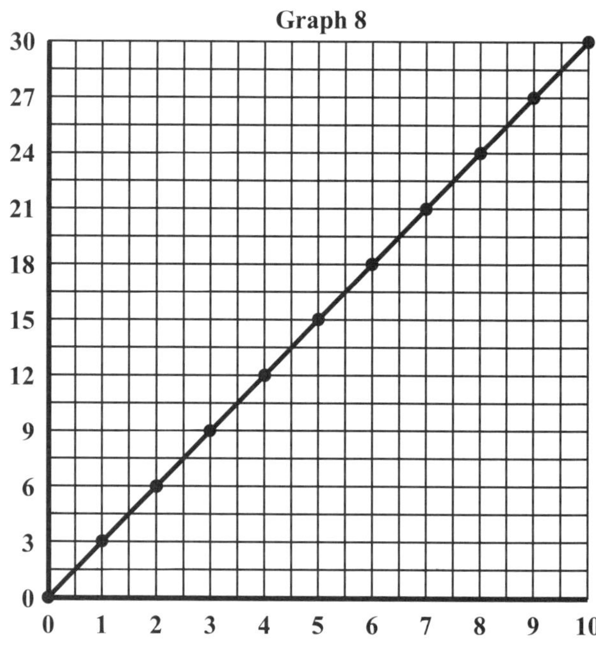

Discovery Template 39
Connecting Slope to Real Data

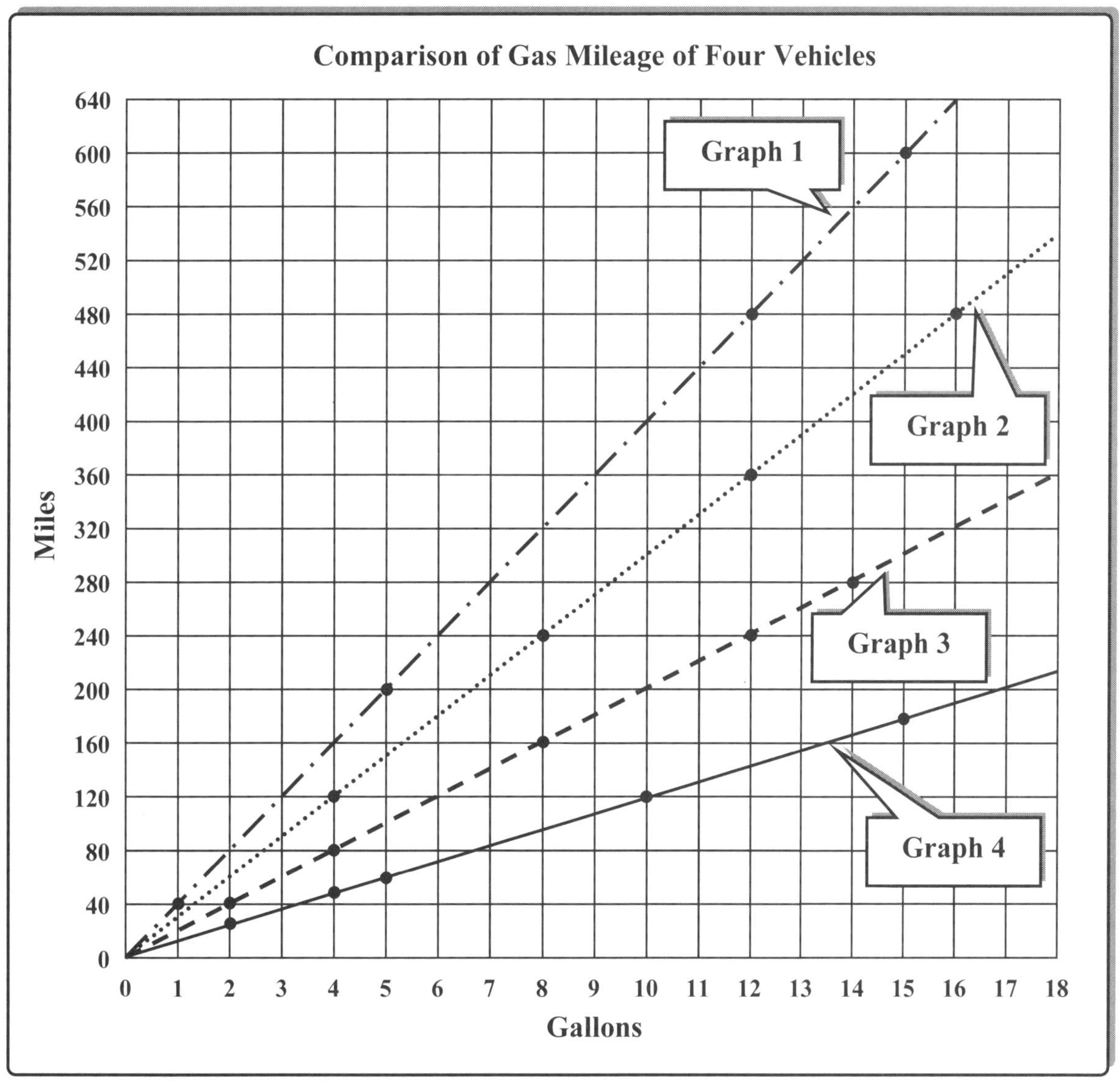

Discovery Template 40
Scatter Plots

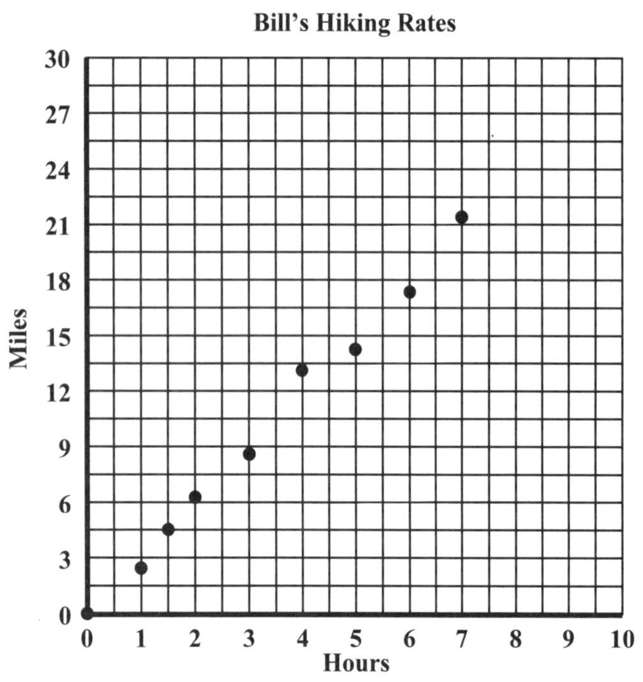

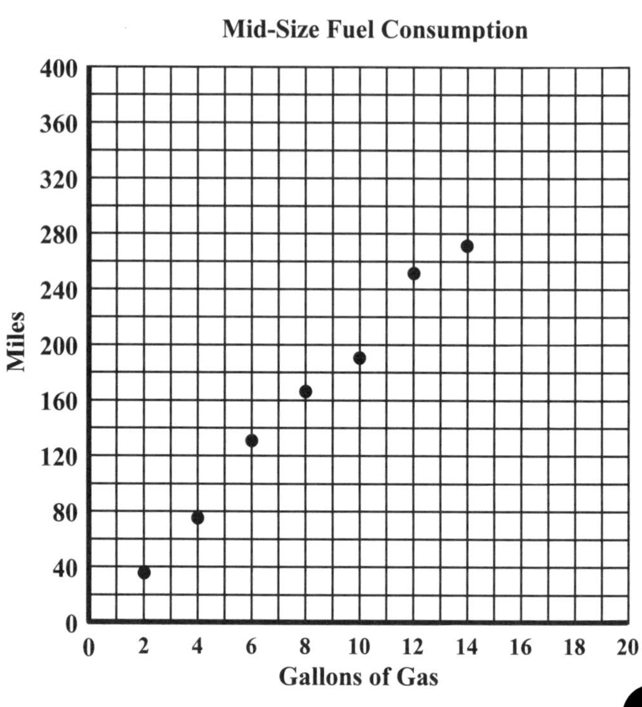

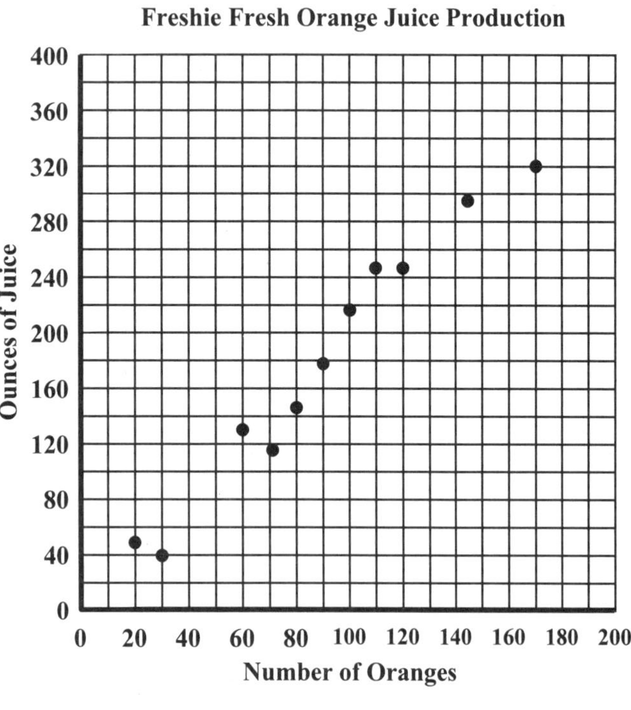

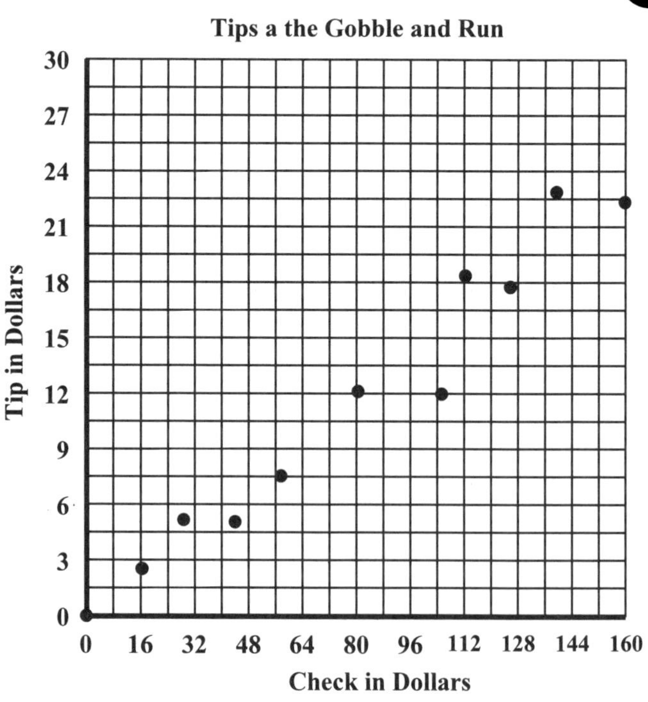

Discovery Template 41
Guess My Rule

Data Source 1

1 2 3 4
5 6 7 8 9
10 11 12 13
14 15 16 17 18
19 20 21 22
25 42 50 60 72
80 90 96 100
101 120 150 200 250

Data Source 2	
Input	Output
12	$3 \cdot 4$
30	$5 \cdot 6$
48	$6 \cdot 8$
50	$5 \cdot 10$
60	$4 \cdot 15$
72	$6 \cdot 12$

Data Source 3	
Input	Output
12	$2 \cdot 2 \cdot 3$
30	$2 \cdot 3 \cdot 5$
48	$2 \cdot 2 \cdot 2 \cdot 2 \cdot 3$
50	$2 \cdot 5 \cdot 5$
60	$2 \cdot 2 \cdot 3 \cdot 5$
72	$2 \cdot 2 \cdot 2 \cdot 3 \cdot 3$

Data Source 4	
Input	Output
12	$2^2 \cdot 3$
30	$2 \cdot 3 \cdot 5$
48	$2^4 \cdot 3$
50	$2 \cdot 5^2$
60	$2^2 \cdot 3 \cdot 5$
72	$2^3 \cdot 3^2$

Data Source 5		
Input		Output
12	6	3
21	35	7
48	18	6
50	15	5
60	45	15
72	12	12

Data Source 6		
Input		Output
12	8	24
21	28	84
48	36	144
50	10	50
60	40	120
72	8	72

Data Source 7		
Input		Output
12	6	$2 \cdot 2 \cdot 3$
21	35	$3 \cdot 5 \cdot 7$
48	18	$2 \cdot 2 \cdot 2 \cdot 2 \cdot 3 \cdot 3$
50	15	$2 \cdot 3 \cdot 5 \cdot 5$
60	45	$2 \cdot 2 \cdot 3 \cdot 3 \cdot 5$
72	12	$2 \cdot 2 \cdot 2 \cdot 3 \cdot 3$

Discovery Template 42
Searching for Patterns

Input			Output
A	3	5	15
B	4	7	28
C	9	5	45
D	2	7	14
E	10	9	90
F	8	4	8
G	6	18	18
H	7	21	21
I	12	3	12
J	8	56	56
K	4	6	12
L	9	12	36
M	15	25	75
N	21	49	147
O	16	24	48

Discovery Template 43
Discoveries with Exponents

Data Source A	
Input	Output
2	$\frac{1}{2}$
3	$\frac{1}{3}$
5	$\frac{1}{5}$
7	$\frac{1}{7}$
10	$\frac{1}{10}$
12	$\frac{1}{12}$
20	$\frac{1}{20}$
25	$\frac{1}{25}$

Data Source B	
Input	Output
2	$\frac{1}{4}$
3	$\frac{1}{9}$
5	$\frac{1}{25}$
7	$\frac{1}{49}$
10	$\frac{1}{100}$
12	$\frac{1}{144}$
20	$\frac{1}{400}$
25	$\frac{1}{625}$

Data Source C	
Input	Output
2	$\frac{1}{8}$
3	$\frac{1}{27}$
5	$\frac{1}{125}$
7	$\frac{1}{343}$
10	$\frac{1}{1000}$
12	$\frac{1}{1728}$
20	$\frac{1}{8000}$
25	$\frac{1}{12,625}$

Data Source D		
Input		Output
2	3	$\frac{2}{3}$
4	9	$\frac{4}{9}$
5	7	$\frac{5}{7}$
11	12	$\frac{11}{12}$
3	10	$\frac{3}{10}$
7	20	$\frac{7}{20}$
9	25	$\frac{9}{25}$

Data Source E		
Input		Output
7	5	$\frac{7}{25}$
11	6	$\frac{11}{36}$
8	7	$\frac{8}{49}$
11	12	$\frac{11}{144}$
3	10	$\frac{3}{100}$
7	20	$\frac{7}{400}$
9	25	$\frac{9}{625}$

Data Source F	
Input	Output
Billion	10^9
Hundred Million	10^8
Ten-million	10^7
Million	10^6
Hundred thousand	10^5
Ten-Thousands	10^4
Thousands	10^3
Hunrdeds	10^2
Tens	10^1
Unit	10^0
Tenth	10^{-1}
Hundredth	10^{-2}
Thousandth	10^{-3}
Ten-thousandth	10^{-4}
Hundred Thousandth	10^{-5}
Millionth	10^{-6}

Discovery Template 44
Scientific Notation Randomizer

	A	B	C	D
Ace♣	8.3	Hundred Million	10^{1}	426
2♣	5.4	Ten-thousands	10^{2}	8,920
3♣	7.8	Hundreds	10^{0}	241,000
4♣	1.2	Thousands	10^{4}	3,450,000
5♣	6.4	Tens	10^{9}	2,340,000,000
6♣	7.9	Hundred-thousands	10^{5}	31,000
7♣	8.3	Millions	10^{6}	52,100,000
8♣	4.3	Ten-million	10^{7}	54
9♣	9.1	Units	10^{8}	3000
10♣	1.6	Billion	10^{3}	843
Ace♦	7.6	Thousandths	10^{-2}	0.43
2♦	9.1	Hundredths	10^{-1}	0.002
3♦	8.8	Tenths	10^{-5}	0.1
4♦	2.5	Thousandths	10^{-1}	0.00345
5♦	1.4	Hundred-thousandths	10^{-3}	0.00012
6♦	3.4	Millionths	10^{-2}	0.03
7♦	1.2	Tenths	10^{-4}	0.045
8♦	4.1	Ten-Thousandths	10^{-4}	0.00032
9♦	5.6	Thousandths	10^{-5}	0.76
10♦	1.2	Hundredths	10^{-6}	0.432